PROLIFIC PREAMBLES

PROLIFIC PREAMBLES

A Digital Diary of Musings, Memories and Miles Between

SHANNON HOGAN COHEN

DECKLE WAY PRESS

Prolific Preambles: A Digital Diary of Musings, Memories and Miles Between
Published by Deckle Way Press
Del Mar, California, U.S.A.

Deckle Way Press
1155 Camino Del Mar, Suite 116
Del Mar, CA 92014

HOGAN COHEN, SHANNON, Author
PROLIFIC PREAMBLES
SHANNON HOGAN COHEN

ISBN: 979-8-9913234-4-4, 979-8-9913234-6-8 (paperback)
ISBN: 979-8-9913234-7-5 (hardcover)
ISBN: 979-8-9913234-5-1 (digital)

Library of Congress Control Number: 2025916120

LITERARY COLLECTIONS / Diaries & Journals
TRAVEL / Essays & Travelogues
BIOGRAPHY & AUTOBIOGRAPHY / Women

Cover Design: Julia Kuris, designerability.au
Interior Layout & E-book formatting: Amit Dey (amitdey2528@gmail.com)
Publishing Management: Susie Schaefer, finishthebookpublishing.com

QUANTITY PURCHASES: Schools, companies, professional groups, clubs, and other organizations may qualify for special terms when ordering quantities of this title. For information, please visit www.shannonhogancohen.com

To the brave.
To the bruised.
To the ones still becoming.

CONTENTS

MESSAGE FROM THE AUTHOR

Welcome to *Prolific Preambles,* a collection born from the transformative power of reflection and the raw intimacy of a decade-long journey toward self-discovery, contemplation, and the ever-evolving nature of love, loss, and understanding. What began as journaling, an instinctive act of self-preservation, evolved into a profound process of introspection, growth, and healing. These pages are more than just words; they are fragments of my life, threaded together through the lens of experience, resilience, and the relentless pursuit of meaning.

This collection began ten years ago, in the quiet margins of my everyday life, capturing thoughts in motion, heartbreak in real time, and questions I didn't yet dare to speak aloud. But the seed for this kind of expression was planted much earlier. In sixth grade, my adored father had just passed away from cancer at the age of thirty, and I was struggling to make sense of a world that suddenly felt too heavy. My teacher, Ann Bass, noticed. She slipped a poem titled "*The Weaver* " by B.M. Franklin into one of my assignments, her red-inked scribbles guiding me gently through each stanza. That poem, about trusting a larger pattern, even when life feels tangled and unclear was the first time language offered me light in the dark. Mrs. Bass taught me that words could carry us when we don't know how to move forward. That lesson never left me.

Writing became my sanctuary—a place to wrestle with truths, to make meaning out of chaos, and to soften the sharp edges of memory. Over time, those private reflections became more than a coping mechanism. They became a mirror, a map, and a record of progress. The bulk of this book is a mosaic of that growth: raw, unfiltered, and unafraid. These pages chronicle the process of dismantling false identities, confronting uncomfortable truths, and finding light even in the shadows. Here, vulnerability meets resilience, and moments of stillness give rise to truths that demand to be written.

I invite you to step into these contemplations to linger in the moments that speak to you, challenge you, or unearth parts of yourself you thought were long buried. *Prolific Preambles* began as my digital diary, a warm-up act for my thoughts, an introduction to ideas that no one around me seemed to want to hear, or that I didn't yet know how to say aloud without sounding a bit unhinged. I chose the word "prolific" because it captures the overabundance of my ramblings, reflections, and revelations—never-ending, ever-evolving, and stitched together with preambles that frame the deeper stories to come.

Anyone who knows me is aware of my affinity for alliteration. *Prolific Preambles* isn't just a curated collection; it's a lived experience. A space where ideas could take their first breath, where meaning began to take form, and where I tried to navigate the messy landscape of life by writing through it. It was a way to offer solace, provoke thought, or remind myself and now you that we are all, in our own way, searching for something in the preambles of our lives.

To help guide your own journey through these pages, the book is divided into eight thematic sections: *Self-Discovery, Personal Narratives, Grief and Growth, Reflections, Travel, Love and Connection, Letters and Musings,* and ending with *Poetry;* each tracing a distinct arc of human experience: grief, identity, longing, healing, love, and transformation. These are not tidy chapters, but living, breathing constellations of thought and feeling. Interwoven throughout are over one hundred personal narratives and poems drawn from my digital diary, carefully curated to highlight honesty, rawness, and resonance. These entries are random rants and fragments of truth captured in real time, before I had the language to make sense of what I was living through.

Each section stands alone, yet together they create a map, not of where I have been, but of how I have come to find meaning in it all. Each one reflects a phase of my growth and offers its own invitation: to pause, to ponder, and to see a little of yourself in the words and pages that follow. May they remind you that your own story is still unfolding, and you are far from finished.

SELF-DISCOVERY

Mapping the Inner Landscape

This section captures my earliest musings, my attempts to understand my inner world, my contradictions, and the unraveling of identity beyond the roles and expectations placed on me. These thoughts are often raw, sometimes uncomfortable, but always sincere. Understanding myself has been both a discovery and a struggle, and this section marks the first step in that lifelong journey.

Peeling back the layers of who I thought I had to be revealed a quieter voice I had long ignored, my own. In these early entries, I begin to question the scripts I inherited and the personas I perfected to feel safe, loved, or enough. You will see me stumble, reach out, resist, and occasionally retreat, but also start to reclaim pieces of myself I had silenced for too long. This is the excavation site where the dust of expectation begins to lift and something truer begins to take shape within me.

My love of storytelling started in childhood, sitting beside my grandmother as she read to me, each word opening a door to another world. Her voice, calm and wise, instilled in me the belief that stories are important that they help us understand life and each other. As I grew older, this love grew into a calling. The gatherings I organized and the spaces I created were all driven by a desire to keep storytelling alive. Because sharing our experiences isn't just about connecting, it's about moving humanity forward.

This section is both personal and communal.
A beginning.
A remembering.
A return to voice.

OWNING MY STORY

What can I learn from my life?

Many of the things I once felt ashamed of are now what I'm most proud of. Vulnerability isn't easy in a world that demands composure, but it's been my way through. I'm still learning and evolving but understanding and untangling the emotional and psychological messes of my life has become my purpose and my passage out of "Numbville," the fictional town I created to survive the unbearable after losing my dad.

Revealing pieces of myself through entries in my "digital diary" became a lifeline, a place to reflect, to heal, and to extend my hand to others. By sharing the truth of my journey, flaws and all, I've tried to offer a mirror for those navigating their own storm. I hope that, by providing glimpses of my journey, someone else might find the courage to face their own.

As a child, I enjoyed reading and writing, but I would also lie in the grass, watching clouds drift by, curious and filled with wonder. That same curiosity lives in me still, now from airplane windows high above, reminding me there is always something greater than myself. Yes, I'm a proud member of the Cloud Appreciation Society, complete with a pin.

The last thirty-plus years have been a messy, winding, and at times numbing experience. I've come to understand that love and loss are intertwined, and that joy and pain often walk side by side. The relationships that shaped me, people, places, and even ideas have brought both beauty and heartbreak. And I'm still learning to hold that truth.

Writing is my attempt to look back, reflect, and make sense of the fragments to understand the why behind the patterns, the wounds, the resilience. I don't regret where I've been. Instead, I've learned to listen to the discontent when it appears, to not let it linger or harden me. I've begun to meet myself with more compassion.

Merging the justice-seeking girl I once was with the still-feisty but more forgiving woman I've become hasn't been easy. Journaling daily has helped peel away the layers of protection I built long ago, layers that once kept me safe, but later kept me stuck. I now see these past decades not just as survival, but as a roadmap toward presence, purpose, and peace.

Leaving Numbville meant grieving not only people but the losses of identity, community, and clarity. It meant naming the things that shaped me—abandonment, manipulation, narcissism—and choosing to alchemize them into insight. The real challenge was believing I could. That I would.

What began in 2012 as private personal narrative entries and relentless research evolved into something more profound when, in 2021, I spent 558 days in a doctoral program studying intergenerational trauma. I wanted to understand not just myself, but the way pain echoes through families. With the help of Tristen, my trusted therapist and friend, I dissected the layers, personal, ancestral, and societal.

We are wired for story. It's how we connect, make meaning, and heal. Through shame, grief, and hard-earned clarity, I have cracked open and slowly stitched myself back together. Each chapter of my life has taught me something: childhood brought curiosity, adolescence brought challenge, young adulthood required independence, and midlife offered reflection and reclamation.

This process has revealed universal truths: the ways families fracture and repair, how grief manifests in different forms, and how silence and survival often go hand in hand. But perhaps most importantly, it showed me the power of naming things; to own your story without shame is to step fully into yourself.

Living in Numbville taught me what it means to feel cut off from life. Getting out meant choosing to feel again, choosing to reclaim my agency and transform survival into wisdom. That choice, again and again, is what healed me.

If my story resonates with yours, let it be a sign. You are not alone. My journey isn't a prescription, but a possibility. A way through. And maybe even out.

As Edmund Hillary said, "It's not the mountain we conquer, but ourselves."

WELCOME TO NUMBVILLE

Reclaiming my life wasn't about cleaning up a mess; it was about stepping into a mystery. A journey without a map, without applause, and often, without words.

For years, I had quietly dreamed of being a writer, a storyteller, even a poet — someone who could use narrative not just to entertain, but to enlighten. In childhood, my mistakes were often framed as flaws, rather than lessons. Misbehavior led to soap-in-the-mouth punishments and warnings spoken through clenched teeth. It was an era when *children were supposed to be seen and not heard,* an especially harsh command for a girl born curious and quick-witted.

But somewhere deep inside, I knew: my missteps weren't shameful. They were signposts. My life, even in its chaos, was carving a message I was meant to decode.

As a girl, I would play school with my sister in the basement. I always insisted on being the teacher. Back then, I didn't realize I was rehearsing for something real, testing out the tools of understanding, truth-telling, and guidance. I was preparing to teach myself.

No one in my family talked about dreams. That kind of thinking belonged in fairytales. But my inner world was alive with possibility. I invented an inner guide, a gutsy voice that showed up when I doubted myself. She whispered what the adults wouldn't say: that I was capable, that I could become. I named her Rosie.

Rosie was my internal warrior—part goddess, part gut instinct—and she helped me survive when logic fell apart. She reminded me that I could reroute at any time, even after I'd gone astray.

Then, life happened.

At eleven, I lost my father. He was thirty. Grief opened something in me that never closed again. My so-called normal disappeared overnight, replaced by a world filled with unspoken sorrow and emotional neglect. The adults around me didn't know how to help. So I stopped expecting them to. Rosie tried to stay with me, but I drifted. The pain was too loud, and the silence too constant. I built a fictional escape hatch, a town of my own invention.

I called it Numbville.

Numbville is a place we all visit, though few admit it. It's the quiet town people arrive at when feeling becomes too dangerous, too exhausting. A refuge for the emotionally overdrawn. A hiding place for the heart.

Population: unknowable.

Rules: come and go as you please.

But most who come… stay.

When I arrived, I was welcomed by blank stares, small talk, and weary smiles. The town was filled with people like me, people who had been abandoned, misunderstood, or burned out from trying too hard to fix what hurt them. Most of them weren't angry; they were just… done.

Done trying. Done feeling. Done hoping.

The mayor, a charming divorcé with hollow and haunting eyes, greeted me like an old friend. "We don't solve things here," he said. "We shelf them."

A waitress at the local diner whispered her story to me between coffee refills. She had been bruised by every man in her life. "It's quieter here," she said. "Less disappointing."

I stayed. Not because I loved it, but because numbness, for a while, felt safer than truth.

And Rosie? She was furious.

She stormed into my dreamscape and shouted, *"This is not living." This is rehearsal for regret. You're meant to feel it all, not sleepwalk through someone else's script.*

I argued with her at first. I told her healing was hard. That clarity felt cruel. That I couldn't possibly go back and untangle it all. She didn't flinch.

She simply said, *"Begin where you are." Leave Numbville. Not just for yourself, but also for others who have forgotten there's another way of living.*

The truth is, Numbville exists inside many of us. It's the place we go when life overwhelms, and emotions feel unbearable. It's a coping mechanism turned personal prison.

But here's what Rosie finally taught me: We don't have to be lifers!

It takes grit to leave the town you built to protect yourself. It takes heart to live fully again. But somewhere out there, or maybe in here, others are waking up too. They've built their own Numbvilles. They're yearning for connection, for courage, for something real.

Maybe, just maybe, we can find each other.

And, together, we can return to life.

WHEN TRUTH DISTURBS THE PEACE

A Reflection on Colette, Legacy, and the Courage to Choose Yourself

Some women walk the well-worn paths, and then there are women like Colette.

A writer, performer, and sensualist who defied convention, Colette lived boldly, curiously, and unapologetically. Her pen carved space for truths many women were too afraid to name, and her characters, so often mirrors of herself, pushed against the edges of polite society with poise and ferocity. Her novel *The Vagabond* isn't just literature, it's a reckoning. Through Renée Néré, a woman who leaves a faithless husband and makes her living on the stage, Colette explores a question that still presses against the walls of my own heart: How do I remain true to myself in a world that would prefer me silenced or softened?

Renée's refusal to be "kept," to be rescued or reduced, echoes a restlessness I know well. Like her, I've stared down the comfort of what's expected and chosen the ache of the unknown. Not because it's easier, but because it's mine. Because freedom—absolute freedom—requires choosing selfhood over safety.

And then there's *Gigi*; young, observant, being groomed to play a role for which society has written a script. But in the end, she rewrites that script, choosing love and partnership on her terms. That moment of claiming her agency is one I recognize in my bones. Like Gigi, I have unlearned the rules written for me and decided to become the author of my own story.

As Colette once wrote, *"You do not go from one happiness to another, you make your happiness. And sometimes it's a lonely business."* I have found this to be achingly true. Telling my story, unplugged, unfiltered, and in my voice, has not always made me likable. But it has made me whole. That's the heartbeat behind *Love Me,* a collection born from lived experience, from burning bridges to save myself, from rebuilding without apology, from releasing the burden of pleasing and performing. *Love Me* is not just a title; it's a dare to myself. To stop waiting for permission. To name what hurt, what shaped me, and what I now choose. To speak from the inside out, without softening my truth for someone else's comfort.

There's power in claiming your narrative without apology. There's power in saying:

This is who I am. I will not shrink. I will not mask my truth to make you comfortable.

Like Colette, I am a woman shaped by experience and sharpened by introspection. Like Renée, I am a vagabond of the soul, unsettled not by dissatisfaction, but by curiosity, longing, and a desire to know life on my terms. Like Gigi, I am no longer being prepared for a life that pleases others. I am preparing to live my own. But claiming yourself comes at a cost, especially when truth interrupts the illusion of a family's carefully managed silence.

When a long-held secret, especially one involving abuse, addiction, or trauma, is unearthed, it often triggers psychological seismic shifts not just for the individual who reveals it, but across the entire family system. These shifts can be uncomfortable, threatening, and in some cases, relationship-altering.

In families like mine, silence was the mortar that held the illusion of harmony together. My father, charming to some, chaotic to others was an alcoholic. When the poison was in his veins, he could be cruel, especially to my mother. He died young, just thirty, of cancer.

He was my hero, and still is. But, like all heroes —and really, all of us —he was flawed. That doesn't take away my love for him. I've learned I can hold two conflicting truths about my father and still love him deeply. I can acknowledge the harm and honor his goodness. I can carry his memory and his legacy forward with complexity, not erasure.

It took nearly twenty years before my mother finally spoke her truth. Not in anger. Not with bitterness. Just with clarity. I had offered her the space; one I wish someone had offered her sooner. But the truth is disruptive. It doesn't tiptoe in. It arrives like a tremor, shaking what was once buried beneath layers of protection, denial, and fear.

When her story in S.H.E. Share Heal Empower, Volume One, came out, it wasn't her voice they turned on. It was mine. They blamed me for giving her the microphone, for "convincing" her, for disrupting the myth we'd all been taught to protect. They said I did it for attention. For gain. As if truth had to be justified, as if healing were a crime.

What they didn't understand is this: I didn't invent the pain. I inherited it. And by speaking it aloud, I refused to pass it on. Some family members stopped speaking to me. Oddly, they still talked to my mother, whose story they may quietly have resented her for sharing but never challenged her outright, only me - I became the scapegoat, the breaker of spells, the one who pointed to the cracks in the stained glass and said, "We are allowed to see this clearly despite their denial."

But clarity has a cost. And courage has consequences. Still, I would do it again because I've learned that not everyone wants freedom. Some prefer the familiarity of silence, even if it stifles them. But I made a choice: not to be loved for who I pretend to be, but to be known for who I truly am. And in the wreckage of broken silence, I found something that felt like peace.

This fall, I'll spend forty-five days in Paris. A pilgrimage of sorts, not just to learn the language but to live in it. To follow Colette's footsteps, sip from the well of creative unrest, and write without constraint. To honor the voice I've fought so hard to reclaim. Because if I've learned anything from Colette, her writing, and from my own unraveling, it's this: there is no shame in the wanderer's path. Only truth. Only beauty. Only becoming.

PERSONAL PREAMBLES

Let me be honest: I'm not writing as an expert in psychology, grief, or personal transformation. I'm writing from lived experience, shaped by curiosity, pain, and the ongoing work of becoming. Nor did I emerge from some mystical encounter with a wild woman archetype in a foreign land. While I honor ancient healing traditions and have taken sacred pilgrimages that awakened parts of my soul, the words ahead are not born of a single epiphany. They come from years of quietly—and sometimes chaotically—sifting through my own mess.

Much of what I've come to understand has come from relentless self-reflection, a few trusted therapy sessions, and a deep dive into the study of intergenerational trauma and identity. It's not for the faint of heart. Trauma lives in all of us. For me, it's been a strange teacher—frustrating, revealing, and oddly personal. And while I've often questioned whether my pain was too selfish to matter, I've also come to respect it for what it has taught me about endurance, empathy, and the complexity of being human.

I've read the books. The ones stacked in my "babe cave" on reclaiming your voice, your power, your peace. I've filled hundreds of black-and-white composition notebooks with theories, questions, lists, and long-winded reflections. I'm addicted to Uni-Ball gel pens and carry paper and colored Post-its everywhere. My thoughts zigzag, and I pity anyone trying to organize them. I'm told I see too many sides of every issue. I say, "It depends." Context is everything.

I hold high expectations—sometimes impossibly so. I worry about wasting time. I follow my husband around, turning off lights. (Thanks, Mom.) I'm playful, too—that's from my dad. I call myself a recovering academic, now living creatively on my own terms. I take vitamins religiously but avoid exercise. When I travel, I miss my body pillow, Phil. I hold grudges, or perhaps I remember what people have shown me. I rarely forget a hurtful comment if it pierced my character. Still, I'm told I seem calm, even chill, until I'm not.

I wake up curious and go to bed wanting more. I feel everything, even when I don't show it. I can be intense, but I rein myself in for growth. I rely on coffee, crushed-ice Diet Cokes, Pinot Noir from Oregon, and Sancerre from France. Insomnia and I are old companions; melatonin and magnesium are my bedtime rituals.

My own encounters with trauma felt normal until I started naming them. My great-grandmother Alvina had two nervous breakdowns but was considered "fine." People around me have quietly fallen apart and rebuilt. I worked with Hospice for a decade. I've seen death up close. It still jolts me. And yet I've talked myself—and others—off countless emotional ledges.

I love neuroscience, epigenetics, evolutionary biology, and molecular collisions. I'm also a card-carrying member of the Cloud Appreciation Society. Beach walks at low tide settle me. Stars make me feel small and right-sized all at once.

I often wish we could rearrange time and preview consequences. But the uncertainty is part of what shapes us. I've learned to coexist with the unacceptable. It doesn't mean I condone it, but I can hold a contradiction. Tranquility is my yearning. Relaxation is my struggle. I continue to examine the parallels between the girl I was and the woman I am, contrasting their emotions, reactions, and coping mechanisms to better understand how I love and live now.

I'm constantly evolving. The problems I face, my girlfriends often do too. I want to shout from the rooftops that self-doubt is normal and discomfort isn't weakness. It's usually the soil where resilience grows. I've come to validate my own story, my emotions, and my survival. That's where my strength lies in owning, not overcoming.

This time around, I've permitted myself to write slowly, with less pressure and more presence. I've traded speed for intention. I'm letting this unfold, word by word, embracing my new mantra: *slow and steady wins the race.*

FLING IT OR FACE IT?

There are days I wish I could send people an invoice for wasting my time. But would that be *nice*? Thanks, Mom, for raising me to always be. For years, I leaned too far into being polite, biting my tongue, smoothing things over, and giving people the benefit of the doubt.

But life has a way of wringing out wisdom. And lately, I've been shifting. Gently, but firmly. I'm learning to choose people who align with my future—not my past.

The days of tolerating bad behavior for the sake of peace are over. Passive-aggressive digs, manipulation, sweeping things under the rug to keep the illusion of harmony? Not on my watch. If someone's disrespect is loud, their apology better match the volume, or don't bother. I'm done cleaning up messes I didn't make.

Let's be real: people who fling their baggage instead of facing it are just avoiding their own emotional work. It's easier to lash out than to sit with discomfort and ask what needs healing. Owning your mistakes takes courage, and not everyone's ready for that. But I'm no longer carrying the weight of someone else's unfinished business.

I've made peace with being alone. I've stopped chasing approval from people who don't understand me. I don't owe anyone an explanation for how I live. Let them pound sand, I'm living by my own rules now. I've weathered my own storms. I've owned my chaos. And now, I choose peace, truth, and people who take responsibility for their impact.

This is my manifesto... raw, real, and right on time.

PAUSE AND PAY ATTENTION

As I pause and reflect, I realize how fast I often tore through life, especially in my younger years. Only now can I appreciate how much I missed by rushing forward, always looking toward the next thing. If I could advise my younger self, or even myself today, it would be to slow down, notice the small things, and let my senses guide me.

There were so many moments I could have savored if I had paused to pay attention. Life seemed about reaching goals, hitting milestones, and moving quickly. However, in doing so, I often overlooked the beauty that was hidden in plain sight. I now understand that our senses are the gateways to the mind, profoundly influencing how we perceive and experience life. We connect to ourselves, others, and nature through seeing, hearing, and feeling the world around us.

Today, I remind myself how different life feels when I walk through the world with my head up, noticing the changing flowers along the sidewalk or the birds perching on a lamppost. A hummingbird's brief, weightless hover can be a fleeting but profound moment of stillness, but only if I can catch it. I notice how these sensory experiences ground me, helping me feel connected to my surroundings and more at peace within myself.

There's a strange paradox in our hyperconnected world, while technology keeps us connected, it also creates a dangerous disconnect. It's so easy to fall into the habit of staring at my phone, missing the world unfolding before me. I don't want to fall victim to that, to allow technology to rob me of the richness available in these simple, sensory moments.

Slowing down and resisting the pull of distraction takes effort, but I feel more alive and in tune with myself when I do. I remind myself and would tell my younger self as well, that life is not just about significant accomplishments or grand moments. It's the little things, the sensations of everyday life, that shape how we feel and who we are.

Pausing helps me fully experience life, noticing not just the grand beauty but also quiet miracles, like the scent of rain on the pavement, a butterfly sitting on a pink hydrangea, or the way sunlight filters through the leaves. These moments bring me joy, balance, and connection. They are always there, and I need to take the time to notice them.

I want to live more consciously, slow down, and experience the world with intention. I want to remember that being present is a gift I give to myself, one that fills me with a sense of belonging and wonder. Life is happening all around me right now, and I don't want to miss it.

ASPIRE TO INSPIRE

There has always been a special place in my heart for storytelling. It has given me a safe space to listen, learn, and laugh. My grandmother often read books to me when I was a child. This experience left a lasting impression on me. We shared a bond through the book that no one could replace. The pure anticipation of the story, the message woven into the text, and the time we spent learning together.

As I reflect on those times, they taught me many lessons and strengthened my belief that every story has meaning and purpose, whether it is written or spoken. I have always felt a special closeness to the storytellers in my life, admiring how they want to share their history with me. Protecting this shared experience was a duty, but so was learning the hidden lessons that might apply to my own life. It opened the door to healing, knowing that someone has walked this path before me. A support system and confidant appeared, someone who shared my storyline, but with a different cast of characters and background in their tale.

Lastly, the overarching themes that emerged across generations, and how history tends to repeat itself. It was my duty to learn from my foremothers' and forefathers' mistakes, not repeat them. This will only happen if the story is shared. It has been said, "A story is how one constructs their experiences."

Allow me to introduce my cornerstone and guiding light: my grandmother, Rosalie Marie Hogan. She was born on January 2, 1929, and passed away on May 15, 2014. It hurts me to know that I will never hear her voice again, fight with my husband and aunt over her Lebkuchen cookies during the holidays, taste her chicken and dumpling soup, smile at her red lipstick, or argue with her about what a woman's role is in this world... and the list goes on.

I take comfort in the fact that she will continue to inspire me in many ways, and I will pay it forward to others. Her legacy will live on through those acts that make me smile.

She grew up in the village of Reese, Michigan, a farming community of close-knit people who value their families, work, and homes, and she lived there her entire life. Reveling in the fact that life stayed the same and going about her daily routines shaped her for over eighty-five years. I enjoyed asking her questions about life, her childhood, and how hard it is to mimic her crumb topping on my apple crisp.

She would beam with pure joy when asked to share stories of her early days. "Working on the farm, playing baseball with the boys, the aroma of fresh cut grass, ice skating in the wintertime, enjoying the simplicities of life and not taking them for granted but always appreciating the 'little things' that matter most," she would say.

Her path in life was set early and quickly: graduating from high school while pregnant and marrying the man who challenged her on the basketball court. This same man had his own struggles, but she remained the cornerstone of the family until his death in 1984. They led an ordinary but stable life and valued the social network they built within their community of friends and family. With three children, she refined her skills as a homemaker.

She could have taught classes at the Culinary Institute. The scent and taste of her freshly baked bread and homemade strawberry jam would make you want several pieces. Her house was immaculate. My mother mentioned many times, "we could eat off her floors as children" because her house was spotless. She had a gift for creating a warm environment for her grandchildren, and each one has heartfelt memories of all the hours spent coloring, playing cards, and watching her preserve the fruits and vegetables of the season.

If we let it, life also has a way of precluding us from our dreams. Her aspirations were to be an astronaut or a professional softball player. My younger sister remembers falling asleep during the summer evenings with the radio tuned into the baseball game. No one ever saw her favoritism toward a team or grandchild . . . and goodness knows we all thought we were her beloved!

The part of my grandmother that no one noticed was her quiet confidence. Life threw her a terrible curveball that pushed her to the sidelines. She lost her mother, husband, and son within three years. The timeline below shows her journey into seclusion. Her mother, Rose, died in August 1983; her husband, Leo, passed in January 1984; and her thirty-year-old son, Tom, left us in August 1985.

The courage and resilience she kept deep inside were silent. I always marveled at how she must have understood what pain feels like and how emotional energy can drain you, yet she kept going because life doesn't pause to mourn with you. Still, she did not share her pain with a therapist, a group of girlfriends, family, or coworkers. She faced it alone, and no one knows if she found it unbearable. She never revealed it, and when I asked, she would say, "I did what I had to do," which was to move on.

That she did. For the next thirty years, she made a conscious choice to live her life on her own terms. Often, family members would encourage her to be more social or travel, but that wasn't what resonated with her. She was happy with her daily routine and appreciated the peacefulness surrounding her.

My respect for her grows as I reflect on her life. She did it her way. Understanding who she was, the self-reliance came from within her, not from anyone else. She trusted her inner compass, which held, "I am the keeper of my own destiny." She would persuade no one, only herself. She would challenge no one, only herself. And she was a builder. Tenderly, she instilled poise in others by modeling her own self-assurance through her actions. Let us all learn the lesson that "quiet confidence" can leave a mark if one is insightful enough to recognize it.

CONFESSIONS OF A RECOVERING PEOPLE-PLEASER

For years, I lived under the weight of others' expectations—bending, shrinking, and reshaping myself to make those around me comfortable. I believed keeping the peace and making others happy was the measure of my worth. But eventually, I reached a breaking point. That was when I realized: in trying to please everyone, I had abandoned myself.

This is a brief snapshot of the moment I began waking up to myself, the moment I stopped chasing approval and started reclaiming my voice. I'm learning to set boundaries, honor my truth, and live a life rooted in authenticity, not applause.

Let it be known: every people-pleaser was once a parent-pleaser.

People-pleasing doesn't appear in adulthood out of nowhere. It's not manipulation, it's survival. For many of us, it begins in childhood, born out of trauma or emotional neglect. When the adults in our lives were inconsistent, critical, controlling, or simply unavailable, we learned that to receive even scraps of affection or attention, we had to adapt and become who others needed us to be. But the cost? We lost sight of our true selves.

For me, that meant burying my needs and silencing my voice for years. It has taken time, therapy, and relentless self-work to find that voice again. I've had to get comfortable with discomfort, learning to disappoint others rather than betray and avoid abandoning myself.

At my core, my true self has never disappeared. I call her Rosie, after my beloved paternal grandmother. Honoring Rosie is my way of reconnecting with my wholeness. She reminds me that no matter what has happened, the most genuine parts of me are still here, waiting to be seen, heard, and valued.

As a child, I learned to make others feel safe, calm, and in control, even when I felt the opposite. It was a protective response. However, people-pleasing is draining. I've realized it's a trauma response, not a personality trait, and my healing started when I shifted that love outward to inward. It was empowering to finally identify my needs, express them, and release the shame that came with doing so.

Disappointing others no longer terrifies me. Walking away from disrespect no longer paralyzes me. These are now acts of self-respect, not rebellion. Reclaiming my identity is still an ongoing journey. Breaking free from patterns that once kept me safe is not easy, but it is liberating. With every choice to prioritize my truth, I find more peace and strength.

Healing isn't linear, but it is transformative.

You, too, can break the cycle. You can create a life grounded in self-respect, not self-sacrifice. It starts with choosing yourself, not once, but over and over again. And let me tell you, that choice? It's wildly freeing.

GRIT VERSUS QUIT

There are moments in life when the lines blur, when what looks like dignity may be delusion, and what feels like courage teeters dangerously close to collapse. We often romanticize perseverance, assigning nobility to the act of pushing forward at all costs. But beneath that sheen of strength can lie exhaustion, denial, or a desperate refusal to let go.

Reading *The Undefeated,* Hemingway's short story about Manuel, an aging bullfighter past his prime, sharpens this tension. Manuel chooses grit; he steps into the ring again, battered and overlooked, because his identity is tied to the fight. Quitting would feel like vanishing. But should he have laid down his cape after winning his titles, letting the silence of dignity speak louder than the crowd? That same question haunts the story of Muhammad Ali. How long do we keep fighting simply because we don't know who we are without the fight?

I've found myself at this same crossroads more than once clinging to projects, relationships, and roles long after they've stopped feeding me. Grit kept me going, but lately, I've been asking if letting go might be its own kind of strength.

Dignity, in its purest form, is grounded in truth. It's knowing who you are, what you value, and what you're willing to stand for, even in defeat. Delusion, however, wears a similar mask. It says, "Keep going. You can't afford to stop." It's the voice that won't let you rest for fear that rest equals failure. It urges you to keep performing, even when no one's watching, or worse, when you're the only one still clapping.

Then came another perspective and voice, Annie Duke's *Quit,* a book that challenged me to look more closely at the other side of the equation. A professional poker player, Duke argues that we've vilified quitting, casting grit as a virtue and quitting as a vice. But quitting, she says, isn't weakness, it's strategy. It's wisdom. It's knowing when the odds no longer justify the investment. And perhaps more importantly, it's trusting that your identity isn't tied to how long you stay, but how well you choose when to go.

Courage lifts you from bed when grief weighs like lead. It whispers, "Try again," even when the odds are against you. But walk far enough down that road, and you might find collapse creeping in, and often invisible. Collapse doesn't always look like a breakdown. Sometimes it's numbness. Sometimes it's silence. Sometimes it's showing up, smiling, and slowly disintegrating inside.

We live much of our lives at this edge, especially those of us who were taught to survive before we were taught to feel.

To fight before we learned how to rest.

To endure rather than to examine.

To do rather than to be.

And yet, it's at this very edge—where identity is both forged and frayed—that we can start to see ourselves clearly. Not as heroes. Not as victims. But as humans, with beating hearts, bruised dreams, and an ever-present hunger for something softer than survival.

To know when to press on and when to lay it down, that is not weakness. That is wisdom. That is dignity, without delusion. Courage, without collapse. And, as I have learned, my grit is good, but only without losing myself in the fight.

TRUTH TELLER

The only people who get mad at me for speaking my truth are those I learned are living a lie. I will keep telling my truth without needing to prove myself.

A relationship close to me is teaching me great lessons. I have learned a lot about this person by how they leave things. There is a pattern. For me, maturity, mutual respect, and reverence aren't always possible but are available. I am doing the best I can considering the circumstances and walking with peace, knowing I did speak my truth and will not disrespect myself for the sake of the other person, even if it's a family member; too many years of accepting the behavior and letting it slide knowing it did not sit right with me.

I have buckled down on my boundaries as a form of self-love and reminded myself that time is valuable, and my feelings are valid. Those who love me will respect that. Being at peace for me means I no longer need to prove anything to anyone. Whether I speak my truth or not, I no longer need outside validation to tell my side of the story, even when I hear rumors that tell an untrue version. I used to guard my heart, but now I guard my peace because I truly know my peace is worth more than proving myself to anyone.

I know how hard it is to plaster a smile on during "Hallmark holidays" and feel like you are playing the role. The need to play or appear happy and vibrant to make everything seem acceptable and normal.

As life continues to educate me, I have been listening closely to its lessons. There is no more acting. I am learning I never have to play a role when I am around *my people*. There is only the rawness and honesty of me. My self-speaking truth is grounded in goodness and healthy reality. The years of me selling my image at the expense of my true feelings and needs is over. The limited times my old role needs to be activated. I play it quickly. Then go back to my people who don't expect me to play pretend anymore.

As a sidenote, I never lost real friends, real opportunities, or real relationships when I started standing up for myself and setting clear boundaries. What I did lose—manipulators, narcissists, and energy vampires who destroyed my mental health.

CONFLUENCE OF CHOICES

Grandma Rosie often said, "Life is about choices, dear." I always thought this was a simple, logical statement. My father's mother was a unique woman with quiet confidence. She chose a solitary life after her mother, husband, and son died within three years. The calm and peace she showed in her decisions was inspiring, even from a young age. My reclusive grandmother, without realizing it, gave me a valuable life lesson. Watching her interact with family and friends as forces beyond her control shaped her life, she taught me an important truth. People don't need to understand your choices; it's not their journey. This wise advice comforted me when I faced major life decisions. As I reflect on my grandmother's guidance, it was monumental and has created ripple effects in my life.

There I was, standing in front of friends and family at my bridal shower and I could not speak. Something inside me snapped. I was trembling at the idea of getting married in ninety days. Looking forward, I imagined a long life with an individual who I knew deep down did not understand the intricacies of me. My intuition had frequently raised yellow flags prior to this evening. I ignored these cautions while still knowing our relationship was impaired. However, the vibrant, red flag was flying high at my bridal shower. I was flush and full of panic when I was supposed to be full of excitement!

A little background about our relationship. I have moments of madness, but for the most part, I am a loyal and loving person. Early on, I observed that my adventure-seeking ways and expressive personality did not fuse well with his straightforward and systematic approach to life.

I like to be spontaneous and act silly. My fiancé was rigid and serious.

I am a free-spirit and do not like to be confined. My life doesn't always have a plan of action. I value order and routine, but I also require freedom and spontaneity. It became apparent we would agree to disagree. At the beginning, it worked, his yin and my yang. But over time, our differing views divided us. This man I was about to marry, would be a wonderful husband to someone, just not me.

I had two choices:

- Marry a man who I love more like a brother than a lover.
- Cancel the wedding and explain to him, it's me not you.

This internal conversation transpired in my head regularly after I agreed to marry. I could not turn it off. I was confused, but I knew what I needed to do.

Why do you stay? I think you should just get married. No! You know you're not ready. You'll be sorry. But I love him and his family. Oh come on, you know the truth. Stop kidding yourself. You want different things out of life than he does. What happens when you marry him? Trapped. Be honest with yourself and him. I feel suffocated. I feel guilty. I feel fearful. I feel commitment. I feel I failed.

He and his family were generous and gracious to me over the course of our relationship. I am endlessly grateful for their big-heartedness. The respite and restoration they provided was honorable. But it could not trump the feeling of being trapped between the safety and protection of the known versus the fear of the unknown.

Leaving was not easy.

I can't begin to tell you how many times I had to give myself a pep talk about believing this was the right decision. My mental chatter was dizzying. I second guessed myself regularly. Family and a few friends supported me. However, they didn't understand why I was breaking off an engagement to a kind, warm and thoughtful individual who adored me and would provide a secure future. Many "friends" disappeared. You find out who your true support system is when an engagement ends and sides are chosen.

I had to pause for a moment and remind myself, these judgmental individuals were not participating in our relationship. I cared deeply for my ex-fiancé and his family. I did want to impose animosity or hurt to anyone.

Yet again, I had two choices:

- Try to explain my inner adversity and motives for the breakup.
- Trust my intuition and ignore the naysayers.

My grandmother was right in saying people like to provide commentary. Only "I" need to understand my choices, not others. People like to offer unsolicited comments, many times these remarks reflect *their problems,* not mine.

I now position myself in a way that allows me to be myself. No longer settling for anything less than what I believe I deserve, even if it means walking away from an "ideal situation."

Change brings opportunities to bloom, and this occurs when I venture outside my comfort zone. Respect for my beloved grandmother grows as I reflect on her life. She made a final life choice when she left this world. For which, people could not take comfort in her approach to dying. She did not succumb to modern medicine and left this life, her way.

Listen to your mental voice.

Take a chance.

Make a change.

Be true to you, the choice is yours!

BUDDHA BABBLE

My expert editor… my Shero, who is invisible to you. She is remarkably patient, guiding grammatical errors to their correct usage, while bringing reasoning plus artistry to my madness. Illuminating the meaning of my thinking along the way.

We share an inner giggle when my lively mind becomes overly philosophical, meandering, spiritual, and sometimes even transcendental. Once this occurs, in no sequential order, it means I have activated Buddha Babble.

She warns me to minimize the babble and deliver clear and concise verbiage. This is a constant struggle for me. I enjoy verbosity. Philosophy and critical thinking excite me. Human behavior and the meaning of life entice me. My mind, like my writing, is always in flux. It is constantly shifting which creates esoteric thoughts that often come across as didactic and hard to identify with.

When and if, my perplexing rambles materialize, she reminds me to eliminate the free-wheeling, free-style sort of writing that can be challenging to follow. "There is a power in presenting direct development," she frequently repeats. Quite simply: less Buddha Babble.

My expert editor has a flair for bringing flow to my phraseology. Her heroic modifications create a meaning metamorphosis and allow skillfulness to shine. Simple tips and sensible excisions make my Buddha Babble comprehensible. She has a knack for underlining areas where a reader may struggle, which forces me to reframe the structure of my sentence and deliver a straightforward sense of understanding.

I am grateful to have my invisible hero slashing sentences and properly placing commas. Without her expertise stylistic snags, redundancies, and run-on sentences could be victorious. She gently prompts me to be transparent and use more direct ways of expression.

An incurable lust for learning guides me on the journey of exploring my mind. It is important to show true mettle in my writing and continually evolve. I am fortunate to have my invisible hero, a compassionate teacher who brings enlightenment and order to my endless Buddha Babble.

THE MAKING OF ME?

Throughout my life, I have unraveled and unearthed many layers of my identity. A constant work in progress is what my life feels like. Yet somehow this shapeshifting seedbed of personhood often brings me back to a concrete self.

The perplexity of my existence fascinates me. The continuum of my personal identity is the journey I am currently on. I am asking myself *what makes my childhood self the same person and me*? Considering I have had a lifetime of changes transpire, from my cells to my values. Harvard psychologist Daniel Gilbert captured this question brilliantly, "Human beings are works in progress that mistakenly think they are finished."

To understand this paradox perfectly, I recognize it will not happen. There will never be a theory to examine or an experiment of logic that will ever offer a lucid explanation. We will grapple with this puzzlement until the end. Rene Descartes, the French philosopher, and mathematician previously explored existence and the nature of reality by way of Plato to no avail, yet we continue to study their rationale. A responsible thought experiment is attempting to discover me. The ultimate question is will my results bring me closer to the illumination of my perennial question of *who I am*?

As I continue to parcel myself out into various social, biological, and psychological contexts, my identity will constantly be in flux. What I hope to unveil is my interpretation of my agency through the conception of who I am. This is a complicated biological fact of my character. My basic biological understanding is radically different than the emotional, intellectual, and social spaces I inhabit. My objective will be to interpolate between these various modalities of my being for my further identity development.

BLUESTOCKING SOCIETY 2.0

Our lives are shaped by our connections to each other, past and present.

I am interested in the lessons we can learn from the lives of the great creatives, people who exemplified the pursuit of mastery and embodied a bold point of view.

The concept of coming together and sharing ideas with like-minded people excites me. I have imagined gathering around an elongated wooden table with tapered candles flickering and a glass of red, robust *vino* in hand while deliberating the art of life and living. My invitees would be the provocative Gertrude Stein, an American writer of novels, poetry, and plays; Virginia Wolff, an English writer and one of the foremost thinkers of the twentieth century; and finally, the mystifying Anne Morrow Lindbergh, an author, aviator, and the wife of fellow flyer Charles Lindbergh. Each of these legendary women has left an imprint on my psyche. The stories they told make us question societal standards and challenge our sense of normality.

A few years back, I came across one of those words that just tingles the mind: bluestocking. I was immediately smitten with the term and subsequently, its meaning.

Bluestocking is an unusual word that brings different images to each of us. I decided to ask my friends and family for their instant impressions. One of my valued female friends thought of Christmas, while another believed it to mean blue panty hose. My teenage son was confident it was an elderly man with suspenders. They were all pragmatic answers, and it was entertaining to watch each person's reaction once the actual meaning was revealed. The definition provided by various sites on the web is: an intellectual or literary woman.

The word bluestocking came into existence in the mid-eighteenth century. A group of women in England decided to replace their customary evenings of idle chatter and card playing with "conversation parties." They would invite celebrated men of letters who would share their experiences in life and learning. This exposed the women to higher levels of thinking. A regular invitee named Benjamin Stillingfleet would wear his inexpensive, tattered, blue stockings to the meetings. This shocked the women since men generally wore black silk stockings. But these polite ladies looked beyond Mr. Stillingfleet's clothing choices. His lively conversation was their fundamental focus.

Countless individuals during this era considered it inappropriate for women to aspire to learning. These shortsighted people sarcastically began calling this learned circle of ladies "The Bluestocking Society," or so the story is told.

However the name was acquired, I applaud these women who were intent on having their intellectual and literary interests satisfied. A spark within me was ignited. My curiosity instantly took on a new sense of eagerness and enthusiasm. I wanted to mimic this meeting of minds by creating a similar concept.

I found my small community lacking venues for artistic and literary exchange. Or perhaps, I could not locate these groups within my social circles. What I did find was talk of fashion fads, parenting guidelines, and the vitriolic reality television digression. Yet while these trivial topics were discussed, my imagination would take me to that elongated table with the flicker of a candle, a glass of wine . . . I knew creative souls were out there. I needed to find them. To converse and construct together. To be daring and deep. To share similar storylines.

While raising my two sons, it became essential for me to find dynamic conversations. I wanted to inspire and be inspired. The idea of linking women together through shared experiences was my plan. I wanted to create a forum where we could gather and grow together, sit and search for solutions, relax and reflect while chatting about life, love or lunacy.

I was determined to start my own bluestocking society, with a modern twist. I would invite a "bluestocking" from the community to lead each discussion and share her life experiences to a group of interested ladies. I encouraged my friends to participate, and they called their friends to join this intimate social gathering. The objective was to have meaningful discussions about various topics and issues—something more than the typical kitchen table conversation. It quickly became a quarterly parlor series with a different topic on each occasion. This was not meant to be a lecture series.

The conversations hinged on individual strengths; they were "life talks" that provided information and camaraderie. I named the get-togethers *Living Legacies.* During each session of our parlor series, we learned from our foremothers' strengths and shortcomings.

Each *Living Legacy* parlor series provided a unique and authentic space for women to gather. The evening would begin with socializing while indulging in sweets and sipping a glass of wine or hot tea. I would warmly welcome our living legacy and the ladies in attendance. There were stories of resilience, personal triumph, survival, and the many joys inherent in each of our lives. We walked away mentally nurtured and energized by the life lessons everyone offered. It became a place to build a movement of shared understanding where relationships will grow, alliances will be forged, and ideas will be nurtured.

The idea of stories and sharing experiences is so simple and universal, yet it has become a lost art across generations. That is why the concept of women gathering and exchanging ideas must continue for centuries. You can create your own "bluestocking" society, and together we can inspire one another. Invite your own Gertrude Stein, Virginia Woolf, or Anne Morrow Lindbergh — trust me ... they are out there! The challenge is to find them. We creative women come in many styles and silhouettes. It is our passion, our drive, and our willingness to be different that stay consistent. In the spirit of our female predecessors, we need to celebrate nonconformity with our own versions of the bluestockings—The Bluestocking Society 2.0.

PERSONAL NARRATIVES

Stories that Shape Us

If *Self-Discovery* is about internal exploration, *Personal Narratives* ground those realizations in lived experience. These stories are the foundation—the moments that have shaped, tested, and compelled me to reexamine my beliefs. I share these individual experiences to establish context and create a space of relatability. My hope is that in these pages, you might see reflections of your own journey as well.

Our stories are where the soul meets the street. The following entries capture the messy, beautiful collisions of real life—family dynamics, exploring and understanding intergenerational identity, trauma breakthroughs, and the quiet moments that somehow leave the loudest echoes. Writing them was not always easy, but it was necessary. They are the threads that connect me to truth, to memory, and to the complex, ever-learning terrain of being human.

Parallel to this personal unraveling was my academic journey—an intellectual exploration of how technology is transforming the psychosocial experience of being human. As I studied the changing relationship between intelligence, identity, and innovation, I started to ask deeper questions: What happens to our sense of self in a world increasingly influenced by algorithms? How can we maintain agency, authenticity, and emotional integrity in a digital age?

This section reflects both the internal and academic sides—a mirror of my becoming. A woman learning to understand not only herself but also the world around her as it changes, and how to stay whole amidst that transformation.

HAPPY HEART, HELLRAISER!

For much of my life, I believed I was the flexible, accommodating person everyone liked, who fit neatly into any room, adjusted seamlessly to every expectation, and wore the "golden girl" label with quiet pride. Well, most of the time. I had invested so much of myself into this image that I convinced myself it was real, but the cracks began to show as I kept squeezing wisdom out of life. It wasn't that I lacked good qualities or authenticity; it was just that this version of myself wasn't whole. And as life's pressures and truths collided, that carefully constructed illusion shattered. Suddenly, all my unfinished business, my raw edges, unmet desires, and unspoken fears were exposed vividly in living Technicolor. Not just to me, but to everyone around me.

Many times, I've wrestled with being labeled a hellraiser and hurricane.

But could they be happy ones? Could these titles reflect more than just chaos and disruption? Could they capture moments of authenticity and growth?

The words hellraiser and hurricane held allure and accusation, an odd mix of pride and guilt. But the truth is, I've always felt a pull toward this paradoxical path that blazes with intensity and sometimes leaves a little chaos in its wake. This isn't about being reckless for the sake of it; it's about living with unapologetic authenticity, even when that means unsettling the status quo or stepping on the toes of convention.

For a long time, I questioned what it meant to carry joy in one hand and disruption in the other. Was it selfish to walk my truth if it sometimes broke hearts, including my own? Or was it brave—necessary even—to ignite the fires that lead to meaningful change? I've come to believe it's both. Living this way means confronting the uncomfortable, leaning into the storms I stir, and finding clarity through the mess. It requires me to take responsibility for my impact on others while refusing to shrink or silence my voice.

In my journey, there have been moments of laughter that lit up entire rooms and connections that cut straight to the soul. There have also been stumbles—when the fires I kindled burned too hot, leaving ashes where I'd hoped for warmth. Through it all, I've learned that to be a happy hellraiser is not about inflicting pain but about radical self-honesty and embracing both the joy and the consequences of walking my own path.

I'm learning to balance this role, striving to bring more love, compassion, and growth into the storms I create. I'm also learning that it's not my job to carry others' expectations or to brew the tea that keeps everyone happy. That burden was never mine to bear. And in the end, perhaps that's the heart of it: finding happiness in stirring things up but knowing when to bring peace. It's a stance that takes courage, tenderness, and a relentless desire to keep growing. Maybe it's not for everyone, but it's the only way I know to live fully and with all my heart.

MY TRAUMA TAUGHT ME . . .

One day I woke up different. It had been a long time in the making forty-seven years to be exact! Years of over-functioning for others together with compassion fatigue forced me to reevaluate my sense of self. Well, maybe a few therapy sessions helped, too! I was officially finished trying to figure out who was on my side, against me, or who was walking warily down the middle because they did not have the guts to pick a side. I was done with anything that did not bring me peace or pleasure. The damaging people in my life were given tighter boundaries or purged. Their negative energy would no longer infect my peace, nor would I allow their bitterness to penetrate my positivity.

Awakening to trauma is painful and scary. For me, it has been an isolating experience. Feeling the feelings and not becoming the emotions is harder said than done. When I began my healing journey, it was almost overwhelming to see how trauma manifested everywhere in society, mainly within my family system is where I saw it front and center. I continue to witness my trauma, allow it to be present then release it without judgment. This process of reconciling my resentment started to change my life. To be honest, it was not just one day that gave me hope to move past the generational gook. It was a collection of days that forced me to see through the darkness and allow my light to triumph. Realizing life is too short of leaving the key to my happiness in someone else's pocket was a delightful feeling.

Trauma is an intelligent process. It took time to understand its impact on me and my actions toward myself and others. I believe we all can relearn and unlearn our past behaviors. I try to describe the effects of trauma is when our inner emotional world becomes the outer emotional world. Which often leads to hurt, traumatized people hurting and traumatizing people. The fragmented worlds of emotion we live in are invisible forces. The nature of trauma is multifaceted. This inner and social disconnect or dislocation of psychosocial integration is what I want to explore further, both in myself and its effects on others.

With my continued research toward my dissertation in the field of epigenetics and inheritance of trauma, I have been introduced to leading experts. One of them being Dr. Gabor Mate, a palliative care physician who devotes his energies to addicted men and women. Watching a documentary recently on the Wisdom of Trauma with Dr. Gabor Mate and other experts in the field such as Thomas Hubl, I learned that trauma causes us to live in survival mode. A hypervigilant state where we are 'looking over our shoulder' always believing people are out to hurt us equating to a lack of self-trust.

Both Mate and Hubl talk about trauma and recognize it is a colossal and complex dilemma. Having abandonment issues and dealing with the death of a parent at a very young age has caused suffering in ways I could not have imagined. Yet, I became adept at masking and ignoring the pain; outrunning or pretending it did not affect me.

To heal from trauma, we must learn how to trust ourselves again, return to our bodies, and forgive ourselves for what we did while we were in survival mode. I will continue to explore my journey with trauma and the disconnect we face in the realm of pseudo-connectivity in our technological age. Our society fails to talk about trauma and what drives people into addiction and emotional pain. We live through a time when there is a desperate need to escape the isolation and dismay of our daily lives.

I entered and found safety in my fictional town of Numbville in the hope of finding solace from my imbalanced feelings. This place I escaped to avoid the desperate feeling of dismay in my daily life. As the highs and lows of my life felt overwhelming. The inside and outside noises around me dulled when I was in my place of refuge. No one bothered me in Numbville. I would watch the world and all its players like a variety show. My limited participation in life was half-hearted like never being fully alive in my own body. I found comfort, safety and security staying within the confines of this walled city I concocted.

Healing our collective trauma is a process that will take time and energy. I am hopeful that my journey of integrating my intergenerational and cultural wounds will be an example for others to follow. For the longest time, I felt my muddled mind was mental illness, yet this could be a genetic flaw from my father and mother. I also learned that parents who generate trauma were traumatized themselves, repeating the cycle they once learned as children. I will delve deeper into this when I discuss the epigenetics and inheritance of trauma biologically.

For example, I had a father who was an angry alcoholic who abused my mother while intoxicated. My mother was emotionless and lacked the parental tools to give me love and attention. What my trauma has taught me is that my parents did not intend to traumatize me. Both my parents did the best they could with the level of awareness they had at the time. As I continue to uncover the underlying dynamics of both individual and collective trauma, I will heal not only my own deepest wounds but access my higher potential not to allow transmission of this trauma for future generations. To me, that is a beautiful thing trauma taught me.

HEALING HAPPENS WITH CONNECTION AND CHANGE

Within my research, I continue to reveal how being trauma-informed is vital for your relationship with yourself but with all your interactions. This wave of information has stirred many ripples through my shared ocean of awareness with all those pertinent in my life.

Understanding my trauma has given me the strength to continue my voyage of learning, investigating, and healing trauma not only in my mind and body but to have an awareness of the need to heal trauma in social structures and the world around me. I hold a vision of a world that breaks free of the cycle of trauma and becomes more open and inclusive. Yet, I honestly realize it starts with me.

As I have allowed my wounds to teach me about listening, self-love, and compassion toward myself and my past, it has also reminded me of the preciousness of life and those I love. My truth has opened my heart and, by osmosis, the heart of my husband, Tim. Together this innate wisdom is starting to shine through both our wounds. Healing happens in connection. For the past twenty-four years, our relationship has been a safe space for me to grow, evolve, and authentically express myself. For that, I thank my good-natured hubs. I truly believe one of a couple's goals should be where both people work to heal childhood trauma and feel completely free to express what they think, feel and need.

A form of love language is having empathy toward your partner's trauma. Relationships scared me growing up. I did not trust that those close to me would not hurt me. This is because those close to me did hurt me growing up. My father died when I was eleven. My mother abandoned me soon after by marrying a man who verbally abused me, my mother, and sister and who once tried to physically attack me. I was never afraid of him and always fought back.

This early trauma inhibited my development and did not promote vulnerability. I entered survival mode, and my nervous system was always in fight and flight. This hyperarousal became an ongoing pattern until I accepted how unhealthy it became for my mental and physical well-being. When I had children in my mid-twenties, I recognized and began healing this transgenerational trauma I had been carrying for years.

The unconditional love that I was not offered was something I desperately wanted to give my children. I did not want them to have the unhealthy interior structure I carried into my adult development and form a portion of their identity that I did, emotionally distance myself from those who loved me. Cue Tim. My kindhearted husband was not there to just make me happy. Instead, he provided a safe space and a relationship opportunity to grow, evolve, and authentically express myself without judgment. He listened to my plight and related in ways I would learn later that were similar. He trusted my parenting process despite his broken family system. We were committed to breaking the trauma cycle.

The more of our past Tim and I carry into the present, the less available we are for connectedness. We wanted to reciprocate and healthily resonate with our children. Without empathy and understanding of our pain, we would more likely project our interior conditions onto each other and our children. Our collective trauma awareness as a couple has been a gift that continues to give not only to ourselves but to future generations. Therefore, this transgenerational shift has helped us both to reset ourselves back to our innate sense of individual wholeness, despite the myriads of circumstances both of us were born into. What a great way to make inner harmony and build a perennial healing bridge for our two sons.

BRIDGING THE BURN

I knew what I needed to do. I had to enter deeply into the roots of the *I am* to learn the reasons for my resentment. I longed to experience happiness and this profound awareness of the terrain of my interior world. People around me were not on the same journey. This is where the resentment started to seep in. The powerful pull of me talking through my trauma was not only healing but altered the course of my life. I profoundly grew, and this changed me.

Now that I found myself on the precipice of a new me, I wanted to offer possibilities to others on how they, too, can shed light on their dark. I was excited to share my ways, and we together could directly address generational and cultural traumas to heal ourselves and those broken family systems we all came from. Well, not so fast—people I realized don't like change.

Your negative energy will not infect my peace; hopefully, my positive energy will rearrange your misery. I saw this meme on the internet and smiled. Recently, I am learning how to reconcile my resentment.

After years of over-functioning due to my childhood trauma and abandonment, the overzealous feeling to be needed and loved by others is done. I am finished with my people-pleasing behavior. My therapist told me I have compassion fatigue. Is that a thing? I always felt if I can overcome my darkness, why can't everyone else? I can help them. I can only love and help myself. They have to do the work to heal their own wounds.

What I have learned is that some people just don't know anything different than to be miserable. They've been doing the same thing for so long that doing something new is foreign. I have tried for years to aid those who can't seem to find their way out of the dark, to no avail.

After attempting to show them through my own experiences that change doesn't cause any relief at first, but rather an upheaval and discomfort to what we are used to. It does not look attractive as self-work, rather hard work. To rid the negativity, I had to learn where it came from— internal dissatisfaction.

The change will shake everything we know apart. People don't like change. For me, evolution has allowed me to grow and expand. It has taken time for me to become ok with not being liked. Despite my loving or kindhearted nature, I finally understand that I cannot please my way into collective acceptance. My real ray of sunshine does not affect them as they are used to the rain. Being okay with shining regardless of their dark cloud status is my challenge.

As I am learning to cheer those who do not embrace change in any way, I also notice their little successes and remind them that they will and can snowball into real change eventually, if they choose. My resentment has come in many forms, but I will save that for another time, or maybe my 'tell-all' memoir. What I can share in a general sense is the pacing of progress for others has been my Achilles heel. Others' pacing has painful for me to watch, as I want them to level up, and when they don't, I run interference. This rescuer mode is wrong, not healthy and has caused compassion fatigue.

Those days are dwindling. It takes time to undo my past of why I felt the need to people-please and have expectations of others. I hold myself to high standards and life has forced me to level up, so I expect everyone else to. This thinking is selfish. Understanding my past played a significant role in this dysfunctional behavior. It is not up to me to save anyone but only myself. If they don't choose to, *all I can be* is a role model from a distance, as they see the efforts I make to attain contentment with my chaos. They make their own choices. *All I can do* is shine my light and not allow their misery to infect my peace. This is easier said than done.

In reality, by reconciling my resentment I have learned the best lesson. Other people changing or even liking me for my Pollyanna ways is a bonus. Me accepting my messy self is the real prize.

HOW TO HANDLE?

From the moment I opened my eyes each morning, I found myself slipping into the role of caretaker for too many years to count, not just for my husband, but for my children, now ages twenty-four and twenty-five, my mother, and my sister. Mothering became second nature, extending far beyond its intended boundaries. I nurtured, soothed, mended, and protected.

Often, at the cost of my own needs and identity as I took on the emotional and physical burdens of everyone around me. But was this my fault? Or was it learned behavior passed down through generations?

For me, healing has been vital. I have been deconstructing myself for the last twenty years, mainly after the children were born, around the ages of two and three, as I realized there were some behaviors from my past that I did not like. As an advocate of breaking generational curses, I have gone against my bloodlines and those of my husbands to heal from the trauma, so my children never have to. They should not have to carry my extra baggage; they will have their own. Prioritizing my family before myself has taken an emotional toll, but someone wise once told me, "You know you have a big heart when you feel bad for doing what is best for you."

Another part of my problem is that my delivery may not always be gentle when addressing the situation, but I always attempt to acknowledge their perspectives. They may feel uncomfortable or defensive about past behaviors, so they prefer not to revisit the issues. My mother, in her defense, has been open to feedback and engaging in difficult conversations. My sister often forgets her behavior, which she often blames on me, as being overly critical and constantly dwelling on the past. I am always intrigued by people who do not own their own behavior.

My husband has always been a unique case, as it took time for him to finally acknowledge the past pain caused, as he wasn't interested in having conversations about it (probably living in Numbville, too), which doesn't work for me or a partnership.

But how do I stop my enabling and mothering? I don't want to rupture relationships that mean so much to me, yet I can no longer continue in this role that has bred resentment and frustration. It's a delicate balance that requires careful consideration and honest communication. Let me explain how I arrived at this crossroads and what steps I am taking to redefine these relationships more healthily.

First, let's start with my two twenty-something sons, who have developed high emotional intelligence and a deep understanding of accountability and communication. They navigate their relationships by talking through problems, paying attention to others' needs, and staying aware of their roles in these interactions. They know who they are as individuals and don't rely on others to build them up, avoiding the need to needle or seek validation from those around them. Additionally, they are excellent listeners, always present and engaged in our conversations, making our interactions meaningful and supportive.

Trust me, they have imperfections—we all do. However, I am trying to make the point that my sons view life through a lens that is larger than their world. They possess an innate ability to make others feel seen and heard, engaging with people in a way that transcends self-interest. Despite their flaws, their capacity to genuinely connect with and understand those around them is something I deeply admire.

On the other hand, my mother and sister seem to struggle to be themselves. They often adopt the behaviors of those around them, as if seeking validation or direction externally rather than finding it within themselves. This tendency contrasts with how my sons navigate the world, making my role in these relationships more complicated and, at times, burdensome.

I have struggled with each, feeling the weight of trying to prop each of them up and defend them for most of our relationships. In my efforts to support my mom, sister, and husband, I often found myself taking on responsibilities that weren't mine, becoming the emotional anchor, they seemed unable to be for themselves. This dynamic has been exhausting and left me questioning how to continue in these roles without losing myself. The personal toll has been, in part, a choice I made, one rooted in a desire to help and protect them.

However, untangling myself from these roles has been a significant challenge, especially when trying to do so without undermining their character. I want to step back and allow them to stand independently, but finding the balance between supporting them and maintaining my well-being is proving difficult.

Over the last few years, the logical next step involved setting more significant and better boundaries with my mom and sister and holding myself accountable to these new limits. This process has been in progress, and after plenty of uncomfortable conversations, I believe they both now understand where I stand moving forward. This headway has brought a sense of relief and clarity, at least to me. However, it leaves me with the challenge of addressing the dynamic with my husband and navigating our marriage moving forward.

For far too many years, I allowed the same hurtful behaviors to continue, speaking out about the injustices but accepting minimal consequences. I carried the weight of these burdens to protect my children from the dysfunction of my husband's family and the unresolved issues he has yet to face, and maybe never will, it's his choice and journey. My priority was always keeping our family together, especially after losing my father at eleven and experiencing my mother's emotional abandonment when she remarried a narcissist who was verbally abusive toward both of us. After four years of marriage, I encouraged my mom to divorce him, along with support from other family members.

However, now that I am on a healing journey and have taken the time to process my experiences with the help of a therapist, I have written a life review that has brought me new clarity. I understand the importance of recognizing and reconciling past pain, as it naturally comes into our current relationships. This has happened with my husband; his unresolved wounds from how his parents have affected his relationship with me and our children. I can no longer be his lighthouse, guiding him through his darkness, because this dynamic has created an imbalance in our relationship. While he wants to ignore and not revisit his past transgressions toward me, I need him to acknowledge how they show up in different forms.

I'm at a crossroads because I'm unsure how to handle this situation. My husband doesn't want to relive the past, even though the same behaviors resurface differently. When I address these issues, he becomes defensive, accusing me of living in the past instead of focusing on the future, where he wants to evolve and move forward. It's a tricky balance, wishing to heal and grow together but feeling stuck in a cycle that can't be broken without acknowledging the unresolved pain.

The crux of the situation at hand is the tension between my desire to address past issues and my husband's focus on the future as I continue to struggle to help him understand that one cannot fully engage in an emotionally intelligent relationship without first dealing with the pain from one's past. He doesn't see that his behaviors often mimic those of his childhood role models, patterns that have gone unresolved for too long.

I can no longer keep "teaching him" how to navigate the emotional dynamics with those around him, including what I need from him. It's exhausting to be the one continually guiding him when I need a partner willing to confront and heal from his wounds instead of avoiding the work and leaving me to do the heavy lifting.

We have had countless heartfelt conversations, and he understands how I feel and my wish to no longer hold onto his feelings or anyone else's as we move into the future, only to act out of love and accountability. I will stop self-abandoning and seeking their approval or acceptance. If they want to connect with me emotionally, they must participate, put in the effort, and stop engaging in emotionally immature behaviors. The internal work is tough but fulfilling.

As I stand at this juncture in our marriage, I realize that the path forward requires us to actively engage in the work necessary to heal and grow. I can no longer bear the weight of doing it alone, nor can I ignore the impact the unresolved past pain has on our present. It's time for both of us to step up, confront our respective histories, and rebuild our relationship on a foundation of mutual understanding and emotional intelligence. This is how I need to handle my frustration by setting clear boundaries, insisting on shared responsibility, and ensuring that we contribute equally to the emotional work required to truly move forward as equal partners rather than remaining stuck in the patterns that have kept us apart.

STILL SEARCHING… LONGING FOR ANSWERS!

Fair warning: the thoughts in my mind often spill onto the page. In them, I find myself caught between two worlds—capitalism and death—struggling to understand what it means to be alive and truly living. I have one foot grounded in logic, acknowledging the fragility of the body and the mysteries of the mind. The other reaches for something more, something unseen but undeniably felt, while recognizing that even the space I need to write is sustained by the currency of this world. I live with quiet conviction in my values and a sense of confusion about life's mysteries, yet I believe this keeps me humble and drives my ongoing growth.

Can this be the whole story of humanity?

My father died when I was eleven. He was only thirty. That loss opened my eyes to a world most children never have to see. It wasn't just the grief, it was the confusion of it all, how someone so lively could... disappear. I learned early that life isn't guaranteed, and love, no matter how pure, can't always save you.

After he died, I needed a mother who could hold my pain and reassure me that even though the world had fallen apart, *I was still safe*. But she couldn't. She had her own unspoken fears and her own broken pieces. She never quite found the confidence to be herself, so how could she model that for me? So, I became that for myself. Protector. Performer. Provider of comfort… for others, primarily. Because when you're not seen, you learn to be *useful*. You figure out how to read a room before entering, to fill in every emotional gap, to be the strong one, the funny one, the capable one. Even if no one ever asks you to be.

And now I find myself fifty-one years into this human journey, with a body that holds both wisdom and weariness, and a heart that's become more tender, not tougher, over time. I learned early on that my thoughts could consume me; so, I began writing, and when I felt uninspired, I would read. Both writing and reading have been two sides of the same coin for me, helping me understand that words have the power to both drain and replenish my mind. They offer a balance during times of chaos and calm that swirl within and around me. I continue to trust the process of expressing and discovering myself, as it always guides me back to who I am and helps me make sense of the world around me.

I continue to recognize and acknowledge that my journey of self-expression unfolds within the system of capitalism, an imperfect system, yet one that provides me the space to step back and rediscover who I am, as well as the room to explore my inner world. Capitalism and its framework have kept me captive, chasing, and consuming until I faced the one truth I could not escape: we have no idea what happens after death. I've learned to play the game, perform roles, meet expectations, and climb the ladder. Yet, the more I achieved, the emptier I felt. No title, house, or handbag ever filled the part of me that yearned for *meaning*— for the soul, for the kind of fulfillment that comes from being, not *having*. Consumerism both traps and liberates, creating a tension that I've learned to live with.

As I remain in the hive of busyness, caught up in commerce and the currency of survival, death also keeps me on the edge of everything, humbling me with its unknowable horizon. The market and moments beyond price will always coexist within me, nourishing each other in quiet reciprocity. The few moments that cannot be bought and that sustain me are:

- The gentle, sacred act of mothering.
- Love has both fed and carried me through moments that money could never buy.
- The excitement of arriving in a new country and realizing I know nothing, yet everything that matters is universal.

- The electric connection of randomly meeting someone who also wants more from life, who refuses to sleepwalk through it, who questions what they're told and who they're told to be.
- Nature soothes my soul with its healing rhythms, textures, and untamed spirit.
- The act of reading and writing, which offers a power of pause.

I don't mean to suggest that I have a perfect plan or a flawless idea of the afterlife. I was raised from Kindergarten through 12th grade to believe in God and the Lutheran faith, wearing monogrammed sweaters and reciting scripture in chapel. But by high school, I was already getting in trouble for asking too many questions — questions that made adults uncomfortable. The kind that revealed cracks in certainty and chipped away at the polished surface of doctrine. I wanted to believe, but I also wanted to *understand.* And no one seemed to have the patience-or the answers, for that kind of hunger.

So, I kept searching. Not just for answers, but for something deeper…. for *more.*

And that's what I mean when I say I don't believe this is it. I don't mean heaven as real estate in the clouds. I mean the *next level* of the game—a level where collaboration replaces competition.

Where interaction doesn't spark conflict but curiosity. Where agency is not rebellion, but a birthright. In this "more," there is no passing down of behavior issues or inner decay through generations. There is only the quiet joy of growth and breaking free from past pain. Not because you're forced or broken, but because you *want* to be more. And that desire, that hunger for growth, is the force that keeps this higher realm together.

Sometimes I wonder if Earth is just a testing ground for something greater. A tough proving space for souls that feel there's something better waiting—not as a prize, but as a return. Not forward, not backward, but *deeper...* and ongoing despite the tension of death, taxes, and uncertainty.

Maybe those of us who feel the ache most, who grieve loudly and love even louder, are the ones remembering. Maybe the future is calling us back. And maybe this longing... it isn't emptiness at all. Maybe it's a memory, or perhaps it's me being a lifelong learner and an amateur scribbler with insatiable curiosity and interest in what I don't know.

MY NEXT CHAPTER

As I finish my last week at Union Institute and University, graduating with a Master of Science in Organizational Leadership, I reflect and smile. My curiosity has always led me to explore the nature of existence, the human heart and its depth, and the mind and its malleability. I have worked in the corporate realm, culinary world, nonprofit sector, and as a freelance writer. Still, a puzzle piece has been missing. Obtaining my master's degree has helped me strategize and visualize my next subject of study. The knowledge I have obtained, coupled with hands-on learning experiences and research, leaves me wanting to further my education on the fundamentals of technology and its advances that affect humanity.

Next stop: Gonzaga University! Starting September 1, 2020, I enter the Leadership Studies doctoral program and confront questions of humanity with critical thought and moral conviction. However, to begin, I have had to accept that this journey is an ultra-marathon. I will be fine-tuning my normal operating procedure. Embracing my ambition while modifying my behavior in brevity is what this next chapter looks like. Considering my typical sprinter style, the next four-year journey will influence my standard strategy and approach. One of life's ironies is how things can happen when you aren't paying attention. Well, my life philosophy is slowly shapeshifting into, "It's a journey, not a destination," as I keep discovering many things I have done in my life were "endpoints versus experiences."

Intellectual stimulation has always been an emotional experience for me, and something will only be a deeply emotional experience for me if it engages me intellectually as well. I relish information that offers insight into human nature and expands my mind. Gonzaga's mission aligns with my approach, and this excites me. I seek to gain knowledge, impart it to others, and glean new insights in return. As a lifelong learner, I believe education is a multi-dimensional approach. The information collected is not only for an individual's advancement, but also for influencing others and society as a whole. As a researcher and graduate student who relishes knowledge, I am eager to educate others on the impact of artificial intelligence (AI) and how our actions and inaction toward it will alter future frameworks.

Please join me on the journey, as I offer insights into my own quest on how to slow down and change course. As I gradually reclaim personal perspective, together with bringing an awareness on how our collective humanity and emotional intelligence relates to technology. My future posts will investigate the benefits, risks and responsibilities that come with machine learning and AI. I will explore the promise and peril of AI and ruminate on what I learn while obtaining my PhD.

DECONSTRUCTING DISCONTENT

I discussed the abstract with Dr. Jeannot in my PhD program at Gonzaga University. The weekly lectures always addressed several highlights based on readings in our Ethics and Leadership class. Which is forcing me to think about my continual yearning to "question everything."

The core principle of philosophy is to find meaning in life. Past and present philosophers have offered refreshing ideas on how to live a happy and good life. My esoteric professor was never concerned with technical concepts or strategies for leadership or development but instead categorized our thoughts into thinking more critically. His messaging is a covert dissecting of our daily behavior. At the same time, he catalyzed the conversation for us to cognize the meaning of our valued insights on life and happiness, death, society, and the universe.

The idea of questioning everything can seem strange. It can also aggravate when applied to a child who won't stop asking "why?" However, my inner five-year-old will not succumb to adulthood and continues to poke and prod. My twenty-five-year-old son finds my behavior exhausting at the dinner table.

I can't help myself. It should be a general requirement to ask questions as we go through our everyday lives. There is hope that the answers may offer a new, refreshing perspective and way to live. The point of continually asking questions is not necessarily to find answers. Often, when I ask and receive an answer, it generates more questions. Yet, this is when I believe we genuinely begin to understand something.

Let's look at life. The goal of school (this course) was television shows, documentaries, books, songs, podcasts, and anything else that conveys information about a subject matter. It is the idea of storytelling. Which is, ultimately, answering a question that may or may not have been explicitly asked, but it is a response nonetheless.

Questions have a place in every aspect of human existence, from how long I bake chickens to the square root of twenty. They can be ridiculous or meaningful, simple or tricky; yet either way, they are a vehicle that allows information to be transferred from one person to another.

Questions can create breakthroughs or devastate relationships. Asking questions can often give answers but will always give just a little more than that.

To question is to consider. To consider lends toward understanding. Therefore, by asking everything, I am looking to gain a better understanding of everything. Many people may agree that understanding things in general is good. Many ancient philosophers believed that death was the end of human consciousness. Some believed in the afterlife or immortality, and many did not. They all agreed that our minds are temporary forms that will one day break down. We must acknowledge our interconnection with each other. If we take more time to ask questions, we can learn from each other, which is a rational approach to me.

I believe we each create and control our destiny—the values we place on how to get there change based on the individual. My inner drive for inquiry is partly to pursue personal greatness and partially to overcome suffering and weaker traits by learning from others. Hardship is what molds our character and makes us better. For me, dissecting the pain in my life creates meaning. The secret to life is how to obtain happiness. My discontent is still being deconstructed.

Stay tuned on how I handle that difficulty moving forward.

THE HUMAN RECOVERY PROJECT

How can we reclaim ourselves in the digital age?

I think about this often. As technology accelerates, shaping our behaviors, interactions, and even our sense of self, I find myself questioning: *Are we losing touch with what it means to be human? Are we unconsciously trading depth for convenience, connection for illusion, and self-awareness for algorithmic influence?*

Through my own self-guided research—beyond the structured walls of academia—I continue to explore the profound intersection of identity, technology, and trauma. I am particularly interested in how digitization influences not only our individual psyches but also the transgenerational transmission of trauma.

How much of our emotional inheritance is being reshaped by this constant digital immersion? Are we healing, or are we simply numbing in more sophisticated ways?

To be human is to seek understanding of ourselves, of others, and of the ever-evolving world around us. Storytelling has long been a vehicle for this understanding, offering us windows into one another's inner worlds. When we share our stories, we grant access to our vulnerabilities, our histories, and the very essence of what makes us human. But as the digital world continues its relentless expansion, we must ask: *are we losing access to ourselves?*

The rapid acceleration of technology is reshaping identity at a fundamental level. While digitization has granted us unprecedented access to knowledge, connection, and self-expression, it has also altered the ways in which we experience reality. It influences not just how we communicate, but how we process emotions, how we form relationships, and how we heal or fail to heal from the generational traumas that have long shaped us. The question is no longer whether technology is changing us, but how and whether we are conscious enough to guide that transformation in a way that benefits humanity rather than diminishes it.

One of the most concerning effects of this shift is the increasing detachment from our emotional landscapes. We have built a world of instant gratification and algorithmically curated experiences, where distraction is endless and deep introspection is optional. The mind, overstimulated and overwhelmed, often retreats not into reflection, but into avoidance. As a result, we have seen the rise of what I call *Numbville,* an internalized psychological refuge where we escape to avoid dismay, disappointment, and discomfort. It is a state of being that, on the surface, feels like self-preservation but ultimately erodes our ability to connect, to feel, and to process the deeper existential questions that define our humanity.

This phenomenon is compounded by the transgenerational transmission of trauma, both personal and collective. Trauma is not just experienced; it is inherited, encoded into our very biology, shaping our neurological responses and psychological frameworks. But when this trauma is processed through a world increasingly detached from embodied human experience, where the digital self-eclipses the physical, it creates an unprecedented challenge: we are carrying the wounds of the past without the emotional tools to heal them.

Instead of facing our pain, we scroll past it. Instead of wrestling with discomfort, we filter it. Instead of engaging with complexity, we reduce it to soundbites and reactionary debates.

What, then, does it mean to reclaim our humanity in this era?

The *Human Recovery Project* is my dissertation attempt and effort to explore this critical question. It is an inquiry into how the interplay of trauma and technology is shapeshifting our identity—biologically, psychologically, and socially—across generations. It is a call to consciousness, a blueprint for re-engagement with the self, and a reexamination of how we can move forward in a way that fosters both individual and collective well-being.

To advance, not just ourselves, but humanity, we must first recognize that healing cannot happen in a vacuum. Just as trauma is transmitted across generations, so too is resilience. The key lies in creating spaces that allow for deeper reflection, meaningful discourse, and the intentional reintegration of emotional intelligence into our digital lives. We must develop practices that tether us back to our physical experiences, movement, nature, storytelling, and face-to-face connection while simultaneously harnessing the best of technology to facilitate healing rather than hinder it.

Humanity is at a crossroads. We can either continue numbing ourselves, further detaching from the richness of our existence, or we can actively participate in our own recovery. The choice is not just individual; it is collective. It is about redefining what it means to be fully alive in an age that increasingly tempts us toward disconnection. It is about remembering that technology should serve humanity, not replace it.

Our stories, our experiences, our traumas, and our triumphs are the raw materials of identity. But if we are not careful, we risk becoming strangers to ourselves. The challenge ahead is not just to navigate the digital age, but to do so while remaining deeply, authentically, and unapologetically human.

PEOPLE MATTER

The world is changing.

Whether you think our current COVID-19 crisis is an overblown hoax or the great equalizer of modern society, we can't deny this crisis has suddenly and dramatically altered the state of our lives.

So what do you do? How are you coping? What does social distancing mean to you? Are you sheltering in place?

This short narrative is not meant to be an antidote for collective helplessness and/or further confusion, but rather a message of comfort to our collective human fragility. During these tumultuous times, I often think of my friend Clara Knopfler, who is under mandatory lockdown in the assisted living community where she lives. Clara survived the Holocaust with her mother. She chronicled in her book, *I Am Still Here: My Mother's Voice,* accounts and pieces of her past.

I have been fortunate to observe firsthand how Clara is slowly healing the world with her message of hope. Her mission is to educate others, advising everyone around her to be aware of what is happening in the world. She captures the attention of each person she meets with her stories of survival. I spoke with her a few days ago and her hopefulness is contagious.

Hope can also counterweight the heavy sense of our relationship with the unknown. We hope, precisely because we are aware that terrible outcomes do happen. Everything is possible and often probable, whether it is good or bad. However, the decisions we make impact our desired outcomes.

Can a cosmic timeout offer insight into the miracle of our reality?

Maybe I am overreaching but it does intrigue me on how easily the evolution of our existence can be taken away. It is a choice to understand our capacity to transcend suffering. We can find true freedom and survive trying times by not only helping ourselves, but others. When we begin to explore how easily we imprison ourselves in our own minds, the healing begins. As we look within during this public health crisis we are living through, let's understand and pay attention to the signs being shown to us find freedom from our muddled minds.

Life is both beautiful and bittersweet. Our physiological precariousness to our survival can be sobering. We are forced to learn how to be vulnerable in order to keep our sanity. Thank goodness for technology and its ability to globally connect everyone.

How lost and alone would we feel if our devices were "timed out" too?

Our unique human paradox is living more empowered lives with those we love, even in the craziest circumstances. As we feel our way through this new era, when both hope and fear are at a global high. Let's never forget what Clara endured.

An ornamental plaque perched up on her desk reads *Learn from the past. Live for the moment. Hope for the future.* We must regularly remind ourselves to recognize the love, wisdom, beauty and truth in all people—during times of chaos and crisis.

MY INNER STORYTELLER

The weight of this journey, this habit of carrying others' expectations and bending to their needs, left me on the edge of something resembling ruins. My soul felt cracked and bruised from years of being contorted and reshaped. I reached a point where I could no longer keep up the facade. The demands of being someone to everyone had robbed me of being true to myself.

And now, on the verge of a comeback—a return not to what I was but to who I truly am—I face an unexpected obstacle: my old identity, the very version of me that has weathered so much to feel loved, valued, and needed. It clings to me, insisting I stay where I am, whispering that this is where I belong, that I can't possibly change now. There's comfort in the familiar, even when that comfort comes with chains.

Yet I know this shift will ripple through my relationships. As I shed the layers of what others have known me to be, I recognize that some may feel unsettled or threatened by this change. The balance of those connections may falter as I let go of the parts of myself that once catered to others at my own expense. Some relationships may evolve with me, while others may resist, and in this transition, I'm learning to accept that I can't control how others will respond. I can no longer silence these fiery feelings that have grown fiercer and fuller.

But in this moment of reckoning, I feel an undeniable pull to shed that skin. Deep within me, a voice continues to call out, urging me to stop fighting myself and start honoring the part that knows I am enough just as I am. To have a bright and true future, I must relinquish the weight of others' expectations and trust that my own will carry me where I need to go.

This is my swan song, a final bow to the version of me that once served a purpose but now holds me back. The path forward requires courage, not to be more than I am, but to be exactly who I am. So, I let go of the need to be everything to everyone, and in doing so, I am finally free to become fully, unapologetically, myself for my own good and for the future self who deserves to live untethered.

STRIPPING THE SOUL

My first introduction to Bell Hooks was nearly twenty years ago when I read her book *Feminism for Everybody.* I was captivated by her sharp intelligence and sincerity regarding how patriarchal culture prevents men from understanding themselves and connecting with their feelings.

This inspiring book and Hook's words helped me find the language not only to guide my husband in expressing his feelings. It sparked a fire in me to raise my two sons with empathy and the understanding to hold onto the core truth of who they are in a world where social norms and male dominance are taught to oppress and control. It took me years to discover my feminine identity while patriarchy swirled around my personal and professional life. Authors like Bell Hooks provide a path for amateur writers like me to feel valued, and to believe that my ideas are worth writing down.

Gloria Jean Watkins, who writes under the pen name Bell Hooks as a tribute to her grandmother Bell Blair Hooks, shows how to be a clear, easy-to-understand writer. Her writing is compelling, and as she reminds us, "there are writers who write because we need to make sense of the world we live in; writing is a way to clarify, to interpret, to reinvent." Yes, Ms. Hooks, I could not agree more.

I respect how Bell Hooks does not avoid difficult conversations.

Writing has transformed her, allowing this lively woman to uncover something new about herself. Hooks has taught me to focus on discovering my identity through writing and using my words to break free from my shadow self. I like when she writes, "My granddaddy would say there is light in the darkness, you just have to find it." Like Hooks, I also kept a diary when I was growing up. As she states,

"This record of confession brought me face to face with the shadow self, the one we spend a lifetime avoiding."

I read the chapter "Writing from the Darkness" and highlighted many of her sayings. The first was "It was though I lived in a constant state of siege" . . . a process of unmasking, stripping the soul, making me feel naked and vulnerable. Even though the experience was cleansing and redemptive," she goes on to share how writing was a "therapeutic process of retrospective self-examination and an engagement of critical self-reflection."

In short, this American author, professor, feminist, and social activist is dedicated to restoring people and transforming systems through her words. I am inspired to continue my journey in this Ph.D. program, utilizing the framework from my research and the insights of the excellent writers and critical thinkers I continue to read each semester.

AN IMPERFECT PARADOX!

I live in two different worlds. One, which I consider my traditional world, is where I share with others and is not separate from them. The other is my isolated and imaginative world, where many creative acts of craziness happen.

Ultimately, this duality of my worlds is intimately and intricately connected. They converge. They merge. They propel me into chaotic states with lofty thoughts and questions. A bifurcation of brilliance valuing the dichotomy of me.

With plenty of my questions going unanswered, I continue to contemplate and consider the why, what, and how. This desire to cultivate my curiosity and quest for a deeper understanding of life's meaning separates me from wanting to participate in the mundane and familiar.

How do I learn to live out this delicate dance and intermingle my madness within a traditional world? If I knew the answer, you would not be reading this.

My mind is a mysterious machine. My condition is a conundrum. My circumstance leaves me frustrated. I relish silence yet require the noise of modern life. An imperfect paradox.

A new acquaintance recently asked me if I am an introvert or extrovert; I couldn't tell, they said. Does it really matter? I wondered. Whether I'm social or anti-social, or if I prefer being around people or alone, I flip-flop between both. I'd say I'm a social introvert. I enjoy hanging out with others, but after a while, I get drained and need some alone time.

Oscar Wilde once said something along the lines of how healthy it is to spend time alone. One needs to know how to be alone and not be defined by another person. This resonates with me.

It will be a challenge, but I plan to cross-pollinate—between both the conventional and the ephemeral. As I explore my insights on what it means to lead a good life—intellectually, creatively, and spiritually—answers may emerge as I live into them.

I no longer claim the contradictions in my life. I create space and time for both, and when I do, my soul smiles.

TAMING A MONKEY MIND

At a family dinner a few weeks ago, my father-in-law asked, "What are you up to now?"

I expressed with an enthusiastic, almost childlike tone, "I'm working toward completing my two-hundred-hour certification to be a Registered Yoga Teacher."

The puzzled look on his face spoke volumes. He continued to appear perplexed while stating, "You're always moving from one thing to the next. Will you ever be content with where you are?" My immediate internal reaction was: *Holy smoly, you glum guy! Why can't you be happy for me or say, "How nice," or even, "Good luck?"*

Thank goodness my teenage son noticed my flummoxed expression and decided it was time to talk about his day and informed everyone, "I am so annoyed with my teacher. Can you believe it? She marked me late again!"

Immediately, I felt unsettled, questioning myself, *Am I everywhere and nowhere at the same time? Do I need to settle down and find one thing that makes me happy?* I took a deep breath, located my inner Zen zone and thought, *Who cares what he thinks!*

Yet, it still made me ponder . . . *What makes me think I can teach yoga? I get nervous speaking in front of people . . . But I am quite flexible, and I have practiced yoga for years. Why shouldn't I teach? I confuse some of the poses sometimes but that's why I am learning to teach. The best way to learn is to teach. What the heck . . . I want to evolve as a person.*

I *am* going to do this! I *will* be a yoga teacher!

Through the years, learning about restoring my own mind and body control has proven successful (especially at family dinners). I realized guiding others to do the same would be gratifying, no matter how farfetched it sounded at the time.

About a year ago, I met an inspiring yogini named Lila who projects enormous amounts of love and light. When I am on my mat, her yoga sessions feel like a spiritual service with a splash of soothing and a twist of settling into each pose. The energy she exudes is contagious.

Coming out of my comfort zone is awkward and nerve-racking, but extremely empowering once I mentally and physically get past the first few uncomfortable moments. Having learned Lila was co-leading the upcoming teacher training classes, and with the support of my husband and girlfriends, I enthusiastically signed up. In the back of my mind I knew that dreary comments would be forthcoming from some family members, and even then, I asked myself, *Do I jump from one activity to another? Was this the right decision?*

The answer came quickly. *Yes, it's the right decision. You made this choice for a reason. Live into your answer.*

I am curious about almost everything: nature and its existence, the human heart and its depth, the mind and its malleability. Over the years, yoga has provided me a safe place to explore all of these. It has been and continues to be an ongoing journey of self-study and life study.

Maybe I should have replied to my father-in-law: *The same is lame to me.*

However, yoga and my Midwestern roots have taught me to pause and be polite before I verbalize something that may only be hurtful and not helpful.

I enjoy constant tinkering and *thinkering*. Layers excite me. Exploring the physical, mental, and spiritual aspects of myself has been a constant in my life, as far back as I can remember. I have been many things and will continue to be many more.

Having worked in the corporate world, the culinary industry, and the non-profit sector for many years, I still felt something was missing I needed more. I returned to school to study Clinical Psychology, but it turned out not to be my true passion. These pursuits never fully engaged me. The activity I choose must captivate me completely; otherwise, my attention and mind drift. I thrive on diversity in my life. I enjoy keeping my mind flexible while refining my human heart and blocking out negativity that others may emit due to my choices.

My experiences have taught me many things about myself. The most important lessons turned out to be finding out the three *C's* of where I cannot be: Confined, Cramped, and Constricted. Just the thought of any of these three adjectives makes me cringe.

Today, as a freelance writer; wife; and mother of two teenage boys; a wanderluster; a yogi; gardener; librarian (I have a Little Free Library); wannabe ballroom dancer; and an individual who likes to drink wine and eat stinky cheese, I am exactly who and where I am supposed to be, in this moment.

When Lila, my mentor, mentioned to the class the other day, "Quiet your monkey mind," I could relate. The Zen Buddhists refer to this notion as the constant chatter of the mind, also known as the monkey mind. Unsettled. Restless. Fidgety. My mind is continuously in motion, which is why yoga has been beneficial for me. It forces me to focus on the present and the task at hand, which is staying in the posture while discovering my breath.

Practicing yoga has helped me to power down and reel in my racing thoughts. My mind and movements are like those of a monkey... in perpetual motion. My personality traits can be mischievous, curious, and playful. My thoughts and actions, at times, have the tendency to mosey into places they do not belong.

I like it this way. It is who I am.

That same class, Lila gently repositioned me, as I was not following her cues. Everyone, except me, was on their left side, in Supine Twist, while I was doing the Twist and Shout on my right side, with my leg crossed the wrong way.

It is taking time, but I am learning to quiet my monkey mind. With improved self-governance, there is hope that teacher training will transform my fear and encourage me to pay particular attention to the cues in both life and yoga, while remaining inquisitive and engaging.

It is a struggle not to limit my own activities and advancements. When fear sets in, it is easy to shut down. Did I mention, I get anxiety speaking in front of groups? Each class, I look my fear in the face, recognize my monkey mind, and feel grateful for the yoga community that accepts me. I continue to acknowledge my anxiety, which is a huge first step, and feeling the fear is not fun. But I asked myself, "What's the worst thing that can happen? I mess up and start over." Oddly enough, in Lila's class yesterday the theme was *I do not need to be perfect, just fearless, and resilient, and me.*

My intentions for this teacher training, and in my everyday existence, are to remain active in untangling the wild nature of my monkey mind. Never tame it, but allow this delicate balance between the mind, body, and spirit, freedom to roam and run in its cleverness and curiosity. While acknowledging my boundaries are self-imposed, I will endeavor to swing with the monkeys in the jungles from tree to tree wherever the next vine takes me.

FORGIVING FAULT LINES

I always pursue truth despite the discomfort it sometimes causes. It has been fun finding the courage to own the various stages in my storyline.

Just last month, I returned from a four-generational trip to Ireland, Germany, and Switzerland. This was the first time all twelve of us had travelled together. The range of personalities participating pushed both edges of the spectrum. Ages stretched from the eldest at eighty to the youngest at fifteen. Our time together, short as it was, taught me something about myself. I must forgive the faults of myself and others.

As the trip unfolded, many family members freely displayed peculiar behaviors. They were not concerned with needing to be perfect—so why should I be? Throughout the journey, we explored the scenic peaks of Ireland and Switzerland multiple times. My eyes were drawn to breathtaking scenes of massive rocks jutting sharply from the earth. My heart longed to follow their beauty to the horizon. I felt the wisdom of these ancient mountains speaking directly to me, offering truths like a storyteller sharing insights through timeless traditions. The quiet environment, with only the wind whispering through the mountains, was the perfect moment to look inward. The stunning peaks made me reflect on my urge to excessively perfect situations. It seemed like the right time to acknowledge my imperfect family and confront this personal flaw.

My inner landscape, a metaphor for my emotional and spiritual state of being, longed for introspection with each encounter. As my mind wandered inward, these natural surroundings provided a space for meditation, silently teaching me how to stand fearless amid an unreliable world and all its unforeseen elements.

Multiple mental and emotional snapshots were taken during these immediate and intense connections. I was mesmerized by the mountains and their majestic stance while admiring all their frequent cracks and crevices. I did not recognize it at the time, but this feeling of pure connection with unfiltered nature was what I needed. I am a meaning-seeking individual, and sometimes my way of thinking against the backdrop of life's idiosyncrasies cannot be explained. "It is not the mountain we conquer but ourselves," said Edmund Hillary, whom I greatly admire, a New Zealand mountaineer and explorer who became one of the first climbers to reach the summit of Mount Everest.

I must nurture myself into acknowledging and accepting my imperfect beauty while giving myself and others permission to be jagged like the awe-inspiring mountain ranges.

It has always been essential for me to make the most of my experiences. I have an innate desire to analyze, fix, solve or attempt to make sense of them. Over the years, this personal philosophy has tricked me into thinking flawlessness and dwelling on something too much or too long are positive attributes. The climbing contest of "Mount Perfection" has been personal, within me. However, my interpersonal relationships have taught me that we are all connected through our fault lines.

Many truths were revealed during our family time together. It was remarkable how each of us unveiled various foibles, yet we managed to carry on and snicker at the "blunder of the day" during dinner each night. It is easy to see others' faults. The inability to accept disorder and imperfections in my own life has always been a deficiency of mine.

During the trip, I was reading *On the Move* an autobiography by neuroscientist Oliver Saks. This unconventional man sums up many of my heartfelt beliefs on what life and living are all about. He penned the following, "I have been able to see my life as from a great altitude, as a sort of landscape, and with a deepening sense of connection of all its parts." Many experiences in my life continue to shed light on my insatiable thirst and desire for growth, while solving the many mysteries of me.

Ever since our trip ended, I have been reminding myself to do the best I can every day by improving upon what I learned the day before. What I have realized is that no one is faultless and there is no need to be faultless. Seismic activity is good for my soul.

Who knew that an experience with my clan and the countryside abroad could bring me closer to myself and the mountains? I will learn from my mistakes and welcome life's winds and winding paths. They will balance both my perfectionism and imperfections. This will be my true source of interconnection—appreciating the asymmetrical landscape of my life.

LOYALTY VS LIBERATION

What is the intersection between truth and silence when it comes to family, when I'm no longer willing to protect the peace for others at the expense of my own? When will I finally be free from the burden of carrying the truth while others roam freely under the guise of it being "all good"?

I've come to see that the space between truth and silence is where I've lived for far too long. It's a place of quiet suffocation—a place where I swallowed discomfort, buried reality, and carried the emotional weight of others so they could remain comfortable in the illusion. I used to think silence was noble. That holding my tongue meant I was protecting harmony. But now I understand that wasn't harmony—it was *avoidance*. And I was the one absorbing the cost of it.

I've spent years being the keeper of unspoken things. The emotional buffer. The one who sensed everything, said little, and paid the price silently. But the truth is not an attack, it is just inconvenient for those who benefit from denial.

And now, I no longer ask, *"What will happen if I speak?"*

I ask, *"What will happen if I don't?"*

Because I see now that my silence has been subsidizing other people's stories. Stories that paint over pain with politeness. Stories that protect reputations instead of relationships. And I'm done being part of that performance.

Crossing the line from loyalty to liberation has cost me deeply. It has reshaped relationships, created distance, even silence where there was once closeness. I've had to ask myself: *Is this selfish? Is speaking my truth and choosing myself too high a price to pay for peace?*

But here's what I've come to believe: selfishness and self-preservation are not the same. Choosing myself doesn't mean I don't care. It means I finally care enough to stop abandoning myself to belong.This is not about revenge or drama. It's about release. I'm no longer willing to be the one who makes everyone else feel okay while I stay stuck in what's unspoken. I'm not carrying the truth alone anymore. If others aren't ready to face it, that's theirs to hold—not mine.

I choose truth as my compass now. And I choose silence not as surrender, but as sanctuary. A silence that honors what's real, not what's convenient. Because I've finally learned: protecting peace should never come at the cost of betraying myself.

PEN AND PAPER OPTIONAL

I relish information and the process of obtaining it. For me, the important aspect of collecting information is the way I acquire it. A recent conversation with my tech-savvy son has me reassessing my process.

The astute observation he shared was simply stated. If I used a computer all the time to retrieve information, I would not need to go to the library, travel across the country to learn about different cultures, or use a pen and paper to jot down my thoughts and observations. If I want to find material on my current topic and finish my writing projects faster, use a computer for the entire process.

Interesting idea. I contemplated for a few days about his comment. Was he right? Do I give in and use my supercomputer as my only source and way to possess empirical evidence?

In his technology-based world, information retrieval time is more advanced and faster compared to my deliberate time spent researching in the library, learning through shared stories, or reading my handwritten notes from reference books. The endless supply of information he taps into daily is instant. The supply of information I locate is often contingent on the library having the data or records I am inquiring about. The computer, public library, and my travel are all sources of information that are measurable and specialized, yet he pointed out that computers are faster for finding information, period.

This may be a deeper social phenomenon.

A new wave of information is always forming, oftentimes faster than we can absorb the material generated. I do not want to miss new theories and ideas that are being presented online, nor do I want to be without my ballpoint pen and notepad while accessing information at the local library. However, I explained to him that life is hands-on learning. We must never forget to value one of our deepest needs as humans, to connect with other Homo sapiens. Shared collective experiences are important. One-on-one interactions with a librarian or classmate are just as significant as connecting to the World Wide Web.

Technology, in a short time, has and will continue to change our social arrangements. It is evolving more quickly than libraries are being built and books are being printed. How much is too much? We do not know, but we have the choice to participate or not. It is up to each individual to determine what level of high-tech knowledge works best for them.

Technology is evolving more quickly than humankind. It is forcing all of us to listen, learn, and eventually adapt our ways. As technology advances exponentially, humans evolve linearly – biologically, cognitively and socially. Is my brain and our systems keeping up with the tools being built?

My note taking and means of accumulating data is clearly "old school" compared to my son's peer group. This may always agitate me. I want to scream, "Sweetheart, you don't understand. For me it is the experience of obtaining the information. It is like a great love affair, getting lost within a world of thinking and feeling, a sense of accomplishment when piecing the intellectual, multi-dimensional puzzle together." This is in all probability the same sensory experience he obtains from his input/output method.

Looking directly into his big, brown eyes, my verbal response to him was simply stated. "My thought process is immensely more complicated and complex than the binary code your computer uses to produce facts and figures. My life experiences are unique to me. The memories gathered and cross-cultural connections formed when I travel are exclusive to me. My deep conversations with diverse people are pertinent to only me.

It all measures up and counts as valuable information that in my mind is worth gathering the untimely old-fashioned way. The library and discovering new cultures abroad are where I gather information toward the subject matter being presented. My experiences in life have helped shape my ideas. The computer will continue to be the conduit used for transporting my thoughts to a larger audience and for research, should the other retrieval practices come up short."

My son continues to think my methods are outdated. Oh well. I know his note-taking skills are nonexistent, so it is a stalemate. I will continue to marvel at this wonder we call a computer, which aids me in typing these sentences and guides me when I am locating a subject, even when the library is closed. I will never cease to write down my thoughts with a trustworthy pen and paper or, perhaps, a new digital pen.

In the end, whether I reach for a pen or a keyboard, what matters most is the act of showing up to myself, to the page, to the truth. Pen and paper invite pause and presence; a computer offers speed and structure. Each has its place. Some days, I need the ink to slow me down. On other days, I need the keys to keep up with my thoughts. Both are vessels. Both are valid. The words will find their way, one letter at a time.

THE INTERSECTION OF HUMANITY AND TECHNOLOGY

We are in a constant state of flux, a reality that has become painfully evident in recent years.

The 2020 coronavirus pandemic reshaped behaviors, leaving lasting psychological and societal aftereffects. While the pandemic has faded, its impact continues to shape how we interact in community and professional settings. Enter artificial intelligence, machine learning, and automation—technologies that were already augmenting human capabilities before the pandemic but now stand at the forefront of a new, rapidly evolving era.

History shows that every groundbreaking innovation has been met with fear and skepticism. The radio was once called the "devil's box," predicted to corrupt society. Television was seen as a threat to morality and productivity. The internet was supposed to destroy our ability to think critically. Now, the same concerns arise with Artificial Intelligence.

Will it become sentient? Should we be worried?

I advocate for efficiency, and it is fascinating how often society cycles through this same pattern of resistance before ultimately embracing change. It seems almost a human condition to lament and dramatize new advancements, only to later integrate them seamlessly into daily life, rarely acknowledging the benefits they bring.

Every new technology, like any shiny object, has advantages and disadvantages. Yet rather than mindlessly resisting progress, I wish more people would take a moment to think before they speak to approach these transitional times as opportunities to expand awareness, learn something new, and engage in thoughtful discourse rather than making an enemy of innovation before its full repercussions are understood.

Of course, certain aspects of modern technology do give me pause. Social media, for example, has significantly altered the landscape of human interaction, particularly for youth. The pressure to fit in, the curated highlight reels of influencers, and the unattainable societal "standards" shaped by filters and selective sharing have created a distorted reality. Young people often consume these images without realizing they are merely fragments of someone's life, not an objective truth. We must do better in educating and empowering them to see beyond the filter to develop media literacy and critical thinking skills that allow them to differentiate between authentic experiences and carefully crafted illusions.

Yet, my concerns do not stop at social media. As I continue my studies, I am diving deeper into AI, its evolving role, and other transformative technologies such as CRISPR, a gene-editing tool, and Neuralink, which seeks to bridge the gap between the human brain and machines. Like any innovation, these tools hold incredible potential for progress and peril. They raise ethical questions about the boundaries of human intervention, autonomy, and what it means to be human in an era of rapid technological enhancement.

Our species has survived by being adaptable, agile, and capable of reflection. We are the only beings on this planet who can step back and analyze the long arc of evolution and progress. That is precisely why studying human intelligence—and its intersection with artificial intelligence—is imperative to me. This is not just about innovation for convenience; it is about ensuring that we understand these advancements' ethical, societal, and psychological impacts.

The responsibility lies with us to educate all involved parties about the consequences of these technologies. We cannot afford to be passive observers in a world where humans and artificial intelligence are becoming increasingly intertwined. Through both research and education, my work is dedicated to examining these rapid changes, understanding their psychosocial effects, and fostering an informed dialogue about the future we are building.

It is not only the coursework and research in the Leadership Studies Doctoral Program that intrigues me but also the opportunity to be part of something larger than myself. As an educationalist, I aim to investigate the rapid transformations brought on by technology and how they shape our intellect and collective humanity. The challenge is not just in understanding AI but in ensuring that we, as individuals and as a society are equipped to navigate its influence thoughtfully, ethically, and with a clear-eyed understanding of both its promise and its perils.

Recently, I presented a slide deck on the psychosocial effects of our identity and intelligence, discussing CRISPR's potential impact. Many in my cohort had never heard of it before. They were intrigued, not by the dystopian fears of 'masterclass' engineering or black-market babies, but by its potential to help those born with conditions like epilepsy and depression. Once again, all I can remind people is that there are always two sides to every coin, and it's our responsibility to approach these advancements (which will not stop) with curiosity and critical thinking.

I am hopeful.

THOUGHT PARTNERING WITH TECHNOLOGY

Changing my mind used to feel like betrayal like I was abandoning some core part of my identity. But I've come to see it differently. What if, instead of disloyalty, it's a signal that I'm *leveling up*? That reframing alone has opened a deeper investigation into how technology, especially in our increasingly digital world, interacts with our personal and social identity.

In many ways, our relationship to technology mirrors our relationship to ourselves. When a computer slows down, we don't hesitate to update it. We run diagnostics. We optimize. We fix the bugs. Why wouldn't we afford ourselves the same courtesy?

These days, I'm doing exactly that, challenging outdated beliefs, adopting new perspectives, and indeed, updating my internal software. In this process, ChatGPT has become a surprisingly essential tool. Not a replacement for my intuition or lived experience, but a *thought partner*. One I can challenge, brainstorm with, and even debate to better understand what I truly believe.

That is where AI (artificial intelligence) enters. The conversations around it are heated, and rightly so. People are both fascinated and fearful. We talk about its brilliance and its blind spots, the speed it offers and the trust it demands. Yes, there are risks – privacy concerns, misinformation, the potential to lose touch with our own critical thinking.

But let's be honest: if you carry a phone, your data is already a part of the trade-off. And if you lose your critical thinking because of a computer-generated response, maybe you never truly had agency to begin with. Technology does not erase conviction – it simply tests it. The responsibility to think for yourself, question what is presented and stay anchored in your values has never been more important, but the choice is yours.

I do not outsource my decisions. I shape them with input from my own experiences, trusted voices, and technology like ChatGPT that helps me sharpen my sentences and thinking. With ChatGPT, I've developed a process, a kind of internal dialogue, where I refine my thoughts, write with greater clarity, and organize my ideas with greater precision. It's not about agreeing with everything it offers; it's about using it to fine-tune my own voice.

Being an independent thinker doesn't mean doing everything alone. It means having the discernment to choose the right tools and the right collaborators, human or otherwise to grow. I still hold on to my agency, my conviction, even my sassiness and stubbornness, because they define me. But now I allow space for recalibration. That's not weakness; that's wisdom.

In both my physical and digital worlds, I engage with minds and machines that don't think like me. Some echo my values, while others don't, but each interaction is an opportunity to refine my understanding. I don't want to lose myself to algorithms mimicking human bias or to the avalanche of content flooding my feeds. That's why I stay vigilant. I protect my values. I question everything. I reflect deeply.

And when the noise gets too loud, I turn down the volume, consult my thought partner, and write my own update. If I lose myself to technology, I was never really anchored to begin with. I remain the author of my thoughts, the editor of my beliefs. And with the right tools, I am still writing my story on my terms. We all need to remind ourselves – agency does not disappear in the presence of innovation, it polishes it.

VISIONARIES WHO REACH FOR THE STARS

It's been said, "The moment you doubt whether you can fly, you cease forever to be able to do it." That spirit—the belief that limits are meant to be pushed—lives vividly in the work of three men who've redefined what it means to dream big: Elon Musk, Jeff Bezos, and Sir Richard Branson. Each of them began in different corners of the business world.

Musk in tech and automotive, Bezos in e-commerce and cloud computing, and Branson in music and airlines. But what unites them is something rare: a relentless desire to reshape the future and, quite literally, leave the Earth behind.

Their companies—SpaceX, Blue Origin, and Virgin Galactic aren't just about space travel. They're about vision, risk, and the refusal to let convention cage curiosity. In a world that often tries to shrink dreamers into boxes, these men have cracked those boxes wide open.

Elon Musk has long been considered a wildcard, a rule-breaker with remarkable range. From PayPal to Tesla to launching astronauts into orbit, he's leaned into audacity. His ambition isn't just technical; it's deeply human. He doesn't just want to go to Mars; he wants to make humanity multiplanetary.

Richard Branson, with his trademark charisma and thrill-seeking spirit, brings joy and daring into the space conversation. His flight aboard Virgin Galactic's Unity in 2021 wasn't just a milestone; it was a message: space is no longer just for government agencies, it's for the bold, the curious, and the civilian dreamer.

Then there's Jeff Bezos, the strategic empire builder. What began as an online bookstore has evolved into a behemoth that influences nearly every aspect of modern life. And yet, even amid Amazon's vast influence, Bezos turned his eyes upward. With Blue Origin, he's thinking long-term centuries ahead, about preserving Earth by moving heavy industry into space.

What I admire most about these three is not just their business acumen, but their courage. They've all faced criticism, doubt, and failure, and kept going anyway. They've dared to ask, "Why not?" in a world full of "You can't."

If I had to choose just one person to have dinner with, who would it be? That's a nearly impossible call. But maybe Bezos—his long game, his methodical thinking, and his ability to build an ecosystem that continues to shape how we live and consume is, frankly, fascinating. Plus, I would love to ask him over appetizers politely, but pointedly, why Amazon needs to take 70% of my book profits every time one sells. Genius aside, someone has to pay for my DoorDash dependence!

In the end, Musk, Bezos, and Branson remind us that progress doesn't come from waiting. It comes from believing, building, and being brave enough to imagine what lies beyond the sky.

RUSHED TO RESPOND

I was sharing casual conversation over a cup of rosehip tea with tupelo honey when a new acquaintance asked me, "Why do you write?"

Suddenly, I felt something I thought was a little odd, an inability to respond quickly or articulate an answer. Cutting the silence, my rushed reply was, "It brings me joy." I noticed the interest in her eyes fade and her focus wane, as she continued sipping her steamy tea. My response must have seemed blasé. I tried again. "I like to create a world with my words." This answer seemed to grab her attention; a bit of sparkle returned.

"So you write fiction?" she asked.

"Not exactly. I dabble in poetry but typically write narrative nonfiction. I enjoy fact-based storytelling, similar to personal essays," I explained.

"Oh, like memoirs," she quickly stated.

"More like diary entries with elements of dysfunction and discovery," I added, attempting to evoke another emotional response and engage her enthusiasm.

We parted ways after an unfinished chat over our love of books, types of fictional characters she connects with, and her new love interest—a poodle puppy she'd named Fifi. With the talk of her poodle puppy, she reminded herself it was time to pick Fifi up from her grooming appointment which left me drinking cold tea while pondering the reasons why I write.

This afternoon chat was illuminating. Her question forced me to consciously contemplate what motivates me to unveil my innermost thoughts and feelings. No one had ever asked me why I write—only what I write.

I like details and, when speaking with others, I often feel rushed to find the right words and explanations. This has always been a problem for me. Ever since I can remember, I have had to hide my emotions and internal dialogue to formulate an answer. Naturally this takes time, and I end up being pressured into rushing my response. I determined this was the challenge I had describing my affection for writing to my new friend.

My mental makeup prefers carefully selected words which are the secret to having profound, powerful dialogue and expressing great stories. This, opposed to rapid retorts that are often nerve-racking for me. Given the choice, I want to write what I have to say, not speak it. That's what makes me a writer. Writing is an opportunity to have conversations with myself, at my pace. I experience contentment when I am given the time to find the accurate words that describe how I feel versus an immediate response just to fill space in a conversation.

Writing truly brings me joy. I feel fully alive when I write. My senses are ignited and intensified. I discover creative courageousness inside. It is fun finding the serenity within as I give meaning to jumbled thoughts, and I admire myself for being brave.

Writing is a platform for me to be me, without disguise. I am powerless when my words are not expressed. The fear of people failing to understand the concealed me can be damaging. I do not want to spend my life feeling rushed into reactive replies. Writing allows me to edit my existence. In constructing a story, I seek to reveal myself, I seek to be understood, and I seek to share. Next time, I will tell my new friend that this is why I write.

GRIEF AND GROWTH

Navigating Loss and Finding Light

Grief is an inescapable part of life, one I have known intimately. This section acknowledges some of my most significant challenges, loss, disappointment, and the weight of carrying wounds, both my own and those of others. I could write an entire book on what it means to deal with unhealed people and the traumas they have avoided. But what I focus on here is the grief itself and the transformation that follows. The painful yet necessary expansion that comes from facing the past, reckoning with loss, and discovering that growth is not always gentle—but it is always possible.

These entries reflect the slow and often unglamorous work of healing – the kind that doesn't announce itself with a breakthrough, but a quiet breath after surviving another day. Here, I confront both the death of my father, grandmother, and the making sense of the why that followed. I examine how grief morphs over time, from sharp and disorientating to hollow and haunting and how, eventually, it makes room for something softer. These pages are not about tying not only grief but personal growth all up with a velvet blue bow. They are about honoring the ache, tracing the scar, and learning how to carry what you cannot fix and the work that goes along with it.

Growth lives in the shadow of grief, and this section is my attempt to stand in both.

LOSS, GRIEF . . . AND GROWTH

Loss and grief are among the most universal human experiences, yet we shy away from talking about the pain of living and losing. For me, sharing stories has always been a step toward freedom, and so is following my heart and speaking my truth. I believe that all of my life experiences—the joyful and the sorrowful—have crafted this "feel it all" perspective in me. Loss and grief will present themselves, to all of us. It's a fact. It's not something we ever look forward to but knowing that loss and grief are inevitable has taught me to face their arrival head-on, however tentatively, and listen for the lessons they hold.

My father's death taught me the fragility of life. That loss, so devastating to my tender young heart, spurred an urgency in me to live and to never take anything for granted.

I was out of the country when my paternal grandmother Rosie died in 2014. I was forty—thankful, at the time, for the maturity I had to better face this loss. She was my pillar of strength growing up. I even named my intuition—that inner voice that reminds me of what is right and wrong—after her. I had visited my grandma Rosie in the hospital several weeks prior to her passing. She hated hospitals and wanted me to take her back to 1886 Daily Drive, her hermitage after her mother, husband, and son died. I remember braiding her steely gray hair and playing cards at her bedside. Euchre was her favorite.

Those last moments we spent together, coupled with all the beautiful memories we had created over the years, profoundly impacted my approach to life. Her death further revealed the importance of appreciating those who matter most—to tell people you love how much they mean to you. With my Grandma Rosie's passing, another hole in my heart formed, right next to the one my dad's passing had left—invisible scars, chronicles of loss, yet reminders just the same of what's truly important. Life pressed on after Grandma Rosie's death, with the added recognition of another significant remembrance to hold dear.

Now eight years hence, another loss: the death of my maternal grandmother, Carol Jean. Whether it was maturity, past experience, or DNA, this loss impacted my life perspective yet again, reminding me of the importance of retaining that same enthusiasm I have always had to dance wildly on the stage of life. At the end of the day, I want to be proud of the way I showed up—of the way I lived in this world and dedicated myself to the kind of life that allows happiness, sadness, and growth to flow through me like a hummingbird effortlessly flying from flower to flower.

However sorrowful or unwelcome, loss and grief have contributed significantly to my life perspective. Acknowledging that along with the joys, excitements, and wonders that life holds, there will also be loss and grief; to not turn a blind eye; to not shy away. Loss and grief are just as much as part of life as joy and happiness – unwelcome, but undeniable companions on the path to becoming fully human. It's okay to feel sorrow, to speak of your pain and fear and to embrace the finality of what is – with tenderness, I have learned, not resistance.

Let's be straightforward, we die a little bit each day, and no one is getting out of here alive. So, why do so many find it morbid to talk about death? Why do we not talk about how heartbroken we are? Why do we have to appear like we have it all together? We act like the hurt is gone, but it never leaves us. It just finds another place to reside within you. Loss and grief are so intertwined with life itself that I sometimes find it perplexing that we can't be more real with its inevitability, the sorrow we feel, and the light that it can often shine upon our existence. Loss and grief don't always apply to death, either. Truthfully, I continually process my losses and grieve daily. They both suck. I have not mastered the means, though I believe I've received numerous blessings in being present in those difficult moments.

Entering Covenant Hospital, for the third time for a family member, triggered some lingering trauma from the passing of both my dad and my Grandma Rosie. I kept thinking these feelings were normal—another disturbing event, same space, just a different scenario—filled with the same shitty emotions one comes to expect with death and dying. *I can do hard things,* I reminded myself.

I am grateful for those last forty-eight hours with my grandmother Carol Jean, also known as CJ to those closest to her. I was able to tell her just how special she had been to me. I replayed our endless moments and memories and even teased her about all the makeup she used to wear. She struggled to speak, having undergone extubation from a ventilator just days earlier. All she wanted was a sip of water. Three ice chips were her only option, as her swallowing ability was severely compromised. I told her to pretend she was having a steamy cup of Tim Horton's coffee. She loved robust black coffee.

As I caressed her unkept and uncolored hair, she reminded me in a very raspy voice of just how not okay she was with the fact that her hair was not curled. We pretended I was coloring her hair and prepping for the party she was to attend. I asked who she would invite, and generously she said all her past loves, including Grandpa Jim. She said, "I don't see why not." They had been divorced since I was four years old. I asked my mother, Joni, to reach into her purse and pull out her rouge-colored lipstick. Speaking loud into my grandma's ear, I affirmed this was not her color, yet daubed the waxy paint to her chapped, dry, thin lips. All I wanted to do was give her back a sense of self during the last twenty-four hours of her life. I did not get to do this for my dad and Grandma Rosie. At the end of the day, I wanted to be proud that I never took a back seat to my pain. At the end of the day, I want to be proud of the way I can endure unresolved grief and loss.

My grandmother Carol Jean was complex, like the multiple modalities she fought until the very end. She lost both of her parents within two years, at the young age of twelve and then fourteen. I can only assume this young, heartbroken girl did not have a therapist to talk to. Her two older brothers, Pete and Skelly, were twenty-plus years older than her. She had a heartfelt demeanor more substantial than all the cards in a Hallmark store. Everyone who met her adored her and said she was a lovely, well-dressed lady.

There were so many little things about her that I will always remember fondly. My grandmother loved her jewelry—invariably decked out with multiple gold bangles, rings, and necklaces—but drew the line at dangling earrings! She would never leave the house without a full face of Mary Kay makeup. My dad, before he died, always teased her about wearing high-heeled shoes with blue jeans. I still smile, thinking about how she would eat off everyone's plate. "Let me just try that," she would say. She and I would often share a bowl of fried chicken livers from a German restaurant in the town where she lived. And I will never forget the coral lipstick stains she left on every coffee cup she touched. There were so many.

Her discomfort in recent years was evident. Her coughing was sporadic from lingering pneumonia, with a gurgle appearing every few breaths. I don't think she realized how angry her body had become, coupled with congestive heart failure. The sepsis and lingering urinary tract infection were far more than antibiotics could resolve. She was fortunate to have had hip surgery after she fell six weeks prior but still struggled with seeing through her cataracts and hearing without the hearing aids she never wanted.

I felt a profound need to provide whatever support I could to help bridge my grandmother Carol Jean's passage from here on earth to the pearly gates she was about to enter. I wanted her to feel special, not frightened and alone. "I fear this," she quietly told me after the nurse left on Sunday night. Despite my seemingly strong façade, inside, I was grieving, sad and already mourning the loss of my thoughtful grandmother—a woman who should have bought stock options in Hallmark Cards, Inc., given the vast investments she made over the years. I will miss her slanted, left-handed script on the beautiful cards she would personally choose and send for every holiday and birthday—along with her quirky little gifts.

On Monday morning, the nurses pulled her feeding tube and removed her oxygen and the remaining antibiotic lines and tubes keeping her alive. Watching this talkative and pious woman wither into the abyss was not for the faint of heart. The morphine injections began every thirty minutes to ease her pain, making the transition to her passing comfortable. Dignity matters. Agency matters. Quality of life matters. I sat there thinking about how we need to do better in society by representing the pleasant as well as the unpleasant. The blurry boundaries of young and old and the paradox they represent are utterly beautiful to me. My grandmother's untanned shapeless skin looked great. I told her she had fewer wrinkles at eighty-five than I do at forty-eight.

The attraction of remembering our loved ones in their vitality of beauty is effortless and soothing on the soul; however, I am fortunate to feel and have the direct experience of dismissing the deterioration of the body as ghastly. Our earthly experiences teach us about the ugly duckling and the metamorphosis into the striking swan. I wish we could stop only admiring youth and its vitality while dismissing the converse as "hard on the eyes." The unpleasantness of anything is uncomfortable. At the end of the day, I want to be proud of the way I fought to flourish. At the end of the day, I want to be proud of how I taught myself a version of strength different from the one the world finds convenient. I want to be proud of how I reframed bravery and made it into something soft—recognizing that the laws of nature apply to all of us. We each will wane and whittle away to saggy skin and bones. I don't want those around me to look at me like I am a grim reaper but rather a divine dying diva who lived a life riddled with hardship and many stretches of happiness.

Death reminds me of how interdependent I am with others around me and the importance of fostering relationships and the bonds each brings. I also realize these interactions are pillars of support during adversity if I allow those closest to me inside the walled columns I construct.

Life doesn't always cooperate. Grief changes us. I do know this. I can honestly confess that the continued deaths of my loved ones, which were significant parts of my life, have led to substantial shifts in my personality. Despite my heartache, I want to choose tenderness. I want to be proud of the way I chose vulnerability. I want to reframe and refine the meaning of life again and again; and I want, with every passing joy and sorrow, to love deeper. Patience with people will always be a work in progress for me, yet my motivation to create meaningful conversations and experiences has increased tenfold. I continue to remind myself of what is relevant and worthy of my attention. Time is a thief. However, I am recharged and ready to take it on.

At the end of the day, I know tough times come daily. Everyone deals with death differently. Everyone's journey to healing is unique. Everyone deals with life and living differently. I know life resumes, and with its continuance, I will continue to experience and grow from loss. I will learn to live with it—reminding myself that loss is a part of life; pain is a part of life. I have and can continue to live on with the loss of loved ones. Those we love never truly leave us, as there are certain things death cannot touch. And for that, I am forever grateful.

Cheers, Grandma CJ, you will be missed and were loved dearly!

THE MYTH OF ETERNAL HAPPINESS

Happiness—destination or disaster?

I have given up on the idea of relentless positivity, the Pollyanna outlook that insists happiness is the ultimate goal. Instead, I'm finding the deeper lessons in my anger, resentment, and moments of hopelessness. In one of my doctoral classes, we discussed the concept of happiness. Everywhere I turn, I am bombarded with messages telling me to be happier. Our discussion made us question the overwhelming presence of social media, movies, articles, workshops, and self-help books, reinforcing that we are perpetually unfinished, always striving toward some elusive, shinier version of ourselves.

Oh, and then there is my personal application of positive psychology, with all the intentional practices I try to incorporate into my life as I cultivate better behaviors to enhance my overall well-being, including being optimistic, taking vitamins, drinking more water, and eating healthier. Then there is the exercise, do more Yoga or Pilates. Look a certain way. Work through your trauma harder. Be more productive. More grateful. More mindful.

In our conversation, we landed on a troubling realization: self-improvement, often sold to us, equates to a happier, shinier, more polished version of ourselves. But who decided that happiness is the ultimate measure of success? The evidence of my own life tells a different story. I learned early on that the world is tragic, brutal—unfair, and unjust. Instead of residing in a fantasyland of Disney ideals, I created my version of Nomadic Nowhere, a space where I could drift through the complexities of life without subscribing to a singular narrative of perpetual bliss, kind of like Numbville, but different.

Recently, I've discovered a middle path, not through naive optimism but through trial and error, suffering, and self-judgment. It's not that I don't believe in happiness—I do. I just don't think or believe that one can always be happy while also embracing the full depth of what it means to be alive. Life's raw, intricate, and sometimes painful moments are just as valid as the joyful ones. There have been times when I wore the mask of happiness, played the role of Snow White, and performed the illusion of peace because it was necessary to survive. But I no longer see that as my only option. Instead of striving for constant joy, I seek moments of happiness as they flit and flutter, much like the hummingbird outside my window—brief, beautiful, and never to be forced.

Philosopher Rumi from the 13th century reminds us that every morning is an opportunity to start anew, to welcome each emotion as a visitor with something to teach. My darker emotions—anger, guilt, regret—are not enemies but respected guests. They don't overstay their welcome, but their presence is instructive.

When my father died when I was eleven, I went into overdrive. I ran from grief, from pain, from the inescapable reality of loss. I devoured books, searching for wisdom, desperate to uncover the meaning of life. But the answer, after all these years, remains unknown. As the Buddha said, "Life is suffering." My job here is not to escape that truth but to evolve through it, to expand in the face of challenges rather than shrink away.

Happiness is not a constant state, but neither is despair. Life is a prism—gray one day, rose-colored the next, shifting with the complexities of my neurotic, overthinking, restless mind. There is no such thing as uninterrupted harmony. I want to feel the frustration, the despair, the fire, and the ice of existence. I don't want to live in an airbrushed version of life where only the good parts are acknowledged.

We talk often in both the classroom and outside of it about evolution as survival, but where does suffering fit in? Is our tendency to self-sabotage a flaw, or does it push us beyond our comfort zones? Does our obsession with self-awareness serve as a tool for growth, or does it keep us trapped in cycles of over-analysis? The answers remain elusive, just like happiness but the questions themselves are worth exploring.

Modern humans have a remarkable capacity for self-examination, yet we often wield it as a weapon against ourselves. We analyze, dissect, and diagnose every emotion, sometimes forgetting that awareness—not happiness—is the highest goal. I no longer pressure myself to maintain a romantic-comedy version of my life, where every hardship is neatly wrapped up in a lesson and accompanied by an uplifting fight song soundtrack like *Rocky IV*.

Instead, I am embracing authenticity. I remind myself that history's most interesting, creative, and impactful people led lives full of doubt, struggle, and inner conflict. I am diving deep into myself, learning to love what I find and gently changing what I don't. I will fail and flail, but isn't that the most honest way to live? Again, here I am pondering but learning to embrace the beautifully imperfect, ever-wandering messy human experience—my nomadic way.

TEMPERING THE TRUTH

I appreciate facts. I also prepare myself for life's inevitable challenges, knowing that misfortune is often just a knock away. Acknowledging this doesn't diminish my fear but helps me feel ready when the hardships arrive. However, conversations with uncertain outcomes—those that stir emotions or awaken unresolved feelings—are often met with discomfort. Death, for instance, is a prime example. For many, it remains taboo, yet it forced itself into my life early, changing the way I see, live, and speak. I've learned to embrace uncomfortable conversations, especially about topics like death. It's a shared experience we will all encounter, so why not find comfort in discussing it openly, together?

As a writer, I observe life closely, trying to make sense of it all. I've lived through enough to know that suppressing who I am to accommodate someone else's discomfort only enables inauthenticity—for both of us. Yet, I often notice that many people resist doing the hard work of facing their truths. They numb themselves, avoid the pain, and blame others for their unhappiness, as though this darkness will dissolve on its own. But it doesn't. I want to tell them the void they feel will remain until they acknowledge their sadness and take responsibility for their choices. Their struggles, however, are not mine to bear.

I wonder why people can't recognize that life's trivialities and frustrations are fleeting and unworthy of the weight we give them. We must face our flaws, acknowledge our behaviors, and move forward. That's what I want to say—figure your shit out and move on. Yet, I've learned that my truth often needs tempering, as not everyone is equipped to handle it.

Navigating truth in relationships requires a delicate balance, especially when saying what you see and feel. After twenty-six years of marriage, I've realized that honesty is essential to fostering trust and connection. But truth must be spoken with care, respecting the other person's emotions and readiness to receive it. Yet, even after years of tempering my words, I sometimes wonder if my efforts have been in vain. If someone still can't process the truth after all this time, it may be time to reconsider how I communicate or even the relationship itself.

I've come to understand that some people struggle with truth because of emotional baggage, trauma, or fear. In such cases, gradual exposure to truth or professional guidance may be needed—something I value, having worked with my trusted therapist, Tristen, for fifteen years. Not constantly, of course—just for maintenance.

Yet, tempering my truth has come at a cost. It has been emotionally exhausting, leaving me with frustration, resentment, and a sense of inauthenticity. I've learned that true relationships can only thrive on honesty, and masking the truth corrodes the relationship and my sense of self. I refuse to compromise my self-respect for anyone unwilling to do their healing and self-reflection. I don't engage in the blame game.

Boundaries and acceptance have become my allies. I've accepted that not everyone can handle the truth, and I've learned to set boundaries—deciding how much energy I want to invest in helping others understand and whether the effort is worth it. Letting go of certain relationships has been necessary, though bittersweet. Life without them feels freer and more refined.

At my core, I will always choose honesty. For most of my life, tempering my truth only got me into trouble—mostly with myself—because I resented others' inability to receive it. Now, I aim for direct but compassionate conversations. It's not easy, but I do my best to express my need for authentic connections and explain why truth is essential to me, even when it's uncomfortable. While many struggle with my honesty, at least I've put it out there. I welcome constructive criticism—I've been a writer long enough to embrace red marks and edits. Growth comes from acknowledging our flaws and transforming them into strengths.

Letting go of the outcome has been one of the hardest lessons. No matter how carefully I deliver the truth, some people may never fully accept it. When that happens, I've learned to release the need to control their response and focus on maintaining my integrity and well-being. I can honestly say that I've always approached these moments with kindness and care.

When truth is withheld for too long, everyone suffers. Masking it creates shallow connections, eroding trust and respect. Through reflection, I've committed to setting clear intentions for truth-telling, knowing that honesty brings clarity and transformation. Whether the relationship deepens or distance becomes necessary, truth lets us make peace with what is.

In conclusion, I crave authenticity and meaningful connection. If a relationship requires me to constantly hide my thoughts and feelings, it lacks the depth I need. Brené Brown, author and research professor is best known for her work on vulnerability, shame and courage, as well as her bestselling book Daring Greatly, which emphasizes that authenticity is essential for deep, trusting relationships, but vulnerability must also be practiced within boundaries. Thoughtful delivery, however, is my Achilles' heel. There's never a perfect time, so I speak my truth as it arises, doing my best to wrap it in compassionate language.

Still, I've come to understand that not everyone is ready for certain truths. Tristen wisely reminds me, "Sometimes, temporarily withholding certain truths can be the kinder approach, as long as you're not dishonest." While it's not my preferred method, I've gone there a few times—though never happily. I am an advocate for honest conflict versus dishonest harmony.

Tempering truth is a balancing act, one I don't always master. But I know that when truth is masked too often, relationships become shallow, and trust erodes. For me, honesty is essential, but it must be balanced with empathy, timing, and care for the other person's ability to receive it. I aim to create space for truth that strengthens connections and fosters growth. Though not always easy, it is, without question, essential.

REPARENTING MYSELF

I learned far too early to mold myself into what others wanted, but now I am dismantling that conditioning and allowing myself the freedom to be who I truly am. I spent almost forty years hiding in Numbville and living in this internal world I had created.

My reparenting journey just began two years ago, and being a patient parent to myself has been messy but manageable. *Reparenting* is a fancy new phrase with a simple goal. It is the act of giving yourself what you didn't receive as a child; therefore, holding space for my younger self often feels uncomfortable as I continue to reconcile resentment and recognize that many of the people in my life did the best with what they knew and had, afraid to face their challenges while often not having the courage to address family members in fear of the discomfort or disappointment it could cause.

For all of us, our parents and grandparents are our first teachers, coaches, and mentors, and we do anything to feel worthy of their love and attention, even when we are held to standards that don't feel authentic, which is where I learned to become what others wanted, rather than who I truly am. Our parents and grandparents were raised in the silent generation, which means they did not talk about mental health issues or family dynamics, or help each other navigate emotions. Therefore, trauma dysfunctions and the inability to regulate emotionally were perpetuated. For me, this cycle needed to stop, and I was not going to allow my children to feel unsafe to express themselves in an environment that encourages open communication and expressing emotions. I wanted them to feel valued and secure, which I did not have.

Reparenting our inner child is essential for healing and growth as adults. This process involves giving ourselves the nurturing, validation, and support we may not have received in childhood. It also means grieving the experiences we longed for and releasing the anger we've held toward caregivers who couldn't provide what we needed. In learning to reparent myself, I discovered the wounds left from my upbringing and the power to heal them in ways I never thought possible.

The first step toward reparenting myself was recognizing that something was missing.

For years, I navigated life feeling like a part of me was unseen or unheard, seeking validation from others in ways that mirrored my childhood longing for approval. This drive to please others disconnected me from my actual needs and desires. My journey of self-awareness began with the realization that the love and validation I had been seeking externally could only be enjoyed internally. Reparenting, I discovered, was not just about healing the past but about learning to meet my present self with compassion and understanding.

As I delved deeper into the process, I had to confront feelings I had long buried. The anger and sadness toward my caregivers for their shortcomings in my upbringing were complicated to face. At times, I found myself stuck in the loop of what-ifs—what if they had been more present, more emotionally available, or more supportive? These thoughts felt overwhelming, but the practice of re-parenting shifted my focus from dwelling on what I lacked to giving myself what I needed now. I learned to soothe my inner child by offering her the love, validation, and safety that had been absent during critical stages of my development. This included simple practices such as speaking kindly to myself, setting boundaries, and honoring my emotions.

Grieving was a pivotal part of this process. I had to allow myself to mourn the childhood experiences I wished I had. Grief is often misunderstood, but through reparenting, I learned it is a necessary release—a way to let go of the pain that no longer serves us. This grief opened the door to acceptance. I accepted that my caregivers had limitations, and although their actions—or lack thereof—left lasting scars, I no longer needed to hold onto resentment. Reparenting taught me that while I couldn't change the past, I could transform how I related to it.

Finally, reparenting allowed me to establish a sense of safety within myself. I became my protector and nurturer, developing the tools to navigate life's challenges with resilience and self-compassion. This process didn't mean erasing my pain of the past but instead creating a safe space within me where my inner child could feel seen and supported. With time, I found that I could approach life's hardships with greater confidence and ease, knowing that I could care for myself in ways others could not. I had proven this time and time again, but I longed for others to take care of me. In the end, it was me needing to love me—and that was enough.

Ultimately, my parents started my story, but I am the one who gets to write the following chapters. Reparenting is an ongoing journey, and the work is never truly finished. However, it is a path toward wholeness. By reparenting myself, I have reclaimed my power, learned to love myself more deeply, and found the strength to move forward with a sense of inner peace. In nurturing my inner child, I have reconnected with the authentic parts of myself that had long been hidden, and, in doing so, I've opened up the possibility for proper growth and healing.

MENTAL POST-IT NOTE

I have learned a lot about people, from what they lack. If they lack accountability, they'll shift the blame. If they lack communication skills, they say you're arguing. If they lack emotional intelligence, they call you sensitive or make it about you. If they lack effort, they're not interested. This hit different.

What is happening here is simple.

A person is not grown until they know how to communicate, apologize, and accept accountability without blaming someone else. I didn't become selfish. I just became harder to manipulate. Never will I confuse the two. I finally figured out and accepted that the only closure I needed was understanding that I deserved better. Simple.

Mental Post-it Note noted.

WE ARE MADE OF STORIES

Not only do we carry our stories, they shape who we are. How brilliant is that? It reminds me of what Carl Sagan once said: "We're made of star-stuff! Some part of our being knows the cosmos is where we came from, and we long to return." Who wouldn't want to be made of a little intergalactic matter?

I'm returning to write Volume II of *S.H.E.* after a three-year sabbatical, alongside another writing project. I happened to be home in Michigan for Mother's Day and also attended the funeral of a longtime family friend, Luella Merkel. She would have turned one hundred in two months. A mother, grandmother, great-grandmother, and friend, Luella was a straight-talking, dynamic dame who had been living independently until five days before she passed. I'm heartbroken I didn't capture her story while she was still here.

Though we hadn't been in touch for years, ever since I moved away from Reese three decades ago. I may circle back and interview her family to celebrate her moxie and mettle. Luella's passing reminded me just how vital storytelling is. Human beings have always used stories to share ideas, pass down dreams, connect with others, and make sense of the world.

When we pause to truly relate to one another, we begin to see the timeless thread that connects us all. For me, stories are narrative medicine. They help me understand myself and the people around me. I've long believed in the healing power of sharing personal experiences. It works both ways, for the storyteller and the listener. The twenty-four women featured in *S.H.E.* Volume I offered their stories with openness and wisdom, helping others navigate struggles of their own.

Interviewing women of all ages and backgrounds has been transformative. Some I've known for years; others I met through a friend or by chance. Yet every story, every conversation, reinforced something I've always believed: we carry stories of love and loss, birth and death, joy and grief. These human experiences are connected in ways that go beyond geography, culture, or age. The women in Volume II—coming from all over the world—will share their unique mix of triumphs and struggles, and I am honored they've entrusted me with their stories.

We define ourselves through the stories we tell: who we are, who we think we are, and who we hope to become. Even now, I catch myself crafting stories about returning to the stage, speaking in public, and interviewing again. Could it be that each woman I meet feels the same quiet apprehension? I never noticed. But I have seen how meaningful it is, how simply being heard reminds us that we matter.

When we find a safe person and a protected place, we can speak our pain—whether physical, emotional, or spiritual. The women I've interviewed, and those I've yet to meet, offer that space not just to me, but to each other. It's in these shared moments that we discover who we are—together.

As I begin this new volume, I know the process will reshape me again. With each interview, I am both revealed and refined, just as the women sharing their stories are. Every exchange becomes its own version of truth.

My hands still tremble and my neck beads with sweat just thinking about stepping into this next chapter. But I'm excited. This is my calling: to champion the strengths and struggles of others. It is, I believe, one of the most profound ways we can gather and share the wisdom of humanity.

Everyone around us has a story, and each one is meaningful. Every story contains a nugget of wisdom waiting to surface and be heard. These stories connect me to the past, ground me in the present, and open a doorway to the future. They link me to the courageous voices behind them and to something much greater, the living universe of stories that surrounds us all.

Cheers to you, Luella, and to all the "supernova storytellers"—never outshining each other, only swirling together in a galaxy of light.

DON'T GIVE UP

We often associate success with the cliched adages of "never give up" and "hard work pays off." This is true for me starting at an early age when both these axioms were taught both at school and home. I was in an operetta in fifth grade titled *Don't Give Up,* and I even sang a solo; talk about impressionable. There is an often an overlooked success attribute called *self-efficacy* we must acknowledge.

According to psychologist Albert Bandura, self-efficacy is a person's belief in their ability to succeed in a specific situation. My question is how we can develop more self-efficacy to reach our goals. How can we ascribe this when it comes to overcoming trauma in our lives? Is self-efficacy similar to self-esteem? Both can be cultivated and nurtured intentionally. I remember learning to ride my purple Schwinn bicycle with the floral banana seat and the bruises and scrapes I gathered along the way. It was definitely worth the time and effort I spent learning to balance, rather than focusing on falling.

As I built speed, the confidence came and the sheer determination that I could conquer this on my own once my dad let go of that white and purple seat. The excitement of me doing it was the motivation to continue proving to myself that I can do anything if I put my mind to it. The adversity I encountered was my own self-talk. All I needed to do was ignore my doubt and stay focused on completing my task—balancing this bike.

Bandura, a renowned psychologist, expanded the definition and described self-efficacy as beliefs in one's abilities to organize and carry out the actions needed to achieve specific goals. Therefore, self-efficacy closely relates to its important counterpart, self-esteem, and both are key pillars of self-worth. I will explore this theory of self-efficacy further by examining how our relationships with ourselves and the beliefs formed in childhood influence how we think, feel, behave, and act.

Throughout my life, self-efficacy has appeared both personally and professionally. It can be seen as self-confidence and a willingness to take risks and recover after failures. It showed up during difficult times, such as my father's death, my mother's divorce, and emotional neglect. For me, self-efficacy has been the ability to rebound and rebuild myself, a way to reframe and teach my inner critic or that internal dialogue we all have, reminding me that we have what we need within ourselves to learn, adapt, and grow.

I want to encourage others to start. Don't ignore your pain. My first step in not giving up was to change my thinking rather than practicing positive thinking. Many people tend to turn to personal development books, motivational speakers, and internet memes to cheer us on. The problem with that is personal development focusing on positive thinking will show a different and positive way to look at situations to change how we feel.

Rarely does it teach us how to cultivate and practice another way of thinking. I believe that self-efficacy is learnable and influential in developing confidence and certainty in transforming trauma. The interplay of trauma and self-efficacy will be part of my continued analysis, coupled with the effects of technology on our identity development.

WHAT DOES YOUR DASH MEAN?

When I go home to Michigan in October, one of my first stops is Reese. The small community I grew up in and where my heart holds many dear memories.

I go to the graveyard on the outskirts of town. Here in this sacred place is where my father's headstone is located under a tall pine tree. As I talk out loud to him, typically through tears, I look at the dash.

The dash between his birthdate and his last day of life. Those two dates are something we all have in common. As I continue to age and acknowledge life in a different lens, the in-between of these two dates appear to matter most.

As we all live this one life, I continue to ask myself and those around me these simple, yet reflective questions:

Are you happy?
How are you going to live?
Are you inspired?

My dad was my superhero. Both he and my mom gave me the gift of life. As many of you know, my father was diagnosed with cancer at the age of twenty-eight and died two years later. Boldly, after his death and into my adult life, with fire in my belly and without a doubt in my mind, I was going to outrun life.

Luckily, I am still running at forty-six years old.

When I am in Reese, several people stop me on the street and say, "Aren't you Tom Hogan's daughter?" They too share how he was one of the most charismatic and fun-loving souls they had ever met. Spirited. Motivated. Fearless. Mischief-maker. I can't help but feel those messages are him saying, *Keep going, Shan . . . you are on the right path. Never give up*!

That is his continued legacy.

As I type, the lump in my throat chokes me up. The tears trickle down. I miss the man, who was my father for a momentary eleven years. This emptiness never goes away; however, his love and memories fill the void. Plus, my two adult sons look and act like him in so many countless ways.

What I have "finally" realized: I have the full capacity and potential to live out my best life. We all do. As I continue to make my dash mean something, never will I squander what has been provided to me.

What are you going to do with this one life you were given?

DEEPER DISCUSSIONS

My husband came home two days ago with a very heavy heart. His SAE fraternity brother, Brian, had committed suicide. He was only fifty years old.

"I feel guilty for not reaching out, I should have communicated more," my husband sadly confessed. Brian's untimely death forced us both to look deeper into our own lives and the conversations we have with others.

When I first met Brian twenty years ago, I was immediately charmed by his mischievous sense of humor and his infectious smile. I vividly recall him telling a story about the time he contended for the title of Mr. Arizona. We were enjoying straight whiskey on the rocks at our local watering hole. Although we were surrounded by a crowd of people, that didn't stop Brian from proudly demonstrating his signature swan-like pose. Everyone present was laughing. Brian's swagger and fun-loving personality made him stand out in a crowd.

Reflecting, I wonder if we were seeing a person who had learned to disguise his difficulties behind a larger-than-life personality. Brian was someone who gave the impression that he had it all together. What was he feeling inside that made him want to end his life?

Acting like you feel one way when you really feel another is exhausting. I speak from my own experience. Growing up, I ached to be understood and accepted for who I was. But rather than reveal my true self—full of pain and imperfections—I became a personality that was not reflective of who I truly was. I would be overly energetic and entertaining. This performance distracted me from the negative environment around me and the private pain I was experiencing.

My hiding days are over. I no longer try to be all things to all people. I wish I could talk about that journey with Brian. I'd tell him how much lighter I feel, not pretending to have it all together. I'd tell him how sharing my pain with others no longer feels like a weakness but has actually become a source of strength. I wonder if he would have felt comfortable enough to open up and share some of his struggles with me.

Recently, Anderson Cooper and Steven Colbert had an in-depth discussion about grief that touched on the countless tragedies both men have experienced in their lives. Their tears, honesty, and openness were refreshing. Colbert eloquently stated, "It's a gift to exist, and with existence comes suffering. There is no escaping that." I forwarded the YouTube link to my husband and adult sons. Colbert's comment had made me pause and ponder. Life is suffering, and that is exactly why I believe we all need to come together.

Just a couple months before Brian passed, I remember expressing to my husband that I was longing for deeper, more authentic conversations. But how do we start asking each other harder questions? No one wants to talk about inner darkness and demons at the dinner table, I get that. Yet in this ever-changing, difficult world we need a place to sort through our pain. We need to talk more about feeling through our hurt. We need more support. How I wish Brian and I could have swapped stories.

As I scroll through many superficial social media posts, I try to remind myself that no one's life is picture-perfect despite what they might portray online or even in-person. These are counterfeit ways of showing up. No one wants to appear weak, so we hide our true emotions.

As we awkwardly dance together on this stage of life, I believe there needs to be more affirmation and applause. Recently, I have tried to ignore my natural urge to offer others advice and simply share my own vulnerability instead. I am in no position to preach or provide expert anything, but I do think we could all work on becoming better communicators.

None of us can escape suffering. It exists and affects us all. Why not allow ourselves and those around us to be more candid about emotional pain? When we stand in our truth, we give others permission to do the same. When we experience physical pain we go to the doctor, don't we? Why should emotional pain be treated any differently?

So next time you are sipping coffee with a colleague or even sitting watching Netflix with your child, simply ask, "How are you doing? What was the best (or worst) part of your day?" Send an email or text to a friend you have not talked to in a long time. Let's engage with each other more! In my experience, when I connect on a deeper level, empathy emerges.

GRIEF NEVER DIES

Sadness can be exhausting. Thirty-five years ago, my youthful father died after a two-year bold battle with Non-Hodgkin's Lymphoma. I was a devastated, and angry. I still am. Yet, as I navigate through life's treacherous terrain, it's his humor and casual way of dealing with daily doldrums I long for.

Over the years, I have learned time has no meaning. Dad's departure felt like it happened yesterday; however, it was three decades ago. Grief is a constant companion. As an eleven-year-old, I was numb to the pain, and now as a forty-six-year-old the pain is still real and raw.

Over the years, it felt like I was hauling a huge weight around all-the-damn-time. I was. I still am. Grief does not go away. Often wondering, does grief get harder? The shock and numbness have worn off. However, the unfriendly reminder death walks beside me every day does not.

Over the years, I would write. I would scribble quotes or reflective thoughts which were intended to inspire and motivate me. This is how I tried to make sense of the world around me. What I learned is there is no making sense of my feelings of grief. We each cope in different ways. What works for one, will not work for another. I do know writing has helped me to process and to move through my grief and resentment.

Last week my kindhearted hubs surprised me with academic regalia. I had graduated with my master's and opted out of the virtual commencement or any type of celebration. Yes, this level of education was a personal goal and major milestone. Maybe I avoided fanfare, because I wanted my dad there. In life, I keep pushing and plodding forward, as I want to seize every day and make the most of life, but mainly—I want to make him proud. I long for someone to tell me he sees me. I want to know he is toasting me, while gripping tight that cold Coors Light somewhere tranquil, flashing his signature mischievous grin.

Yeah, August 30 sucks. Yes, I will eat a slice of Boston Cream Pie. Certainly, I will light a candle and cry. Love is forever, and trust me, grief never dies.

SATURATION OF SORROW

Sometimes I wonder if I am the person I was meant to be, or if the life I've lived is a distorted half-life, shaped by loss and abandonment, a journey in and out of numbness. My existence feels like a mosaic of survival strategies—cobbled together to withstand the saturation of sorrow that has defined my path for decades.

The day my father died, the child I was disappeared. In her place, a hardened version of me emerged—a version built to protect against the looming weight of sorrow, a shadow that would follow me up until I turned fifty. I crafted a persona: the nicest person on the planet, a conscious or unconscious strategy to keep rejection and abandonment at bay. Polished and poised, I exuded calmness, but beneath that facade, I simmered with unspoken rage and contempt, resentful of the perfect, accommodating shell I had become. This guise cost me dearly; it cut me off from genuine human connection and kept me in relationships where I was always "fixing," always helping—unable to be vulnerable, always armoring up.

My most authentic self—the little girl and young adolescent within—remained unseen and unwitnessed. She carried me through, holding the weight of years, her essence suspended in a state of untouched sorrow, leaving me numb and alone. I see now that the only way out of this half-life is through grief, yet I have hesitated, fearing the risk of showing my raw self to those who cannot hold it. I have hidden my inner world, realizing now that those around me are only ancillary characters. The actual journey is my own.

This path toward healing has shown me that I must separate the childhood version of myself from the adult I am becoming. I am learning that it's better to be an imperfect adult than to rely on the perfect, competent child I once was, who survived by interpreting everything as a threat to her fragile safety. Her tactics were fierce, always viewing the present through the lens of childhood trauma—abandonment, neglect, and loss. It has taken years to understand that those coping strategies, once essential, no longer serve me. I am slowly unlearning the mistrust she knew so well, learning to see situations as they are rather than as triggers echoing my past.

For so long, I guarded my interior world. It was tender, vulnerable, and deeply hidden, yet I have come to understand that this is the space I must now open. This threshold in time, this painful yet liberating season, has given me the chance to become my own caregiver to mother the child within. I am learning to hold her, to witness her, and tell her, *I see you. I see all that you have carried.* I understand now that these words, these affirmations, were the ones I craved from my father, my mother, and even my husband. But the truth is, I am the only one who can give them to myself. That is the healing. That is what matters.

Now, my tears feel holy. I am apprenticed to my sorrow, no longer fighting it but allowing it to be part of me. The way forward, I see, is to remain present, to let this sorrow breathe and move within me. This is the only way I can truly stay alive, embracing the discomfort of grief, loss, and abandonment without running from it or distracting myself. Only by embracing my hurt can I transcend it, rise above it, and create space for genuine healing.

This saturation of sorrow has become my salve, my means to finally connect the dots between my past and present. After years of resentment, I am letting the buried child within me rise, no longer compelled to flee, to hide, or to shield my heart. Writing my memoir, capturing my survival, and reconciling with myself—not for others—feels essential now. The endless cycles of family drama, both mine and my husband's, no longer hold me captive. I am blowing my cover, inviting my sons to witness my healing journey. I want them to understand that true freedom comes from radical self-love, from nurturing a fierce love affair with oneself.

The most significant harm I could do to them, or myself, would be to remain needy, clinging, a victim waiting for others to meet my needs. I am here to create a safe space for them, a refuge they can trust, untainted by my unresolved pain. I want them to grow, free from the burden of my unhealed wounds, unshackled from any duty to fill my voids.

This journey of self-reclamation is my own, a labor of rediscovering love, unlearning numbness, and embracing my authentic self. I now realize that the life I choose to build from here is no longer a survival strategy but an intentional act of love. I am moving forward with a heart that knows both the depths of sorrow and the heights of resilience, trusting that I am equipped to hold myself in both.

No longer will I settle for a half-life shaped by old wounds or fears of abandonment. Instead, I am stepping fully into who I am meant to be—whole, alive, and fiercely present. I am here to offer myself the love and acceptance I once sought from others, finding freedom in the knowledge that I am enough, that I am complete. This is my legacy to my sons and to myself, the courage to live, unapologetically and with open-hearted resolve, a life that is entirely, unmistakably, my own.

PIECING MYSELF TOGETHER

There are moments when I catch my reflection and barely recognize the person staring back at me. The journey of self-discovery isn't linear; it's a winding path marked by profound realizations and quiet introspection.

For years, I constructed versions of myself built on fear, desperately holding everything together, trying to appear strong even as I was fragmenting inside. Every choice I made became a survival mechanism, a protective layer shaped by past traumas and unspoken wounds. I built walls, wore masks, and silenced parts of myself that felt too vulnerable. But now I'm learning that true strength isn't about maintaining a perfect exterior, it's about finding the courage to dismantle those defenses.

I'm not the person I was, and I'm not yet the person I'm becoming. This in-between space is uncomfortable, even painful, but it's also sacred. Here, I'm learning to be gentle with myself. Healing isn't about erasing the past; it's about understanding, integrating, and choosing a different path forward.

My faith isn't blind optimism, it's a quiet, persistent belief in my ability to grow. The version of myself I'm nurturing is emerging not despite my experiences, but because of them. Each scar and each moment of struggle has taught me resilience, compassion, and radical self-acceptance.

In his song *Things That I Can't Change,* country artist Greylan James reflects on how life's unmovable circumstances can transform us in unexpected ways. One lyric stands out: "The things I can't change are changing me." These words urge me to pause and echo in my mind, urging me to reflect on who I am, my role in this moment, and the quiet truth that I do not have control over everything.

Strangely this realization is not defeating, its freeing. In releasing the need to control, I have begun to find peace in simply being and in letting change shape me rather than resisting it.

I do know there is no turning back the clock. Yet I often find myself looking back, caught in moments when my reflection feels unfamiliar. Asking myself, "Who the hell is that?"

I'm not who I was, but I'm also not yet who I want to be.

Somewhere in between, I keep navigating my everyday choices born from fear, abandonment, and childhood survival, and the need to hold everything together when it felt like life was slipping through my hands. And yet, this work-this messy, imperfect process of becoming-is teaching me to find beauty in the cracks, to trust the pieces as they fall and rearrange, and to believe that even unfinished, I am whole.

MY TECHNICOLOR DREAM

Scribbled at 2:04 a.m, as the dream won't let me sleep. Because somehow, 30 years later, I'm back there again. Watching the performance. The funeral. The fanfare. And feeling the same quiet scream in my chest.

He died.

And I knew it.

I *felt* it.

But in the dream, and in real life—there was a song, swaying, a show. Young boys collecting coins (odd, right?). A calm mother. People were moving around me like nothing had shattered.

It felt like theater. And I was the only one who didn't get the script. I was the girl in shock,

in awe, and in awe of my own silence.

No one matched the gravity I felt. Not then. Not in the dream. And maybe not for years after. So, what is this dream telling me? What does it want? Maybe it's not about *reliving* it. Maybe it's about *reclaiming* it. My truth of that dreadful day, without the performance. Without the choreography of grief that made everyone else comfortable.

Maybe I'm finally naming something that was never said but always felt. Perhaps this is about validating the profound injustice of feeling invisible amidst my own heartbreak. Maybe at 51, I am now ready to hold that younger version of me and whisper, *"You weren't wrong. You weren't too much. You just felt what others couldn't face."*

This dream didn't come to haunt me. It came to hand me something. A mirror. A pen. A way back to myself. I write. Scribbling my way out of silence. Word by word. Feeling by feeling.

No more performance. Just my truth.

I keep writing—because there's a numbness that never left. A kind of going-through-the-motions that's dressed itself up well over the years, smiles at the right times, laughs at the right jokes, gets the job done. But underneath the mask, it's like I've been living in grayscale. And people don't see it. They see the competence, the resilience, the woman who keeps it all afloat. They don't see the velvet chair I sink into when no one's watching, where I sit in the shadows, watching my own life like a play I never quite got cast in.

How does one live in technicolor when the darkness has been so thick for so long?

Sometimes, I feel the stage light catch me, a moment of joy, of beauty, of connection, and for a fleeting second, it pierces the dark. But then it fades again. And I'm back in the velvet chair, back in the hush, back in the space between who I was before and who I had to become.

People say without saying, *"That was years ago. Move on."* They often say it gently, or with edginess, or even with pity in their empty eyes. But what they don't understand is this: I *can't.* It's not a choice. It never was.

My heart won't let me. It holds that little girl close—the one who lost the one person who made my world feel safe, and never really got him or that feeling back. She's still there. Still stunned.

Still wondering how joy is supposed to feel the same when the ground underneath her never stopped shaking. Maybe I'll never "get over it." Maybe that's not the point. Maybe the point is learning to live with it. To carry the grief with tenderness. To stop trying to erase the ache, and instead, ask what it wants me to remember.

And throughout the years, there have been moments. Bright, breathing, *real* moments that pulled me out of the velvet chair, out of the darkened, dank theater, and back into life. My two sons, my two most extraordinary awakenings. They cracked open my numbness with their smiles and sticky fingers, wide brown eyes, and unexpected laughter. They remind me of him, in the way they move, the quiet way they *see* me, the way they love without needing permission.

It's in them I remember what it felt like
to be loved like that.
To be known without needing to perform.

And my hubs, his patience, his steadiness, his willingness to love me even when I don't always know how to mirror it back. There's a quiet heroism in his loyalty to me. In staying when the joy doesn't come easily. In holding space, when I run and disappear into myself.

Then there's nature, those sacred moments when I am surrounded by something older, wilder, bigger than me, and my grief. The mountains, the ocean, the birds, and the wind weaving through trees. That's when perspective finds me again, reminding me that I, too, am temporary.

That one day, I'll be gone. And maybe, just maybe, someone will sit in their own velvet chair thinking of me, feeling both the weight of loss and the gift of love that came before it.

These technicolor moments, they don't erase the grief. But they occupy it. They soften its edges.

They make it breathable and remind me that my pain did not steal everything. That love still lives within. Even when it arrives in quiet ways. Maybe I won't ever fully move on. However, I am learning how to adapt to it. With the ache. With the light. With the knowing that feeling this much—even still—means I'm still alive.

REFLECTIONS

Thoughts Beneath the Surface

Neither grief nor growth happens in a straight line. Understanding deepens over time, and this section is a collection of those moments when I have paused, assessed, and integrated. These pieces are about seeing patterns, recognizing how far I have come, and understanding that wisdom often arrives through struggle, stillness, and surrender.

This is where the dust begins to settle and clarity, however fleeting, emerges. These reflections aren't about resolution so much as recognizing old cycles, quiet discoveries, and uncomfortable truths that gently surface when we stop running. Some entries were written in solitude, while others were crafted after difficult conversations or unexpected moments. In them, I try to answer questions I once feared asking to better understand myself and others. This section reflects the in-between moments, when we are no longer who we were, but not yet who we are becoming.

REFLECTIONS ON BEING HUMAN

Every day, I wake up and often ask – why. Why this dance across the stage of life?

Why the endless daily swirl of activity? Is it meaningful movement or just motion disguised as meaning? My unflinching routine of a quiet coffee before my 5 am workout, followed by the reading and writing moments that give me the solace and strength to seek the answers I crave, seem only to lose the vitality they offer me as I step into the day. The forced smiles, the small talk, and the never-ending to-do lists exhaust me, yet I am automatically pulled into that vortex.

My obsession with productivity both fills me and depletes me. It is an obsession driven by a senseless attempt to prove my worth to a barely watching world, an obsession that leaves me spinning away from my core. Why must I be relentlessly result-driven, as if the outcome is the only thing that justifies my efforts?

Can I unlearn this? Do I want to?

I feel like I live in a simulation – a beautifully glitchy video game. And I wonder... Am I a non-performing character in someone else's plot, or do I carry the main character's energy?

Do I fully grasp the fragility of my world, from my first kiss to my final breath? I toggle through roles and responsibilities, unlocking achievements as if wholeness were a prize just one level away. Is the game of life predetermined (fixed), or can I hack the code? Is it fruitless to wonder?

Yet still, I have the audacity to ask why. Am I alone in these thoughts? Are there others who share this sentiment as well? Maybe this is why I lean into storytelling. I need to know how everyone else manages their time on this life stage. Are we all dancers in a desperate ballet or awkward tango of life? We are all dancing, but truly, who is leading? Everyone is moving to a rhythm no one seems to understand, smiling like the music is beautiful, like we are at the best dance party ever, when really, we are all just shuffling closer to the crash, to the end.

And yet, we smile. We slap on hope like glitter and twirl anyway. Because if we stopped moving, stopped pretending, stopped laughing at the bad jokes that life tells, what would we have left? Maybe life is a wacky, brutal, absurd comedian. Perhaps we are all the punchlines. But maybe—just maybe—we are also the ones who get to choose whether we laugh, cry, or dance anyway. Perhaps the bravest thing isn't pretending it's not absurd. Maybe the most courageous thing is knowing it is and still showing up in the costume, ready to spin.

I sometimes wonder how I keep going, knowing the ending is already written; knowing I will stop breathing one day, and knowing the story will go on without me. And that is absurd, right?

Absolutely absurd.

I wake up every day inside this strange human skin, knowing that every face I love, every time I hold my husband's hand or hug my two boys, and every voice I cherish will vanish, eventually. Yet, somehow, here I am, still breathing, aching for answers, laughing, longing for more, and fighting for another day.

Maybe that's the rebellion: staring into oblivion's face and choosing to love anyway. To choose joy, anyway. To build something beautiful out of fleeting moments, even knowing they will crumble to dust. Maybe life isn't meant to make sense. Perhaps the absurdity *is* the point.

Perhaps the answer is to dance despite the absurdity.

Because, despite the absurdity, the ocean still crashes, the flower still blooms, the sun still rises, and I still feel all of it. I live not because I will last forever but precisely because I won't. That's the defiance. That's the poetry. That is the magnificent absurdity and audacity of being human.

To be human is to awaken in a blink—a blip of time—between stars being born and stars burning out. We arrive mid-sentence, inheriting stories already in motion, searching for meaning in the in-between. We love fiercely, even knowing it all ends. We ache for permanence in a world of change, gathering moments like fireflies in jars too fragile to last the night.

And yet, we create art, hold hands, bury the dead, sing lullabies, whisper prayers, and ask where all the precious souls go when the body goes quiet. Maybe being human is not about knowing the answers. Perhaps it is about becoming in a place where questions can live with tenderness and wonder. Perhaps it's about embracing the power of finding others who also question and seek greater meaning for themselves and their lives, to better frame the absurdities that life presents. Perhaps it's about welcoming the dance, finding the tune and steps that best suit us, and learning from others who have perfected their own.

I didn't set out looking for her. But somehow, Lou Andreas-Salomé found me, as if holding up a mirror to a part of myself I had long tried to silence. Some women are born carrying a wildness the world doesn't quite know what to do with. Lou Andreas-Salomé was one of those women. And in many ways, I realized after reading about her, so am I.

Lou lived in a world that demanded women be small, obedient daughters, silent wives, compliant mothers. Yet she refused to play along. Lou lived by her own terms: thinking, questioning, writing, unflinchingly carving out a life of intellectual and emotional sovereignty. She walked among Nietzsche, Freud, and Rilke, not as a muse or footnote, but as a mind who challenged, provoked, and changed them.

When I first encountered Lou's story, it wasn't admiration I felt; it was recognition. Across time, across different worlds, I could feel her wild heart beating against the invisible bars of her skin and century. It sounded like my own.

Lou once wrote, "Only those who have the courage to write about themselves can tell the truth about others." Those words burned through me. Because telling the truth, especially as a woman is still a radical, sometimes dangerous act. It's why I write women's stories.

Not to romanticize them. Not to tidy them into palatable myths. But to restore their realness: their flawed, complicated, resilient, furious, tender lives.

Storytelling is legacy work. It can be an act of rebellion against a world that has too often demanded our silence, erased our contributions, softened our rage, or rewritten our daring as deviance. When we tell our stories—fully, fiercely—we lay down steppingstones for the ones who come after us. We show them that living in their whole truth is not betrayal. It is birthright.

Yet, telling the truth often comes at a devastating cost. I have learned within my own first family system that society will punish a woman who refuses to shrink. They are the same ones who have internalized the systems I seek to dismantle. The ones who call our freedom selfish, our courage disloyal, our voices "too much." The echo of those who seek to silence us is loud, but the deepest wounds come from voices and actions closer to home – from the very people we were taught to trust, to believe would understand: our families and friends. Yet they can't. They don't. And theirs is a grief all its own.

The loneliness of being unchosen by one's own is a grief too vast for easy language. It breaks something, but it also remakes something. In the ashes of that grief, something incandescent can grow: *an understanding that living your truth is not contingent on applause, knowledge, or even love. It is an offering to something much older, much larger, a tapestry of women across time who dared to exist entirely despite the cost.*

Writing women's stories and my own is not just a literary act. It is a resurrection. A reclamation. A reminder that our lives were never meant to be footnotes or afterthoughts. We were and are, the whole story. Today, I walk with Lou Andreas-Salomé in spirit. Not because our lives were the same, they were not. But our hunger for sovereignty, unvarnished truth, and living unclaimed by anyone but ourselves is the same. She reminds me that a woman standing alone in her truth is not tragic. She is necessary!

It is worth repeating Lou's words again here. "Only those who have the courage to write about themselves can tell the truth about others." I will continue to carry that courage forward, to dance to my tune—for her, for me, for all of us. And for every woman still fighting to be fully seen, fully heard, fully herself: *You are not alone. We were never alone. We carry each other.*

MY LIFE IN REVIEW

T.S. Eliot once wrote, *"We shall not cease from exploration, and the end of all our exploring will be to arrive where we started and know the place for the first time."*

This quote has long resonated with me—first, because I've always been a seeker: curious, adventurous, drawn to knowledge. But more deeply, it reflects the core of my life journey. The more I age, the more I realize that true growth requires looking back to understand where we've been before we can move forward.

This year, as I turned fifty, I made a conscious effort to review my life, not just glance at it, but to study it. I wanted to know the "place" of my beginning as if for the first time. That meant confronting the parts I had long avoided. It meant seeing myself through a more objective lens. What I discovered surprised me: I am fearless. But that fearlessness came at a cost.

Grief and narcissistic relationships have been my biggest challenges. A personal project gradually turned into a full life review, revealing that many of my relationships were marked by patterns of emotional neglect, control, and manipulation. I saw how often I silenced my own needs in the name of harmony, losing myself while trying to accommodate others.

This honest reckoning became a catalyst. It helped me see my courage often quiet, sometimes desperate but always present. And it gave me permission to make changes that support my well-being, not just my survival.

In my writing space, surrounded by memory and stillness, I often find myself drawn to a photo of my first-grade self. A little girl with shy, big brown eyes, a maroon sweater, and a gentle smile. She had no idea what was coming. No idea her life would change so dramatically.

But she radiated possibility. Looking at her now, I feel tenderness, protection, and a desire to return to her, to me.

By eleven, I was already beginning to sense who I was, but my father's sudden death shook everything loose. That loss was my first experience of devastation, one that would reverberate through every phase of my life.

As I reflect, I often glance out the beveled glass window and watch hummingbirds zip past, protecting their territory, darting with purpose. Their movements remind me of the robins I watched as a child, thinking they were just playing. Now I understand it was instinct and survival. Much like the dynamics I witnessed growing up: flurries of conflict, invisible threats, and the ever-present sense of instability.

Someone once asked me, "Who hurt you?"

I replied, "My own expectations."

And at eleven, you don't expect to lose a parent. You don't know that safety can be taken. That grief can steal your footing, and it did. In the absence of my father, another man stepped in as my stepfather, a figure who brought chaos rather than comfort.

His need for control, for power, overshadowed any hope of genuine care. I watched him erode my mother's confidence, diminish her ability to protect herself and my younger sister. By fourteen, I was always on alert. His anger was unpredictable. While he never frightened me, his presence made our home feel unsafe. I became the quiet protector, the peacekeeper, and, silently, the emotional adult.

What hurt most was knowing my mother chose him. Her loyalty to him over us. That betrayal seeded a kind of solitude in me that no child should have to carry.

By eighteen, the situation had reached a breaking point. My mother, finally seeing the danger, accepted help and left. But by then, my trust had already frayed. The damage had woven itself into the fabric of who I was becoming.

Years later, I married and unknowingly stepped into another storm. My father-in-law was a man cut from the same cloth: critical, domineering, emotionally reckless. The déjà vu was unsettling. His constant jabs and attempts to undermine me echoed my stepfather's behavior. Once again, I found myself navigating emotional landmines, this time with two young boys in tow and a husband unwilling or unable to confront the damage being done.

My protective instincts kicked in. I downplayed my pain to keep the peace. I smiled through resentment. I buried myself in survival, again putting my needs aside. The loneliness of this second round, of seeing the patterns repeat, was suffocating. I resented my husband for tolerating it and resented myself for doing the same.

Here's what I know now: finding your voice isn't the hard part. It's being heard and supported—that's the challenge. Setting boundaries with narcissists doesn't earn you respect; it earns you backlash. And when those around you turn a blind eye, it becomes easier to stay quiet than risk the fallout. Until it no longer is.

Eventually, I had enough. I couldn't keep silencing my truth. I couldn't keep absorbing the damage of other people's insecurities masked as power. Confronting that truth meant confronting the anger I carried toward men who abused their influence, and toward myself for tolerating it.

But it also meant reclaiming my worth.

This review of my life—painful as it has been—became a turning point. I didn't abandon myself this time. I stayed. I dug deeper. I kept going, even when it was lonely and exhausting. Maybe it's age that gave me the courage. Or maybe it was the whisper of that little girl in the maroon sweater reminding me not to give up.

Through it all, I've rediscovered my values. I've learned to listen to my inner compass—the one I've named Rosie, after my fiercely strong paternal grandmother. She speaks the truth. She tells me I'm enough. Most of all, I've learned to love the little girl who once felt invisible. She didn't deserve what happened. But she survived. And now, she is seen. Fully.

CONTROLLING MY CRITICISM

Is it me or them?

For as long as I can remember, I've found myself being critical of others.

It's not always overt—sometimes, it's just a subtle thought or judgment that arises when someone doesn't meet my expectations, whether they realize it or not. Lately, I've started to wonder: Is this critical nature simply a reflection of my high expectations? Or is there something deeper at play?

It's easy to assume that my high standards are the culprit. I've always held myself to a certain level of excellence, whether in my work, personal life, or how I approach challenges. I scoff at desperation. I disregard neediness. I value responsibility, efficiency, accountability, and a strong work ethic, and I expect the same from those around me. When people don't rise to that level, I instinctively feel disappointed or frustrated. It's not that I expect perfection, but I do expect a certain effort—a commitment to doing things well and with intention.

However, as I reflect more deeply, I realize that my critical nature may not be solely about having high expectations. It could also be about control—about wanting things to unfold in a way that feels right to me. When people act differently than I would or fail to meet what I consider reasonable expectations, it disrupts the sense of order and predictability I strive to maintain. It's not just about what they did; it's about how it makes me feel as if their choices or actions are a reflection on me.

This realization has made me ask another question: why do I feel such a need for control?

Perhaps it's rooted in the fear of things falling apart or spiraling out of control if others don't meet specific standards. I've always planned ahead, anticipating outcomes and preparing for every possibility. I am a result-driven individual. When others don't follow through or take a different approach, it feels like a loss of stability. And in those moments, my criticism is less about them and more about protecting my sense of order.

Yet, I can't ignore that this critical lens can be harsh and sometimes unfair. Life doesn't always fit neatly into my framework, and people have different ways of doing things, shaped by their values, experiences, and challenges. I've come to understand that my high expectations—whether for myself or others—are not necessarily wrong, but they must be tempered with grace and understanding.

There's a balance to strike between expecting the best from others and accepting them as they are, imperfect and human. In its raw form, my criticism can be unyielding, but when I pause and give myself space to reflect, I realize that what I want more than perfection is connection. I don't want to be someone who distances herself from others because they don't meet my expectations; I want to be someone who can inspire growth while accepting flaws.

In the end, my criticism may stem from high expectations, but it's more about my desire to control outcomes and protect a sense of order in my life. Recognizing this has opened the door to a kinder way of seeing others—and myself. It's a journey toward balancing expectations with compassion, and in that process, I'm learning to embrace the magnificence and messiness of life, finally at fifty!

WHO IS YOUR EMOTIONAL SWAT TEAM?

During life's inevitable storms, it's easy to convince ourselves that we can shoulder everything alone. After all, who knows your struggles, fears, and triggers better than you? But even the strongest among us have limits. When the mental turbulence becomes too much to bear, having an emotional SWAT team—a trusted circle of people who can step in, support, and ground you—is essential. These individuals offer a lifeline when your emotional bandwidth is stretched thin, and your inner resilience falters.

Your emotional SWAT team isn't about quantity but quality. These are not just friends or family members but those who genuinely see and hear you. They are the ones who can hold space for your pain without judgment or a rush to fix it. Whether it's a trusted therapist, a loyal friend who knows when to listen, or a mentor who offers perspective, these people create a safe haven where you can unload without guilt. Their presence reminds you that you're not navigating the turbulence alone, even in your most vulnerable moments.

It's equally important to acknowledge that assembling this team takes intentionality. It requires identifying those who consistently show up for you and setting boundaries with those who drain you. Consider who in your life provides calm in chaos or asks the right questions when your thoughts spiral. Maybe it's the friend who always knows how to make you laugh, the partner who grounds you with unwavering steadiness, or even a community you've built around shared experiences. These are the people who don't just tell you to keep going—they help you recalibrate and continue forward.

Remember, leaning on others isn't a sign of weakness but strength. It's a declaration that you recognize the value of connection and community, especially when your inner resources are depleted. Your emotional SWAT team exists to remind you of your humanity—that no matter how self-reliant you are, it's okay to lean, breathe, and rebuild with the support of those who love you.

So, who is your emotional SWAT team?

Remember, your emotional team isn't just a safety net for life's challenges; they are a foundation for resilience, connection, and growth—a reminder that we are not meant to navigate this journey alone. Take time to nurture those relationships, and trust that you won't have to weather them alone when the storms hit.

THE ART OF COMING HOME TO MYSELF

Burned out and depleted, I slowly crawled back to the core of my existence. Along the way, I rebuilt expectations for myself—ones rooted in genuine fulfillment, not the impossible standards I once set to prove my worth based on old childhood stories.

Coming home to myself meant embracing who I am, separate from everyone else's narratives. I've learned to unapologetically take as much or as little space as I need because it's mine to occupy. The art of coming home to myself is also about understanding that my mind, body, and spirit need more than just rest to be rejuvenated.

No amount of sleep can compensate if my waking hours are spent maintaining unfulfilling relationships, overextending my energy, denying myself what I truly need and want, or performing to please others. I can't count the times I've caught myself acting differently around different people—whether friends or family—never strangers, oddly enough. While it may sometimes be "normal and necessary" to fit in and get by, at what cost? Deep down, it's exhausting to be everyone except myself.

Certain words, actions, and behaviors can ignite one person and extinguish another's flame entirely. My helpful nudges may accidentally stir another's shadows. So, I've learned to let it be—to let others find their way without interfering unless it affects me directly.

We all walk different tightropes, balancing different demons. Staying curious means gently questioning which parts of my story are my own and which echo others' expectations. Some waves pull us under this vast ocean of influence; others guide us to shore. But it isn't the direction we swim that defines us—it's the stories we tell ourselves while we're in the water.

Think about that—how true!

Freedom isn't just about walking away from what dims my spirit—it's about running toward what makes my soul dance. I'm a fierce advocate for gauging worth by my standards, not someone else's measuring stick.

A wise woman once reminded me, "Don't let joy play hide-and-seek." My journey back to myself reveals all the wisdom I've always had. I just needed to tune in. I love hearing my frequency, not out of ego but out of trust in my instincts and experience.

Unlearning has been my daily job. I'm the detective of my beliefs. Keeping what resonates, discarding the rest. My enlightenment? It's messy but magical. I'll keep swimming against the current, climbing onto shores unknown. Breathless, perhaps, but invigorated. This space is, and has always been, mine to claim.

DRIFT TO THE LIGHT

I have realized that not everyone wants to heal. They like to use their emotional wounds as an excuse to not be fully responsible or find themselves. It feels as if they are basically telling me, "don't expect too much from me and you need to give in to me because I am hurt."

It is crystal clear to me when I meet them. These type of people tell their entire life stories the first time we converse.

They are negative, constantly complain and talk only about the past. I like to call them energy vampires or wounded birds.

It can be very hard if these people are in your close circle of family or friends. In fact, it can be challenging to say no, and "get rid of them." However, I realize if I tolerate them, then I have to deal with the consequences.

They are hard to ignore. The best advice I can offer is what I remind myself: Stay away from these types of people.

Love them from afar.

Over the years, I have succumbed and bent over backwards for them. I felt it was my duty to not abandon or betray them. However, lately my inner Rosie reminds me, *if it hurts, it isn't love.*

Love does not need anything from you.

Find light.

Steer clear from darkness.

UNEXPECTED KINSHIP

Every day walking the beach, I notice a lanky man with tattered trousers, silvery hair, and headphones. While scanning the shoreline, he searches for treasures beneath the sand's surface. An attached mesh bag with a small number of shiny metals hangs from his hip. I often wonder, *Is he here for the tangible or the intangible?*

He steadily swings his detector from side to side in a methodical planned pattern, dodging the movement of the tides. Our paths seem similar, as we both walk parallel to the water with our footprints leaving an imprint behind us. He scoops sand while I soak in the stillness and serenity which soothes and settles my overactive mind and body.

Are we here for similar reasons?

There is temptation to tell him how my daily search takes me into different depths, for different types of treasures. A trove of truth into my existence and understanding of living. If I do, will he gawk at me behind his tinted eyeglasses and think I am a loon?

Like the bleached seabird that looms overhead and makes a laughter-like cry over the crashing waves. As the tides zig and zag, the sand searcher strolls along the shoreline with a spring in his step, on a quest for a reward. I think to myself, we must swap stories. I will explain to him how my daily walk on the beach is my tonic. A place to tame my thinker and refuel. This harmonious haven has become a window into my soul. A place for me to reconnect and reflect, not paramount for a palpable prize. Maybe this is true for the mysterious man who smiles at seagulls and allows seawater to tingle his bare toes.

In the breathtakingly beautiful moments walking along this sandy sea beach, I am roused with the imagery that surrounds me. When Mother Nature speaks, I listen. Her natural acoustics help empty my mind of muddled thoughts. Her winds enchant me. As pitches of sound vibrate through the fibers of my being, I embrace my own sense of space in her existence like the rhythmical manner of the ocean and currents of air whirling around me.

The sand-searcher may or may not be able to answer my inquiries. Since there will always be more questions than answers to last a lifetime, perhaps we could investigate together. My quest for the meaning of life's significance will never end. However, it is in this endless exploration of myself and life, this walk and talk may offer me clues and guide me into the very essence of my being.

Tomorrow, I will tell the enigmatic man who hunts along dry sand about my precious prize tucked tight within me. How the wondrous waves and their power, as they ebb and flow, are teaching me to accept what I do not know. The sand man and I can discover together the mysterious nature of life, the chance of fate, and how the place we both inhabit can guide and beguile us.

The afternoon was peaceful and clear with a gentle sea breeze. I noticed him heading toward me as he smiled and said, "I see you here almost every day." I nodded and without hesitancy, he exclaimed how scanning the shoreline is really a secondary outcome of his daily detecting. "Sand searching for me is a soothing and satisfying experience," he states with excitement. As if he was reading my mind from previous encounters. I smiled with the euphoric enthusiasm of a child.

We immediately established ethereal gifts are truthfully the cache of riches we are in quest of. A shared fondness for the steely, shiny dolphins, who surface and splash. The expansive blue body of water in front of us wanting respect, as she whispers, "it is up to us to learn how to extract her power and convert it as our own." The shattered shells sprawled along the jagged tideline, representing we are all part of a greater living whole, making us think deeper into our own existence.

Together we found assurance and agreed our most profound insights about life may be hidden deep down in the treasure trove of our souls, not scattered on the surface. It was at this moment, we sensed our truths. He repeated, "Never overlook what has been written in the sands of time." My happy heart gave him a smile.

We agreed to chat again. As he scoured the sand with his metal detector and hefty headset, I walked away in an energetic manner. Reciting another one of his remarks, "How life, at times, has a way of numbing and hardening our souls, if we allow it." Now it was the spirit of humanity smiling.

I never want to forget to feel. Flashes of serendipitous magic occur when I strip down and be honest with who I am. I have learned to step outside of the person I've been and remember the person I am meant to be, the person I am capable of being, and the person I am today. This is my lucrative find, thanks to the steadfast sand-searcher named Walter.

My new friend helped me understand the importance of self-discovery. In silence, I shout, "Thank you." This outdoor playground continues to be serotonin for my soul. A spiritual experience between me and myself within the soundscape of nature and those who occupy it.

MY "HYGGE" MOMENT!

Last night, I sat around the table with my two adult sons and husband after a dinner of chili and cornbread. Warmed by a crackling fire and the soft glow of candlelight, I watched as the rain cascaded down our windows. It felt cozy, nostalgic really. I've always savored these quiet moments as a family, fully aware of how fleeting they become as our children grow into adulthood. And so, I did what we have often done through the years when nestled around a table, sated and content, I pulled out a game.

We have always been a board game family—Life and Monopoly are family favorites. That night, however, I pulled out a new game called The Hygge Game. It's a box of three hundred thought-provoking questions designed to spark meaningful conversations. As a storyteller, I love every opportunity I get to delve deep past surface-level conversations and world events, which often leave me unsatisfied.

The box states that The Hygge Game brings people together by encouraging friends and family to share stories and discuss both significant and small aspects of life. While there are various descriptions for the word *hygge,* it essentially means creating a warm atmosphere and enjoying the good things in life. It refers to all things that evoke a feeling of contentment and well-being, like cozying up with loved ones or lighting candles; doing things that feel good. So, The Hygge Game is definitely up my alley. I thrive on spending quality time with the people I love and learning more about them in a cozy atmosphere.

Much to my surprise, it didn't take long for this game to live up to its name as I soon drew a card that made me immediately want to share a heartfelt "feeling" I have for two influential women who came into my life nearly two decades ago. This specific card had three questions, and the third was, "Who was your most memorable neighbor?"

Most of the time, I'm one to sit with my thoughts for a bit before I dive into a response, but in this instance, my answer was immediate... though plural: Ruth and Madaline.

At nearly twenty and fifty years my senior, these women represented a sisterhood I desperately needed when they entered my life. We called ourselves Wacky Wonderful Women. At the time, I was in my late thirties, Ruth was in her sixties, and Madaline was in her eighties. I will never be able to find words to describe how they guided me during that time, but I can say that they refused to let me be anything less than myself and loved me unconditionally as a mother and grandmother would.

They were both Wonder Women, with talents that far exceeded anything I knew. Ruth made the most unforgettable coffee infused with cardamom pods and cinnamon sticks. And she talked to us about which new coding class she was taking, patiently showing us how to use the technology on our cell phones and computers. Madaline found shelter in her garden and baked the most incredible cheesecakes and Heath bar crunch cakes. When we sat at lunch, they would share pearls of wisdom about navigating challenges, making sound decisions, and embracing the passage of time with grace.

Each imparted a wealth of knowledge through their experiences, offering lessons in resilience, patience, and the nuances of life. They infused vitality and shared contemporary insights, resulting in a symbiotic relationship that transcended generational boundaries. I feel fortunate to have had their stories and advice; each story served as a compass, guiding me at a time when I needed the influence of influential women in my life. Our bond contributed to a more harmonious life during a time when I struggled with family drama.

For me, Ruth and Madaline were able to weave a fabric of how interconnected our lives were, creating a connection of care and compassion within our small community. Our relationship offered me a deeper understanding of myself and the world around me.

While I had elders in my life before moving to California from Michigan, I felt a void in my new home State and longed for the communal connections I had back home. The gift of girlfriends has always been priceless for me, and I was missing that. Each of these women emphasized the importance of values, integrity, and the significance of relationships. They fostered a sense of continuity that gave me comfort and confidence in my abilities and illustrated just how important it is for women to empower other women, at any age. The wisdom of others teaches us the timeless lessons that can shape character and provide a compass for navigating life's journey . . . if we take the time to listen and learn.

I recently read a study on the importance of intergenerational friendships and how they can bridge age gaps, fostering mutual understanding and enriching lives. My friendship with Ruth and Madaline is a testament to this. Generations before us have much to offer. It's so important that we give them the space to share.

I do know I often think of Madaline, as she passed at the young age of ninety-three. I know she was wearing her Rich and Rose Estee Lauder lipstick as well as her favorite sapphire blue cashmere sweater. I smile and suddenly realize the need to call Ruth, as she lives in Connecticut close to her family. The last time we spoke, she had been on a ski trip with her adult granddaughter Amy, who calls her "Gadget Gramma." Still an early adopter of technology, she was putting the finishing touches on the house she built, fully equipped with a smart home system she designed to connect and automate all her "gadgets."

I love it when life gives us a little nudge to reflect, to remember, and to be grateful. I'll always look back fondly on all that Ruth and Madaline provided during that time in my life those many years ago.

Looking forward to future questions maybe later this evening from the Hygge cards.

STRIVING FOR MORE

Tapping into who we are and what we want from life is no easy undertaking. There are a myriad of obstacles that can stop us in our tracks at various points—significant events that can change the course of our life in entirely unpredictable ways, as well as everyday life events that simply pile upon one another until we feel we are completely burdened and immobilized by their weight. I know that all too well in my own life.

Finding our authentic selves is a journey that often requires years of work and reflection that not everyone is keen to embrace. It's easier sometimes to sit in what is, to not question, to not wonder, to not rock the proverbial boat, to accept what comes our way without regard to our well-being or desires. I have always fought this resignation, though not as successfully and valiantly as I may have always hoped, ultimately falling back on old habits and acceptances that left me feeling empty.

And yet, regardless of how low my lows may have been at various times in my life, I am a seeker. Self-discovery has always been my North Star. I thrive on deciphering my feelings, addressing my reactions, and assessing my awareness of the world. It's my way of finding my way.

In 2023, this need for self-discovery became more profound than ever. After twenty-five years of attempting to hold my marriage together, which left me feeling alone on an island, not to mention emotionally exhausted from carrying my husband and his "generational gook." I had arrived at an impasse. I was tired of trying to correct course for myself while at the same time trying to right the family dynamic that had hung over us like a black cloud for decades. I was no longer okay with this dynamic being at my expense. I had finally realized that the energy I offered was given too freely.

Things came to a head mid-year, which led to several events that genuinely didn't settle within me until the turn of the new year. It's somewhat ironic that it landed at such a traditional time. Each January marks the beginning of a new year, an opportunity to lay the past to rest and look to the future. And, if willing to do so, a time to reflect. The name "January" is derived from the Roman God, Janus, who was said to have two heads—one looking to the past and one looking to the future. He was the god of doors, gates, and transitions. And, wow, did Janus ever live up to his name!

I am still collecting my thoughts and takeaways from all that transpired this past year. My need to assemble them in a fluid fashion has been challenging, yet never before have I known how important it was for me to do so. It was crystal clear to me that while I had undergone a year of dodging punches, it was also a year of formidable endurance—a year in which I stuck to my moral framework and, as a result, discovered profound lessons in relearning and unlearning who I am and what I want to continue to put out in the world. As a lover of wordsmithing, *resilience* became my word.

While I am ready to close last year's chapter—the final year of my forties—I want to take note of a few of the significant events that gave me a deeper understanding of my past, an experience that I have been searching for years to uncover; an understanding that has illuminated the opportunities I now feel I have for a new beginning. Three were particularly significant in reminding me who I am and want to be in the days, weeks, months, and years ahead.

The first of these was actually a second—the publication of my second S.H.E. book, a compilation of stories from twenty-three women of all ages and cultures who courageously share their heartfelt journeys of discovery, resilience, and perseverance. At first, I resisted the pull to write a second book but relented when I realized I had more stories that needed sharing, voices that deserved to be heard. In taking this leap, I recognized that these women, like the twenty-two featured in my first book, are beacons of light that have helped illuminate my path of discovery—the power I possess. This year, working with a new editor—one proven to be my girl guru in many ways beyond this book—brought greater understanding to this storytelling journey of mine: *we find bits and pieces of ourselves in others, like pieces of a magical mosaic that can help us better define ourselves and strengthen our journeys.*

So, this first event (realization, really) was impactful. It proved that *my long-held belief in the power and healing nature of storytelling is something I know I need to honor.*

The next happening came on the heels of the publication of volume two of my book. This year-long effort culminated in an art gallery event showcasing the works of art that twenty-four artists explicitly created for the featured stories. It was a beautiful celebration of an accomplishment I felt very proud to have completed. Yet, as full as this made me feel, I also felt depleted of energy.

How does that make sense? Feeling full and depleted at the same time?

Well, in the story of my life, I often feel like a paradox or walking contradiction. I am learning it's fairly universal; many of the women I interviewed for my books reminded me that I am not alone in this feeling. *We* are not alone. It's okay to, at times, feel like a dichotomy of contradiction, to feel a push and pull that can seem out of step with the attempts of this push and pull to co-exist. It reminds you that you have dimension, depth, and resources for growth. What I realized, however, was that my feelings of being spent extended far beyond the publication of my book and a simple sense of unrest. It developed deep into my relationships. Being busy simply masked the extent of those borders. When the dust of activity finally settled, experiences I'd had and pushed aside came back to the forefront, forcing me to dig deep into my core for answers and the roots of my unrest.

Some of the many ups and downs I have experienced will be chronicled in a book. For now, I will simply say that I felt overwhelmed, too much so at times, with many situations pulling at me from many angles, asking for more and more and more . . . of which I had nothing more to give. I can honestly say I was at a breaking point—contemplating my purpose in matrimony and life and why my actions matter. I could no longer continue putting everyone else's needs and wants before my own, carrying other's feelings for them, allowing them to skirt their responsibilities, struggling to hold my family together, and parenting a partner who chose to avoid the demons that plagued him.

After several disastrous moments in the last four months of the year, my remarkable therapist and friend, Tristen, listened intently to my turmoil and said, "Trust yourself." Those simple words have haunted me my whole life, yet they have also driven me and been the bedrock of many sound decisions. Trusting myself has caused me to push harder, to be more verbal, and to fight against injustice.

What I trusted was that I needed to be alone. I needed to travel. Travel has been something that has been a part of my life and love since as far back as I can remember and something that I feel privileged to be able to do. As a seeker, travel provides answers and insights that might otherwise go undiscovered . . . gems, forever lost. I have always turned to my love of travel in both times of joy and need, and this past year presented more of the latter.

In the past, my sanctuaries were Bali, Thailand, and other places where calm can reside within me. But this time, the idea of a road trip felt right: an opportunity to detach from the chaos I was swirling in, to give me the time and space I needed to think. I started with fourteen days in the south, traversing through six states in a rental car I coined Chrissy the Chrysler. Throughout my travels, I came to randomly meet charming folks who reminded me of my core without even knowing me. These magical moments of crossing paths are something I relish. It is what led me to embark on writing my S.H.E. books. My editor, girl guru, said it was my superpower. She noted that I had a "magnetic field" that draws people to me to share their stories openly and honestly. I do feel that people cross my path for a reason, and I'm always open to the experience.

This trip proved no different.

I met many people during those two weeks of travel. Whether sitting alone for a morning coffee or in a hotel bar for dinner, my solitude rarely remained. Short pleasantries shared with other travelers coming and going often evolved into conversation, often serving as a mirror to myself, presenting different perspectives on life that challenged my assumptions and prompted further self-reflection. While navigating unfamiliar environments and encountering new challenges, I was again reminded of my resilience and adaptability.

When I have these walkabouts—my personal travels—they often lead to greater introspection, self-reflection, and engagement in activities that bring me joy and fulfillment. They always contribute to a better understanding of myself. I relish meeting new people and hearing their stories; I learn much about myself through them. Taking time away taught me that I needed to step away from social convention and what I believed the world and my loved ones needed from me. It made me realize that I needed to be a better boundary-setter in my personal life.

A few encounters I had over these two weeks were incredibly impactful.

The first took place in Charlotte, North Carolina, at a hotel bar in a far less provocative manner than that line may imply. I settled in at the bar with a glass of Caymus and a light meal, perusing a script I promised a friend I'd review when an elderly gentleman, a retired lawyer, took the stool beside me. Making idle chitchat, he asked what I was reading. After briefly explaining, we extended our conversation to travel and vineyards, both apropos of the moment. Our discourse was easy and fluid, delving deeper into why we relish travel and time to reflect. I found our conversation touching and bizarrely awesome, neither of which I ever questioned.

Ultimately, this wise octogenarian reminded me to be unapologetically myself and never settle for a tolerable level of unhappiness. What a gift! It's not that we somehow don't know this is how we should be; we sometimes need it reflected to see it. I do not question some encounters; I only glean the wisdom gained.

The second encounter that moved me was similar to those that inspired me to write my books, a chance encounter with a woman of remarkable resilience. This meeting took place in Beaufort, South

Carolina. Again, settling into a spot at a bar for a glass of wine and dinner, I happened to sit next to a stylish woman who I quickly learned owned her own interior design firm. Though successful, she shared that her life was anything but, as she was going through a divorce. She noted that the constant search for salvation in her twenty-year relationship left her depleted. We spent three hours conversing, exchanging numbers, and discussing the possibility of including her SHERO story in a potential volume three.

The grand finale of my trek, one that moved me to the brink of nearly falling off my stool was my chance meeting with a prominent literary figure while visiting Charleston, South Carolina. As a nonfiction writer myself, dabbling in biographies, obituaries, and personal narratives for years, fiction has been calling me, yet I keep ignoring it. After thirty minutes of platitudes, talking about family and fun while he sipped his smoky old-fashioned and I my glass of Chablis, he very eloquently offered, "Shannon, go to the edge, then go further. There are no boundaries when it comes to writing or life." Again, we know these things to be true. Applying them to ourselves is another thing. Hearing these words somehow resonated with me in a way I don't think I might have been ready for previously.

The following night in Savannah, Georgia, after dinner with a couple from the Hamptons I had met six months earlier, I sat at the hotel rooftop bar sipping a glass of champagne, ready to call it a night when I met another dynamic person, a therapist at a women's center in Naples, Florida. She shared that she is a married mother of a six-year-old boy trying to keep everything together. As our conversation continued, she revealed that she deeply wished to be more adventurous and to travel more.

"I need more time alone and want to do uncomfortable things, but traveling solo feels scary," she whispered. As I write this, I am pinching myself, reminded of the kismet I felt swirling around me at that moment and how mind-boggling it was.

Shortly after she left, I was still spiraling, thinking it might be the bubbly. I turned to my phone to check my email and found a note from Dollywood's media department, a theme park in Pigeon Forge, Tennessee, confirming they would be happy to host me for a private tour. I had contacted them earlier in the week, expressing my interest in writing a story about women and philanthropy. Dolly Parton is a musical icon and a trailblazer for women. Her challenge of societal gender norms and efforts to break through various constructs have always inspired me. I planned to write a story about her influence as a woman philanthropist and source of inspiration. She is a woman who has trusted her heart and connected with the greater world community through her musical storytelling genius.

As this year drew to a close, I felt grateful for the silence and solitude I provided myself—a space that gifted me my greatest confidant, myself. In a Dolly-inspired expression, I "put wings on my dreams." After my visit to Dollywood, as a way to honor the inspiring spirit of storytelling I believe I share with Dolly, I had the S.H.E. Foundation donate one hundred *S.H.E. Share Heal Empower, Collected Journeys, Volume Two* books to The Dollywood Foundation and Dolly's Imagination Library. I'm excited to be a small part of these organizations' inspiring efforts to promote the power of words and stories as agents of positive change.

Throughout my travels, I felt immensely grateful for all my encounters, conversations, and shared stories. It took just a few strangers to remind me of who I am and how I was built. I have always been curious about what I don't know and the expansion of knowledge, trying to understand wisdom and apply it beneficially. Human behavior fascinates me, especially my own.

I believe the signs guiding my path in life have always been there, but I often doubted their direction. I had stopped listening to my inner Rosie, my inner guide who has always had my back. I named this source after my paternal grandmother. I realized that ignoring her when I needed her most created a huge roadblock. This road trip and the insights I gained motivated me to make a deal with both of us to prevent this oversight from continuing. I know this internal compass is essential to my growth, as I am the best person to understand myself, my disconnects, and my desires.

This second awakening during my road trip made it clear that trusting my heart and recognizing my desire for shared humanity through storytelling are just as vital to me as the air I breathe.

The third important event that emerged is more personal—my marriage. This past year, the chaos of an extended family that had been unmanaged for years, issues and transgressions I always felt I was left to handle finally reached a point where it hurt my well-being. I realized it wasn't my job to carry others' burdens. I wanted freedom from this toxicity. As a result, my husband and I had some very uncomfortable, long-overdue conversations. Thankfully, he was willing to engage and discuss the uncomfortable truths between us, both his and mine. While not easy, these talks have led to greater understanding and closeness, both of which had been missing due to a fractured first family system he grew up in and is still trying to understand.

We have started creating a safe space to question and share. My favorite question lately has been, *how close are these versions of ourselves that we show to our absolute truth?* Along with my own intergenerational identity, I want to explore and become as close to my truth as I can, expressing the person I truly am without conforming to whatever audience or drama is present. I no longer want to hide my many layers. I no longer want to participate in a dance of turmoil, manipulated by pain I didn't fully understand.

This final step in addressing my marriage was what I knew I needed to do after returning from travel. It reinforced the main message: I must honor *myself, fully embrace my authenticity, and find spaces and relationships where I can be myself safely.* 2023 helped me see, feel, and understand where I need to be. I've always been in a state of flux and restructuring, but here's to a calmer and more purposeful 2024, where I'll focus more on myself and my practice of self-writing in my 'babe cave,' deconstructing myself and my discontent, and living with resilience.

WHAT MAKES A WOMAN A FORCE OF NATURE?

Effective communication is the foundation of connection. It allows us to articulate, share our thoughts, and express our internal world clearly and gracefully. This skill is a game-changer, influencing every area of life. In a world full of voices, I recently asked myself: *How often am I truly listening to Rosie, my inner voice?* The biggest shift for me in recent months has been trusting myself, my instincts, over anyone else. I've always been a woman of conviction, but to lead myself and others, I must trust that Rosie knows what's best for me.

Through personal experience, I've seen how being open and expressive draws people in and opens doors to intimacy I never thought possible. The impact isn't limited to my relationship with my partner but extends to my friends, family, and everyone I meet along my journey. When I show people who I am, I create a "sweet spot" a safe space for them to share their truths, too. It's in this space of openness that real resonance occurs.

At S.H.E. (Share Heal Empower), our storytelling is entirely authentic, and the right people connect with messages from the heart. Transparency, authenticity, honesty, and openness are essential to S.H.E.'s success and to building deeper relationships beyond just the community. After all, intimacy requires us to show up completely, bringing all of who we are. The power of shared experiences creates strong bonds, fostering empathy and understanding, but only when we communicate genuinely.

Creating a safe, non-judgmental space allows us to express our vulnerabilities and work through our wounds. We can confidently identify our needs and emotions, knowing resilience will carry us forward. When we stop overanalyzing, stop second-guessing our worth, and instead boldly proclaim, *I give a damn about this— watch out,* we step into our true power. No more looping in insecurity or fear; instead, we trust ourselves. Communication has taught me that connecting with others who have faced similar challenges can be both empowering and inspiring. We begin to tell a different story, one where our voices don't shake, and we wake up with a fire in our belly, ready to share our truths because the world needs our stories.

I become a force of nature when I fully commit to being myself and my purpose. With courage comes rejection, but also resilience. And through it all, I trust my inner Rosie. Mastering communication in all its forms has enabled me to transcend insecurity, fear, and anger, particularly in challenging conversations. My goal is to continually expand my emotional toolkit.

Every time a challenge arises, I remind myself: *I've got this. I've practiced this.* Communicating my needs doesn't have to be hard; it's a natural force within me.

SOVEREIGN SELF

I am going through a major transformation, a messy yet beautiful process. The roles I've long played—caretaker, over-functioner, people-pleaser, wife, mother, creative supporter, the quiet strategist behind the scenes—no longer fit me. I can feel it in my bones. Something inside me is shifting. My internal compass is pointing in a new direction, but the map hasn't fully taken shape yet. And while that feels unsettling, it also feels empowering.

For many years, I placed myself around others—their dreams, needs, and comfort. Now, I'm finally ready to prioritize myself. Not out of guilt, duty, or obligation, but because I *genuinely* want to. Here's what I'm learning: I don't need to see the whole path to take the next step. I can start by creating space, setting boundaries, and saying no to what no longer feeds me, even if it disappoints someone else.

Writing isn't just what I do—it's how I find my way. The stories I've written, both mine and others', serve as guiding lights. They speak of freedom, reclaiming, and returning to authenticity. I return to those words, reading them not just as a writer, but as someone eager for direction.

I'm not stuck. I'm paused. There's a difference. Stuck means helpless but paused means powerful. This is a gestation, not a dead end. Something new is forming. I've carried so much for so long. I've built scaffolding around others' lives. But now, I want to create something of my own, something that energizes me instead of drains me. I don't owe my next chapter to anyone else's vision. My voice, the one I've used to uplift, tell, write, and mother, is asking to be heard *by me* now. I don't need all the answers; I just need to listen. This is the season of my Sovereign Self—and she is just getting started.

THE BOOKENDS OF LIFE

I wrote this as a reminder to myself, and maybe to you too, that in a world full of pressure to be everything for everyone, the only two versions of me I truly need to live for are the girl I once was and the woman I'm still becoming. This is a love letter to them. A reckoning and recalibration. But most importantly, a way to hold both wonder and wisdom at the same time.

I used to think I had to answer to everyone—family, friends, coworkers/bosses/cohorts, acquaintances, and strangers... I twisted myself into shapes that didn't fit, trying to be liked and accepted. But now? I know better. There are only two people I truly need to answer to, my 5-year-old self and my 80-year-old self. That little girl? She didn't care about how polished I looked or how successful I became.

She cared if I was happy. She cared if I was still curious. She wanted me to color outside the lines, ask big questions, sing loud, and wear whatever made me feel magical. She reminds me who I was before the world told me who to be. And that woman at 80? She has seen it all. The loss, the loneliness and heartbreak. The chances taken—and the ones I was at times afraid to try. She is not interested in how many followers I had, how many hours I worked or what I did to leave my mark, or how perfect and put together I appeared. She just wants to know:

Did I live with truth?
Did I make it count?
Did I show up for the life that was mine?

Those two female versions of me, they are my bookends. My beginning and my end. One holds my wonder. The other is my wisdom. So now, when I am faced with choices, when I am tempted to betray myself just to belong, I pause. I check in.

Would my 5-year-old self... light up at this?

Would my 80-year-old self... smile and say, "Well done?"

That's the compass I trust now. Because I don't want to reach the end of my life full of apologies to the girl who dreamed big, or explanations to the woman who knows better. I want to live in between them, with courage, with color, with joy, that doesn't need permission. So here I am, choosing presence over perfection, depth over performance, and truth over approval. This is the life I want, the one that honors where I began and who I'm becoming. No regrets.

Just a story, I'll be proud to tell from both ends.

So, wherever you are right now, in the thick of becoming, in the mess, the magic, or the in-between, remember: You don't have to answer to the world. Just the child who dreamed you into being... and the elder who's waiting to welcome you home. Live in a way that honors both of them. That's the real masterpiece.

WHY I READ AND WRITE

When I read and write, I navigate the labyrinth of life, sometimes tracing well-worn paths, sometimes forging new ones. It's an endless expedition, a lifelong addiction to learning that helps me make sense of the world around me. Writing gives me tangible results, proving that my resilience isn't just about endurance, but also about compassion for myself. Reading reminds me that I am not alone and that others have struggled as well. In their words, a cross-generational conversation unfolds.

When I write, I hover above myself, zooming in and out, both me and not me, a reflection peering through my own eyes but also through another's. I am most myself and least myself in these moments, caught between what I know and what I'm still searching for.

Reading is my ritual, my way of expanding. It broadens my perspective beyond my own experiences. Conversely, writing is where I untangle the knots, transforming swirling emotions, thoughts, and behaviors—both the ones that have served me well and those I need to release—into form. It is where I pause to find the glimmers in the small and mundane moments, where life itself whispers its meaning.

I write to read into my soul for truth. I write to see the story poles of my surroundings, the markers of where I've been and where I might go. I write to make sense of what it means to be here, in this life, in this moment. And in that process, I find my language—the words that help me shape my understanding and my place in the world.

One book that has been a compass for me at many points in my life is *The Alchemist* by Paulo Coelho. It reminds me, time and time again, that all the answers are within me – no matter where I go, "I am home." The universe somehow manages to conspire to help me find my way. If I had to choose a favorite piece of my writing, it would be *Numbville,* a work that lays bare my journey through loss, loneliness, and the slow, deliberate process of coming back to life.

TRAVEL

Journeys Across the Heart and Globe

Travel has been an escape and an education, a way to step outside myself and see the world through a wider lens. In unfamiliar places, I have found both grounding and expansion, new ways of understanding my existence, and the profound realization that geography shifts perspective as much as time does. Whether navigating the quiet streets of a foreign city, standing before landscapes that humble me, or simply absorbing the energy of a place, my travels have shaped my head and heart in ways I could never have anticipated. These pieces explore how literal and emotional movement has defined me.

Sometimes, the movement is external – a long-haul flight, a train winding through grassy hills, a jet-lagged wanderluster meandering down cobblestone alleys. At other times, it's internal – the shifting of beliefs, the stretching of comfort zones, and the unraveling of assumptions. Travel cracked me open and gave me permission to reinvent, to grieve in unfamiliar places, to feel anonymous and alive all at once.

Whether I was traveling alone, with family, or with my son, each trip left a unique mark on my soul. Some of the most surprising wisdom has come from strangers I met – conversations over coffee, shared sunsets with a glass of wine, all these fleeting connections that somehow stayed with me. I have been shaped by kindness, challenged by discomfort, and humbled by beauty. In these entries, you'll see not only the places I've visited but also, each time I return home, how I carry pieces of these experiences with me – quiet shifts, new perspectives, and the undeniable truth that I am never quite the same person who left.

THE WAYS OF WANDERLUST

Oh, how travel has captured my heart!

I have been carefully learning the lessons it provides since my youth. My mother organized trips for me to visit relatives. These safe close-to-home experiences influenced me in a positive way. They made me realize the importance of joining with something larger than myself, larger than my immediate family. It was while I was away from my home base that wandering became a way of life for me. This was the nascent gathering of my connectivity and my burgeoning curiosity.

To roam.

To explore.

To discover.

To learn.

When I roam, with every step away from home, there is a deviation from my norm that takes place and quietly grows with every mile. It makes me feel alive. I've begun to understand there is never a right time to wander. I have to dare to jump . . . and *jump* I do.

When I explore, I collect information.

When I discover, I meet new people. I experience diverse cultures and customs and appreciate the different belief systems in the world and this realization frees me from the trap of the comfort of sameness.

When I learn, I develop as a human being. I acquire new ways of thinking that allow me to see what works and what does not in my life.

I pursue these actions because of my *wanderlusting* ways. I have learned time after time that new encounters and opportunities for growth will never materialize in the safety zone of what I know. My mom packed my suitcases hoping my visits to see my aunt and uncle in Colorado or my grandmother in Florida would bring new perspectives and experiences to my young senses. As a result, I continue to look for unfamiliar circumstances, and now I pack my own bags to explore the globe.

To stall.

To wait.

To stay.

To wish.

When I stall, there is fear of the possibility I will never make memories in different corners of the world. My chances for self-discovery diminish.

When I wait, there is a missed opportunity to participate in this big world I live in. How silly to hold myself back and not go somewhere I have always wanted to go outside the confines of my mind.

When I stay, there is no expansion. If I do not venture outside my fences of familiarity, there is a chance life will become predictable and lack liveliness. I will be happier if I make the choice to go.

When I wish, I am already wandering. I never want my regret to sneak in and steal my travel desires from me. It would be unfortunate to not take chances and later learn I was sorry for not taking them.

These four inactions diminish my existence. They stunt my growth. I will not allow any failure to act—shrink my cultural intelligence.

Traveling feeds my free spirit. I crave the thrill of venturing into the unknown. I long to see new things. I like watching people in their environments. I want to see the differences of their everyday existence compared to mine. I must accept my innermost desire to learn and grow. When I ignore this yearning for adventurous acts, my heart aches. I would miss the richness that I search for and find in each moment of my travels. I would miss the search itself.

I relish smelling a potpourri of aromas while walking into the spice bazaar in Istanbul, Turkey. These fragrances cannot be replicated and are inextricably attached to their exotic location. The colorful stalls overflowing with countless mounds of herbs, dried fruits, and varietals of Turkish delight. The bouquet of flavors fills the air while vendors wait for me to take home their prized merchandises. Apple tea was my singular selection.

The fluidity and finesse of the Romance languages is an art form to admire. I hear varying dialects and elongated sentences. They resonate in my mind when I recall wandering through a café in Seville, Spain, or retro bistros in Buenos Aires, Argentina.

When I see the monstrous Rapa Nui statues in Easter Island, they make me ponder my existence. The various legends connected to these enormous moai figures are extraordinary. Their majestic and mystical habit of standing erect protects the island in ways we can never imagine. They are unbelievably captivating.

The chocolate tartufo in Florence, Italy was an experience that left my taste buds wanting more. This circular, ice cream dessert with its chocolate shell and delightful flavor overwhelms my senses. I crave its creaminess. This delicacy cannot be reproduced in my kitchen, to my great dismay.

The Auschwitz concentration camps I toured in Poland affected me deeply. A reflective sorrow and shock continues to this day permeating through my being. A sacrifice occurred there that I will never understand and not ever forget.

These international experiences continue to influence me and I long for more. I am left escaping the mundane of my everyday thoughts to the wonders of the world I have seen, already anxious for the next adventure. There is beauty hidden everywhere, often in the most unusual places. I must continue to connect with something larger than myself in order to feel alive. I challenge you to pack your bags and find your own ways of wanderlust.

ADVENTURES ON THE AMAZON

I confess, I have a classic case of the travel bug. There is no antidote. I understand the consequences of being infected, with no plans of taming, only tolerating, this disorder.

As I reflect on my time spent in the Amazon, although short, it was the source of many peculiar stories, often packed with surprises. Our family-oriented expedition lasted five nights with plenty of exciting explorations. I was a wee bit apprehensive about travelling into the depths of Amazonia, but energized by the excitement this quest might offer.

We flew into Iquitos, the largest metropolis in the Peruvian Amazon and drove ninety minutes to Nauta, where a riverboat named the Delfin awaited us. My family and I were fortunate to float down the second largest river in the world on an incredible riverboat equipped with the luxuries of a hotel. The idea of being in a secluded and serene setting while venturing into the untamed and natural world was an adrenaline rush.

As the Delfin glided down the mirror-like jungle waterways, I was restless and ready to meet the Ribereños, an indigenous community who call the Amazon River basin home. Flora and fauna were abundant, and time seemed to stand still. My senses were on stimulation overload, as we ventured into Peru's vast Pacaya-Samiria National Reserve, home to sloths and owl monkeys, pink dolphins, scarlet macaws, crocodiles, river turtles, and giant anacondas. The wild scene was complemented by superb birdwatching.

On the first night of our voyage, the captain explained the mythical status of the Amazon, its power within nature, and the spiritual world. "This is extremely important to the native people. A realm they claim to get closer to by utilizing plants that contain certain hallucinogens.

One of the most important persons to many indigenous groups is the Shaman. This individual holds knowledge of local plants and animals and is believed to communicate with the spirit world."

While we consumed a delectable local fish steamed with coconut milk, rice, and beans, I was elated to learn I would be blessed by an introduction to a real-life Shaman the following day. Even if it was a tourist tactic, I was thrilled.

To explore the Aboriginal communities and interact with locals was easily one of my favorite experiences on this trip. I observed and valued how both traditional and modern elements are integrated into their lives. They live in simple but well-kept wooden homes with thatched roofs, elevated on stilts in case the rising river waters come up over the bank. The river is their lifeblood and their respected nemesis, being the source of many dangers.

Watching the women, I could identify with their tasks of taking care of the children, cooking, gathering yucca and other plants with which their ancestral medicine was created. The men, communally known as "forest guardians," they cut down trees to make canoes. They float the Amazon. selling their crops and trade. Young children often join their fathers at an early age to learn how to navigate the Amazon's vast reaches.

One of my most heartfelt highlights from this village visit was when I encountered a group of giggling girls sitting near the riverbank, watching their mothers do laundry. They were around six years old and exuded pure joy. As this magical moment was captured on my camera, I turned the screen to show them their image. Each squealed with delight and ran off. I left the village with a full heart. It was transformative to witness a civilization thrive on whatever food could be obtained through hunting, gathering, and farming for one's family. As we returned to our boat, I noticed our crew embodied the exact characteristics of the villagers: a genuine contentment and solace in their surroundings. I was hoping the mythical spirit of the Amazon would also infiltrate our weary family.

On day three, we ascended to the towering treetops of the Amazon Rainforest, where we experienced the longest canopy walkways in the world. Suspended bridges stretched between fourteen of the area's largest trees. We walked among historic plants and native animals, stopping many times. The pauses were a welcome relief from the heat... I am sure our guide, Juan Luis, stopped so often to ensure we did not need any native plants for heat stroke! After our canopy walk, as we headed back to the Delfin, we spotted pink dolphins. Suddenly, they were real. It took me by surprise. They do exist. These miniature river dolphins glided through the murky waters, their pale-pink skin and bottleneck noses bobbing up and down beside our skiff. Juan Luis explained they are endemic to South America and mainly live in river basins. This Amazon adventure continued to amaze me.

On day four, I somehow contracted an airborne water bacterium that sidelined me for the last two days of the trip. Still, adrenaline-fueled stories kept coming in. Both my eleven- and twelve-year-olds at the time were thrilled to share their know-how about catching a piranha. The fishing guide, named Ra, handed each of them a bamboo stick with a string and a basic hook attached. The lure was a simple piece of raw red meat. A quick lesson in Piranha 101: float the flesh just above the water, and once they bite—yank! The boys and my husband enjoyed their catch for dinner that evening. My oldest quipped, "It tasted like oily fish." Thank goodness, I was on a ginger ale and white rice diet that day.

Later, a nighttime hunt for nocturnal animals took place. The story goes that Juan Luis spotted a dwarf Caiman crocodile and retrieved it by hand to show the boys. My husband was not sure who was more terrified, the boys or the crocodile. After my skittish schoolboys calmed down, the crocodile was released and swam away from their skiff.

The next morning, the boys and my husband took a long hike to the giant lily pads. As they recapped at lunch, the guided tour was worth the mounds of mud on their shoes. They laughed at the exceptionally slow pace of the hike due to the thickness of the undergrowth and the rough terrain. I think at least one shoe was left in the mud, as my husband walked back to the boat with an odd tilt to his gait.

"The Lily pads were unbelievable. I wanted to float on one," my youngest shared. These oversized floating leaves looked quite enchanting from the pictures they showed me, and it seemed it was worth the loss of one Nike shoe.

My intestinal discomfort didn't dissipate after I tasted the tree sap on our jungle trail walk the previous day. The wise captain told me it was finally time to take Cipro, a powerful antibiotic that fights bacteria in the body. He had the medicine delivered by skiff to our remote area, and it almost immediately cleared up the bacteria in my body.

Modern medicine prevailed, even here in the jungle along one of the most dangerous rivers in the world. I told the crew that their successful effort to get me to try the Amazon cure, drinking a liquid-like substance dripping from a local tree must have helped the remedy work for my gastrointestinal issues. The sap, which had a gumwood texture, had a hint of cinnamon. It was exhilarating to eat a completely foreign white substance oozing from between the bark of the tree in the Amazon, especially because afterward, I was able to sit on something other than a latrine for the first time in days.

I see life as a constant adventure, and the Amazon did not disappoint; it simply fueled my passion for continued exploration. I repeatedly pinch (and sometimes scratch) myself, recalling the time spent in the largest tropical rainforest with my disorders, the travel bug being persistent while the other was fading.

FRIENDSHIPS FORMED ON EASTER ISLAND

My two sons and I enjoyed an extraordinary journey with Rapa Nui descendant and local guide, Amanaki Rata.

With sleepy eyes after an overnight flight from Lima, Peru, we were looking to meet our guide Amanaki Rata. While surveying the surroundings, we noticed a poised woman with flowing jet-black hair sauntering through our hotel lobby. She smiled at each person she made eye contact with, including us. We were hopeful this welcome burst of energy was our guide, and she was!

Amanaki introduced herself and asked us each enthusiastically about ourselves. Her voice was deep and strong in a pleasant way. She expressed delight at the opportunity to lead a young mother and two school-age boys. Within minutes, she directed us to her open-top jeep to begin the tour, instinctively checking with the boys to inquire if the washroom was needed. The three of us were quickly energized as we set off on our Easter Island adventure.

This Chilean island, located at the southernmost tip of the Polynesian Triangle, has been the subject of myths and heated debate since European explorers first spotted it on Easter Sunday in 1722. There are many questions that scientists and archaeologists have unsuccessfully tried to answer for over a century. They often refer to Easter Island as an "open-air, archaeological museum." As we traveled along the rugged road on this remote piece of land in the South Pacific, we eagerly looked forward to what was waiting for us. We already knew that Easter Island, or *Isla de Pascua* in Spanish, was famous for its mystery and the many unanswered questions about how and why, over six hundred years ago, the Rapa Nui, the native people, built and carved hundreds of giant, stoic stone statues called moai.

We were hiking the quarries at the Rano Raraku Volcano, where the stone statues were originally carved, when my youngest son asked, "When is lunch?"

Amanaki soothingly said, "Soon!" and questioned my well-traveled boys. "Would you like a traditional meal?"

"Of course!" they exclaimed. "We have enjoyed street food in Ho Chi Minh, pastries in Paris, and haggis, neeps, and tatties in Scotland. We love local food!"

Amanaki smiled and said, "Fantastic! My ancestors ate fish and rats . . . and it's all you can eat!"

They both snickered at the joke . . . but continued walking in silence.

We reached the apex of the quarry, and it was a dramatic, sudden entrance into the past with the ancient idols hidden yet protruding from the ground like they had sprouted from the earth itself. We learned they are composed of consolidated volcanic ash. Some stone busts were covered with grass and moss, while others are still buried and yet to be unearthed. These secretive stones were shaped over a period of five centuries by a civilization that later would destroy them. This baffled the boys. They could not understand why anyone would want to destroy something so enchanting and enormous. More stories were shared, and additional questions were asked. To fully grasp the uncertainty of this island was impossible. There are so many questions about what happened so long ago.

Amanaki explained to the boys about the steep cliffs from which it would have been nearly impossible to catch fish from when the Island was first inhabited. Generational advances allowed fish to be added as a staple in the island diet. Polynesian foods included many varieties of fish, vegetables, and fruit which were wrapped in banana leaves to prevent burning while being cooked over an open flame or underground with hot ashes.

The reminder of food caused a grumble from the bellies of the boys. We settled on lunch at the marina, no rats involved. My little rascals held out hope for ice cream and Amanaki used her leverage to alter their plans for an ordinary scoop of vanilla and urged them to try Lúcuma, a flavored frozen custard made from indigenous fruit known for its pumpkin-like taste. While we sat near the waterfront, the boys asked how these gigantic boulder-like statues "traveled" from the quarry to their ceremonial platforms sometimes as far as fifteen miles away.

"Even the native people are uncertain," Amanaki pointed out. "In every place on the Earth where huge megalithic pieces of statues or stones were transported, the explanation of how they were moved involves the use of logs, ropes and a lot of people. There are over three hundred moai in different states of completion that never left the quarry." We finished our dessert, still stumped by the question of how the stones were created and transported. It was perplexing.

At dinner that evening, we met many people from eclectic backgrounds who had travelled from all over the world to experience the mysteriousness of this island. We instantly connected with a Brazilian family from Salvador. The mother was a doctor and the father an international business correspondent. Their family mantra mirrored ours—work hard and play hard. We had many great conversations about life, living, and love. Their daughter Nina, a couple years older than the boys, became a partner in crime. This tactical threesome would daily meet up after our tours to play cards, wander trails, and search out mischievous things to do outside the hotel. They even assisted the hotel chef in making a Brigadeiro, a Portuguese chocolate delicacy for Nina's birthday.

Each morning, Amanaki would surprise us with a basket of warm papaya-mango muffins made from a secret family recipe that she could neither reveal nor divulge. As we headed towards the most photographed location on the island, she told us how her family is one of the oldest clans living on the island. I had just taken the last bite of my mouthwatering muffin when we arrived at the largest ceremonial platform. The raised stone surface boasts fifteen boulder busts and showcases them against a glorious blue backdrop, the Pacific Ocean. It was breathtaking.

My oldest spoke up, "We visited Stonehenge, but these stone statues are so much better and way different." He and his brother ran off to take pictures of the scenery, which was complemented by an abundance of native island dogs.

I could not take my gaze off the majestic and mystical presence of the moai looming over the ocean. They stand peacefully erect, and I am sure they do protect the island, just as the folklore proclaims. I saw the boys from a distance, scampering as Amanaki motioned for them not to feed the animals any of her grandmother's muffins.

Amanaki felt it was important for the boys to understand the geological history of Easter Island, which was formed by a series of volcanic eruptions. "Rano Kau, the island's most spectacular volcano, is a major archeological site," she said.

As she described the island's delicate ecosystem and how the volcano is the highest point on the island, I was preoccupied with taking in the most spectacular 360-degree view I had ever seen of the largest ocean on the planet. We were standing on the crater rim when my youngest child noticed a sparkly stone protruding from the soil.

Amanaki nodded and explained that natural obsidian covers the island. "It is an igneous rock formed when the volcanic molten lava cooled and hardened into a crystallized structure." Unbeknownst to me, as the sunlight danced on the scattered obsidian rock formations that day, the boys were covertly shoving these treasures in their pockets. They were disappointed when I discovered the volcanic, glasslike material in their suitcase and encouraged each of them to return the rocks to their rightful home. I can honestly say, our stay on Easter Island ended with no stone left unturned and all rocks left in their rightful place.

As we drove back to our hotel, I found myself contemplating the mystery in front of me. To be in the presence of these puzzling giants of stone was intriguing and left me in pure astonishment. I hoped that astonishment would be the treasure for generations of visitors to take home from the island. I hoped the answers to unanswered questions that countless scientists and archaeologists have been debating for years would forever lie deep within their haunting beauty.

Each evening, after supper, we convened in the sitting room of the hotel and talked about our discoveries that day with our fellow adventurers. There would be non-stop chatter, from endless sightings of ancient ceremonial centers to volcanic craters, petroglyphs in slate caves, lava formations, and fascinating clues to the Orongo birdman cult ceremony and, of course, the infamous moai and their mysterious creators. Each day we spent with our spectacular guide, the spiritual energy of the island, and the buoyant curiosity of our travel acquaintances was unbelievably educational and captivating.

On the final day, we were left to explore on our own. The Anthropological Museum was a short walk from our hotel and worth a visit. We saw the only intact moai eye ever found, carved from white coral. Walking back to the hotel, we met our Brazilian buddies and asked them to join us for a Lúcuma cone. As we watched the kids swing and teeter-totter at a local community playground, I couldn't help but breathe deeply to absorb the fresh oceanic air and stare at the one-eyed moai from a distance. I think we all wish these monstrous memes could share the story of their existence, but part of me hoped the mystery would be forever. Sometimes it's the mystery that is the joy, not the answer. It's the journey, not the destination.

We said our last goodbyes to Nina and her parents. As their van was being loaded, they kindly presented each of the boys and me with a Brazilian Wish Bracelet. We were given a vibrant pink ribbon knotted properly around our wrists to ensure the fulfillment of our hopes and dreams. Pink was chosen as the color to represent friendship. All three of us will miss our afternoon gatherings, where we conversed and chatted with the Brazilian family.

Amanaki decided to join us for a farewell dinner at the hotel. After our meal, the four of us sat on the wooden patio around an outdoor fire pit. I savored my last sip of Carménère wine, sensing the energy of the island, knowing its cultural legacy will remain within me for a lifetime.

As we finished reflecting and reminiscing, the flames dwindled, and all of us looked up suddenly, almost simultaneously. Captivated by the blanket of stars sparkling overhead, we became a bit misty, knowing our time together had come to an end. A transformative bond was created. We were fortunate to have shared this invaluable experience with our guide, an outstanding human being and representative of the Rapa Nui community.

Speculation will continue to swirl, and stories will continue to unfold for generations to come about the island of stone statues. However, our time spent with Amanaki will never be forgotten. She made us feel like we were part of her Rapa Nui family. Her countless acts of kindness will live on in our hearts, as will her ancestral stories of the moai. We will cherish our adventure as we trekked to the cave of cannibals, risking high tides, and later enjoying our daily diet of homemade papaya mango muffins with a picnic on the white sand beach where British explorer James Cook arrived. Most importantly, we will always appreciate taking the path less travelled and visiting top-secret spots where tour buses never venture.

Thank you, Amanaki Rata, for a once-in-a-lifetime, unforgettable experience and for bringing us into a deeper understanding of Easter Island's mysterious history while forming lasting friendships.

HEAD TO THE CLOUDS

I smile each time I open the mailbox and spot the National Geographic Expeditions magazine surrounded by unwanted bills and junk mail.

A particular featured location lured me in—Taktsang Lhakhang (Tiger's Nest Temple). One of the oldest private monasteries in the country of Bhutan was constructed into the side of a sheer cliff. This mystical image captured my attention every time I gazed upon the article. I imagine walking beneath the cascading, colorful prayer flags and marveling at the beauty it exudes, nestled between folds of the Himalayan Mountains with plant life peeking through cracks and crevices. I tell *everyone* . . . this is a voyage I must make.

This fantasy became a reality on my fortieth birthday. My compassionate and selfless husband booked an unexpected trip for me to visit this kingdom in the clouds. After years of having my head in the clouds, he felt it was time for me to see this holy site.

I have never been deficient in the dream category. In my reality, dreams, often like travel, take me away to unknown places. Being alone and lost in my thoughts allows me to be free. When I travel, I break free from the confinement of my mundane everyday activities.

So, off I went on my adventure. Flying into Paro Airport, nestled among the steep mountains of the Himalayas, I was terrified as our pilot made multiple attempts to land our plane. Eventually, a change in the atmosphere allowed us to land. I stayed at the Zhiwa Ling Hotel in Paro, one of the world's unique lodges.

In the morning, I met my guide, Namgay Tshering, of ABC Tours and Treks. As much as I enjoy being alone, you cannot travel Bhutan without a local guide. Oddly, his presence and aura did not diminish my sense of freedom. In fact, his spirituality was refreshing and welcoming. As we started our hike up the mountain, I began to relish each and every step. Little was spoken between us, yet I sensed he knew something was happening inside me, here in this pious place, where I am taking the hike of my life.

I find myself eagerly walking into the unknown. I mentally detach from apprehension; as the air becomes thinner, my body aches for the summit. I focus again on my guide. Namgay walks this trail multiple times per week. This is motivation for me to continue. A tea break at the half-way mark gave me the nourishment needed to make the final approach to the monastery. After an additional climb that took us over a bridge and across a waterfall with a 200-foot drop, I could see the mystic wonder in front of me.

Tiger's Nest Monastery was still blanketed in a low-hanging cloud, adding an aura of heaven to this place. To arrive was empowering and euphoric. I was no longer gazing at a glossy picture but positioned right where I had hoped to be, wrapped in prayer flags and feeling the energy of the land and proud of my achievement. I stood in my dream, which had become reality.

We walked into one temple and witnessed the offerings to the deities. Many were wishing for their freedom, yet there I was, thanking the same gods and goddesses, for mine at this moment. There was deep inner contentment as I inhaled the fresh and cool mountain air.

As we readied for the trek down, the fog lifted, revealing the Paro Valley 3,000 feet below. I reassured my fellow adventurers slowly making their way, either on mules or with walking sticks through the switchbacks. The descent provided me with magnificent and unforgettable views that were previously hidden on my way up. I found the rhododendrons, pine trees, and wildflowers to be much more vibrant with oxygen . . . mine!

As we continued to descend, I gained a deeper understanding of my guide. Namgay's knee-length robe, tied at the waist by a cloth belt, and his black dress shoes looked uncomfortable to me. I was thankful to be exempt from the traditional dress rule in Bhutan, a

Kira for women and its equivalent for men, the Gho. My tennis shoes and yoga pants felt like a baby's blanket. Namgay indicated that the national dress code must be worn by any Bhutanese person visiting offices, temples, or attending any significant occasion or celebration. I thought about what he said... a momentous occasion or celebration. This was for me. I celebrated my freedom to travel, the opportunity to self-reflect, and the traditions of the Bhutanese people.

WHAT THE OCEAN TAUGHT ME IN FIJI

Fear is to be conquered and, most importantly, understood.

As I reflect, I realize that many times in my life, I let worry dominate; it was a poor choice. The mere anticipation of different threats often outweighed my hidden bravery. These cowardly acts made me cringe and punish myself each time.

A family trip to Fiji with my two teenage boys impelled me to venture into my abyss of anxiety. A long overdue time to reflect and understand my consternation with the deep sea. My curiosity and cerebral mental states were relentlessly battling for years, along with my maternal instincts to not project my dread of the underwater utopia onto my children. It was this mental turbulence that shifted my desire to dive deeper into the unknown and into my fears of the ocean.

My children reminded me, when we arrived at this island paradise, of my continued goals to "meet" uncertainties, and address them while remembering our mental strength is far superior to our fears. Oh, how they turned that on me! They scheduled us for a family dive the next morning. My children using my life guidance on me was not in the parental manual!

That evening, peering out into this continuous body of water which surrounds most of the earth's surface, I longed for comfort. It was here that I silenced my thoughts and sensed the heart of this vast expansion of blue and uninterrupted horizon "whispering" the following into my soul as I drifted off to sleep with trepidation for the following day.

You recognize your life is similar to my existence.

We both live in a vast world that stretches to boundless spheres.

We have no limits.

We each have waves crashing into our shorelines each day. Some varying in size and shape. Their strength often bruising or flattening our psyche.

We both have been taken advantage of and polluted in many ways.

Our force can never be taken awa;, only we can diminish our current.

It was important that my response be mindful and genuine. This was a unique opportunity for me to share my innermost introspections... with an ocean?

For as long as I can remember, my infatuation with you has left me speechless.

You have always provided peace to my innermost being, despite all the commotion of whitewashing around me and my unease with you.

I have been enamored with your storminess and stillness, which contradict each other.

I have been fearful of you for so long.

Dear friend, never fear me, just understand me. You will be a welcome visitor tomorrow.

As the morning sun beamed through the bleached plantation shutters, I felt an unfamiliar calm despite not knowing what lay ahead. The high spirits of my children were nothing less than contagious, there was something inside me that encouraged me to go further, to dive. The experience was nothing short of empowering. Submerging into the unknown was adrenaline-charged, and I felt a freedom that I had never felt before. I had entered a new world, physically and mentally. The experience was magical, feeling eerily alone even though I never lost grasp of the dive master's hand! We returned to shore, the children reveling in my effort.

Watching the sun disappear into the skyline that evening, I listened to the waves whirl along the water's edge, took a sip of wine, and reclined in my weathered hammock. As I closed my eyes before dinner and silenced my thoughts, there it was again. The heart and verse of this vast expansion of blue, a familiar and faint voice, entered my soul, listening intently.

I entered your world today, although it scared me. I trained myself and adapted my thinking to take part in this underwater playground you graciously offer.

It is your exhilarating environment, a habitat for many, that makes me marvel at your mystery.

Fearing the strength of your tides and where they may have taken me gave me great eagerness and curiosity to continue our underwater dance of discovery. To not panic in your presence but understand you.

I have always respected you and now I am committed to our new connection.

Oh, dear friend, you are an enigma as well.

As I dove into your depths of darkness, my feelings and flights of imagination began to soar. With my adrenaline flowing, I realized that I would survive in this unknown yet natural place you rule over.

Remembering to maintain a calm presence of mind in your remote and uncharted waters was vital. You befriended me while the currents changed and shifted before my eyes.

Realizing that your turn of tidal motions could devour me, and I might effortlessly be lost at sea was a nightmare for me. No longer will this anxiety preclude me from encountering your true natural beauty. My ability to swim was always there. I forgot to move, react, and take action to eliminate my distress and discomfort, to not drown in your mighty wonderland.

As I regained my composure and my consciousness coming to the surface from your core, a lifeboat was visible. I recall how out of proportion this floating device looked against you—this immeasurable body of blue bliss. Your expanse waters enveloping this pint-sized dinghy.

As this boat of bravery approached to hoist and heave me up from my aversion to your choppy waters, a profound point of what you embody erupted within my mind.

There was never a lifeboat.

Oh, dear friend, you finally realized our interconnected essence. I was hopeful you would overcome this sense of sorrow toward me and be free to float within my levels of serenity.

It was you, Ocean, who reminded me of the resilience that resides deep within my soul wanting to be activated and waiting to help.

At that moment, you helped me, not hindered me, with your turbulent waters. I understood that I was bigger than my fears of you all along. As magnificent, majestic, complicated, and chaotic as my existence can be, only I can allow you or my life to swallow me up.

I have always been my own trifecta of support: lifeguard, lifeboat and rescue team. All the training has been programmed innately within me, waiting to be set in motion for all types of stormy conditions that may occur.

My sincere apologies for restricting myself from you. Allowing the false evidence that appeared real within my mind to suffocate and silence me was a profound lapse in judgment.

I am here. Bold and brave. Beacon beaming bright. When our sun sets together, allow me to skip and dance with you into the darkness, into your purple and pink hues, into your undisturbed and unending horizon.

Thank you for teaching me how kindred we are. As the sun skittered along its surface, the Ocean blinked at me with a shimmery glitter.

Oh, dear friend, always remember—together we are infinite!

Sitting together at dinner moments later, my two teenage boys retold stories of our underwater diving adventures. Their amusement and bantering about our experiences together made my heart and soul smile. Poking fun at the fact that I held the hand of our master diver the entire time, or how I screamed when the sea snake swam under the boat prior to my jumping in. Or when I asked what happens if I vomit underwater. If this is what conquering a fear looks like, I am equipped for future frights.

After our dessert plates were cleared and the snickering waned, my earlier surge of emotions erupted again. Exhilaration, enlightenment and harmony—they all will reside within me permanently. I have decided this newfound understanding and the courage to conquer fears is life altering. I was determined to not allow my mental turmoil with all its distractions and detours keep me from this unique experience with myself, my children and the ocean.

The next day, I was back on the dive boat embarrassing my teenage children again—holding the hand of our dive master for the second time.

LETTING GO IN KYOTO

Over the years, life has taught me two things about transformation: either my mind will stretch, or my heart will strain. These alterations explore the significance of harmony within.

On a high-speed train from Tokyo to Kyoto, I told my son that we would be walking Philosopher's Walk, a stone path that runs alongside a canal lined with hundreds of cherry trees. Also known as Tetsugaku no michi, it is named after Nishida Kitaro, one of Japan's most famous philosophers, who meditated while walking this route on his daily commute to Kyoto University.

Our timing was impeccable; in early April, the enchanted cherry trees explode with color. I told my seventeen-year-old son, "There is a chance you might discover the meaning of life."

We were walking in the footsteps of many great philosophers who have plodded down this very path for centuries. He gave me the here-we-go-again look. I could see it written in his rolling eyes, Mom-is-taking-me-to-another-museum. We have a history of travel trade-offs wherein I take him to historical sites, and in turn, I later yield to his penchant of more adventurous locations. I continued and informed him how the path got its name.

When we arrived at the Philosopher's Walk, we were greeted by a mystical energy filled with intense joy and radiance that seemed to permeate the air. I could picture philosophers contemplating the mysteries of life, which strengthened my own critical thinking. My senses were awakened as I listened to the harmonious rustling of the trees swaying and admired the stunning sight of the pink petals fluttering onto the slow-moving water and stepping-stones in the creek beside the path. Perhaps I now understand how it got its name, as it truly made me reflect. Light shone through the ancient branches, illuminating my way, while bumblebees buzzed in my ear, reminding me not to ignore my own nature and to make that vital connection with the ever-present nature around me.

For me, letting go has always been a challenge. I am often in on-the-go mode. Lately, I just remind myself to stay in harmony with my own nature. In fact, Socrates, one of the most recognized philosophers of our time, once said, "Beware the barrenness of a busy life." He reminds me that busyness can leave me feeling unfulfilled.

The idea of simplicity and naturalness surprised me with its straightforward approach to this path of enlightenment. It was refreshing to be reminded of the importance of harmony between oneself and nature. In fact, I believe this is what our ancient ancestors of philosophy discovered. Nature and its healing powers soothe and restore us to balance. Nature and all its wonders have become a mysterious living space that exists, yet we still struggle to define or understand the therapeutic powers it offers. The philosophers of long ago applied these theories to their own lives and have taught them to us for centuries through their writings. Still, I somehow continue to complicate the present with future plans and past regrets, but I doubt that I am alone in this.

An inner peacefulness arrives when I surrender to the present moment, specifically, when I stop and reestablish my place in my natural surroundings. When my distance from nature is realized, coming back to the present requires the ability to let go. However, that moment of realization that you are not in the present takes an alert awareness that is not always around when you need it most. Thus, it takes time to cognitively connect with this unseeable realm and make it a daily priority.

My son interrupted my deep-thinking and reflective moment and made the kind of sarcastic comment that only a teenager can dredge up, "Wow! This place is incredible . . . Not!" He wandered ahead on the square-stoned path delicately covered in cherry blossom petals. A few minutes later, he circled back with a change of mind to inform me of the moss garden, temples, and cafes along this streamside path. He had chatted with a professional photographer who informed him that the canal was built during the Meiji Period to revitalize the stagnating local economy and was used to power Japan's first hydroelectric power plant. He whispered, "How cool is that?" The ability of a teenager to make his mother's heart plummet and soar in the space of a heartbeat should never be underestimated.

As I take the constrained high-speed train along its strictly defined route away from my newfound sanctuary, I have plenty of time to reflect and organize my swirling, unrestrained thoughts. Gazing out the window at Hiroshima, I experienced another Joycean epiphany or moment of meditative awareness—the fleeting, surreal moments walking Philosopher's Walk left a lasting impression on my heart. In my mind, I recognized how its fearless spirit moved me.

As I travel, I learn more about myself and continue to stretch and challenge my thought patterns to find answers in my life, while still taking time to pause and enjoy the fragrant flowers and bask in the sunshine that brought them to me. My natural surroundings hold clues to the meaning of life. It is my duty to trust the invisible force that surrounds me as I live, walk, and exist within its mystery.

GYPSY SOUL

Traveling feeds my soul and fuels my free spirit.

I just got back home from a four-country trip—a real adventure of discovery, not only for the sights and sounds each place offers but also for the chance to be part of something bigger than myself. I feel enriched as I interpret personal meaning, participate in a multicultural movement, and connect with a global community.

As I walked and admired the cherry blossoms on Miyajima Island in Japan, I felt a wave of spirituality and my free spirit smiling deep inside. It is a sacred place, full of magic and wonder. A shrine floating on the sea, many preserved pagodas and temples with lanterns lining the island's banks. Serenity was felt by everyone. Even the native deer roam freely, fearless in the peacefulness of this protected World Heritage Site. It was simply divine and full of history.

The deer made me think of my late father, who loved the native Michigan white-tailed deer, now gone from this world but never far from my spirit. Sometimes, when I travel, I lose track of where I am and how far I've gone to get there. I crave seeing new things and enjoy observing people in their environments.

Before I visited China, I imagined it as a corrupt country polluted by a massive population with social issues, as portrayed in U.S. media reports and news feeds. There may be areas that fit this description, but my experience was completely different. I enjoyed walking the streets near Wangfujing, one of Beijing's most famous shopping districts, located in the Dongcheng District. I discovered local markets selling unusual snacks such as skewered scorpions, mini seahorses, or, for those less adventurous, candied fruit.

As I walked along the Great Wall of China outside Beijing, I found time for reflection. Marveling at the longest man-made structure on Earth, I felt deep admiration for the laborers involved in its construction. The heavy workloads and harsh conditions are unimaginable to us today, comfortably seated in our easy chairs. The Great Wall is also known as "the longest cemetery on earth" because so many people died building it. I paid my respects to the souls of those entombed in the stone and earth and marveled at their achievement. Debunking cultural stigmas is one of my favorite hobbies when traveling.

I am afflicted for life, and the influence of my travel goes beyond the journey itself. I have accepted my innermost desire to learn and grow.

While traveling, my senses are uniquely heightened. A stranger's smile or gentle friendliness comforts me. In Bangkok, Thailand, I was riding the Sky Train, their public transportation system, when a twenty-something woman smiled and gestured toward my hair. It took a brief game of cultural charades to understand she liked my haircut. With renewed energy, I quickly left the train platform, remembering the time constraint I was under. My destination was a single residence made up of various old Thai structures. An American businessman named Jim Thompson built and lived in this impressive home in the 1950s, which is now a museum. I only had an hour before it closed. My hurried appearance prompted a local to help, providing step-by-step directions to get there in time. These moments are what make my heart soar.

I crave the excitement of exploring the unknown. I want to see how the daily lives of people there compare to mine.

Seoul, South Korea, is an unusual place to visit because of the political turmoil caused by its northern neighbor. The worry, fear, and anger from those I spoke to were common reactions to my itinerary. The tense relationship between these two contentious countries initially drew me in yet also made me uneasy. I've never felt that my freedom was in danger, never questioned its continued existence, and never feared losing it. The physical boundary between safety and danger was literally right in front of me. Being next to North Korea was unsettling. As I stood on the Military Demarcation Line within the Joint Security Area, I felt numb, with one leg on each side of a stark and powerful divide. Our guide took my group into the Third Infiltration Tunnel on the South Korean side. This dark, damp tunnel extends two hundred fifty meters beneath the border between North and South Korea. The heavy weight of the land above us was a visible burden, and the dynamite holes in the coal-covered walls were unmistakable. I felt a mix of discomfort from the unknown and exhilaration, which reminded me to cherish the life we have.

I have this urge to trek to the furthest corners of the map.

There is beauty hidden in every corner of the world, and I am open to seeing it. Traveling challenges, me and shifts my perspectives on life. There will always be more to see, more to explore, and more cities to get lost in. As wanderlust flows through my veins, the restlessness of my free spirit will never fade.

"I have not been everywhere, but it is on my list!" cries my gypsy soul.

WOMEN OF WONDER

This is a short tribute to women worldwide.

I just returned from a three-week journey through India, Nepal, and Bhutan. It was a thought-provoking experience comparing similarities within our global community. I am grateful to have met many lovely people along the way.

During my trip, I met four incredible women who left a lasting mark on me. Our short time together taught me something about myself and the female spirit. Their presence stayed with me. I had an instinctive understanding of their lives—an unspoken shared connection—a feeling of very little difference in our stories.

Women are all connected, continuously on a journey of growing our minds, heart, self and way of life. We are delicate and durable. We thrive, survive and struggle every day. We must advocate for all and celebrate the women who inspire other women.

The impactful women I met brought forth an inner brightness that left me admiring their resilience and goodness emanating from deep within. They each reminded me of influential females in my own life. I felt a bridge of connectivity through their heartfelt actions and my whole-hearted associations with my friends and family.

* * *

Jya has a contagious enthusiasm and lives in a small village south of Jaipur, India. There was depth in her embrace and purity in her presence. A mother of four children, she has been married for twenty years and is content with life, happy to be alive.

On this day, Jya had many responsibilities to handle. The goat room door needed fixing, she had to walk to get fresh water, and she made a quick visit to the temple to pay respect to her spiritual teacher—that was her short list. Still, she wanted to make me feel special. It was her idea to play dress-up. Jya led me to her closet and chose various bangles, necklaces, and a pair of ornate earrings to match my gold and turquoise silk serape. Amid the colors, the soft silk, and her kindness, I felt wrapped in love that day. This feeling of warmth made me think of my dear friend Laura.

Over the years, Laura has consistently demonstrated what it means to support family, friends, and the community through both good and challenging times. Her ability to spread goodness in the world is endless, regardless of what's happening in her own life. Every day, she puts her family's needs before her own. She exemplifies tireless leadership in her roles as a wife and mother. I feel blessed to have had her friendship surrounding me for over a decade.

Jya and Laura have set examples for me in my own life. Their actions have shown me the importance of taking time to build relationships and practice kindheartedness daily, despite the chaos in our lives.

* * *

Ankita left me mesmerized with her captivating energy and zest for life. She is the front desk manager at a hotel in Thimphu, Bhutan. As I watched her interact with various staff and guests, she treated each encounter with interest and compassion. I was so impressed with her unique behavior, I asked if we could sit together and chat over a cup of Masala tea. Ankita is a stunning, modern woman. She excels at her job, spends time with her family every day, and continues her education — all with a smile.

As I watched Ankita and sensed her care and concern for others, I remembered my neighbor Ruth. Oh, how I longed to sit with her one more time and enjoy her delicious cinnamon coffee while absorbing her wise ways. Ruth moved to the East Coast over five years ago to be closer to her family. We had many conversations about the importance of being the best version of yourself, and those meaningful talks still resonate with me. My dear friend Ruth has a positive outlook, and her insights on life are unforgettable. She showed me what it means to truly live life and not let life live you. Both Ankita and Ruth prioritize their families. Their inner happiness shines through in their actions.

* * *

Ana is eager to build her future, even though her family members have different plans for her. She lives in Patan, Nepal, and is seventeen years old. This determined young woman works with her father in their home business as a cooking instructor—teaching tourists how to prepare traditional Nepalese dishes.

This liberated lady is trying to take the lead in her life. Despite her family's desire for her to marry, Ana is in her second year of college taking classes in hospitality management and has no plans to settle with a man or be confined to the family business.

Ana made me think of my youngest sister, Brittany Jo, who is establishing her own future. My spirited sister is constructing her life one day at a time . . . her way. She graduated from college and found an advertising job in Detroit. She is eager to tackle the world in an unconventional manner.

It seems that personal freedoms are often caught up in traditions. But both Ana and Brittany Jo remind me how important it is to take personal risks and follow your bliss. Each of these young women is just starting their journeys in life—both forging their own paths. I admire their determination and drive to pursue and hold onto their dreams.

* * *

One glance and I could tell a woman named Pushpa represented a strength and depth far beyond my understanding. Her smile illuminated the room when I walked into her spice shop in the Rajasthan region of India. A quiet confidence resonated while she informed me of the various spices from this area. A single glance from her bewitching, deep, brown eyes told me a lifetime of stories in their sparkle.

My great-grandmother Alvina came to mind while listening to Pushpa. She lived for ninety-five years and had the same depth in her eyes. Pushpa's red bindi symbolized a long marriage and commitment, similar to the delicate ring that represented the sixty-eight years of marriage between my great-grandmother, Alvina, and my great-grandfather, Walter.

Echoing the sage, it is not the years in your life but the life in your years that matter. These women remind me that age is more than just a number; it is a deep presence of life. If each wrinkle in the skin told a story, they would have many chapters to share from their book of life. I smile when I think of the lives both women have touched. I will no longer cringe at each wrinkle on my face, knowing they will bring me closer in spirit and strength to these admired women.

* * *

Individually, we live our lives in different ways. I continue to marvel at the graciousness and goodness of the human race and believe we women are at our best when we support and learn from each other. I tingle with excitement thinking about what I have learned from my friends across the globe, and the women who are close to my heart at home.

I will remember and relish all the women of wonder in my life. Their selflessness and support has left an imprint on my soul. Our encounters have expanded and enriched my intellectual and emotional landscape. I feel connected to women around the world, regardless of class, culture or circumstance. As individuals we exude brightness from within and can inspire ourselves and each other. We all share sisterhood living as women of wonder.

BHUTAN BABES

I want to make room for more happiness in my life.
Why?

Because I tend to overthink things. I often overlook the little acts of delight that take place in front of me due to my desire to be everywhere. I am learning that my life does not have to be so complicated and complex. I make it that way.

What made me halt and have this deliberation with myself?

Two little babes in Bhutan. Their presence and playfulness altered my way of thinking.

As I walked out of a local paper factory on a recent trip to the Thimphu Valley in Bhutan, I noticed them in the doorway of a gift shop, grinning. A local man standing nearby mentioned they wanted to play hide and seek with me. Without saying a word, they urged me to discover my younger self again. I felt a sudden craving for inner and outer contentment.

It was easy to participate in a childhood game with these two toddlers. There was no need for verbal communication; the simple recognition of mutual openness was enough. We enjoyed a few fleeting minutes of carefree play. I was completely smitten with our short-lived encounter. These babes lit up my world with a twofold message: life is here for me to appreciate each moment, and I must stop and relish these moments.

This brief experience showed me how I have allowed my responsibilities and routines to take over my inner mischievousness. My inner mischievousness has been latent and wishes to join with my free spirit to run and roam again. These two little rays of sunshine reinforced my feelings of redundancy. I must learn to locate my pause button and incorporate some childlike behaviors back in my life.

When do I begin?

Immediately. Their giggles, innocence, and spirited behavior forced me to reexamine the importance of observing and participating in the pure joy moments each day of my life.

How do I begin?

My first inclination is to stop being so deeply engrossed with the need to be efficient and exact. I am constantly forcing myself to keep routine and order in my life. This overdoing, both mentally and physically, has precluded me from noticing the little acts of delight that regularly take place in front of me.

From this moment, I have decided to change my priorities and perspectives. I am finished with overdoing, overthinking, and overlooking. Enter self-reflection and self-forgiveness. My inner questioning will always exist. However, I will quiet the mental noise that I create when trying to perfect my life. This counterproductive behavior has distracted me from many valuable moments.

I will no longer miss magical moments. The framed image of the two babes in Bhutan on my desk will help me to remember this. I have learned these prized occurrences can happen at any time, with anyone, and anywhere. I will be mindful to not let them fall between the cracks.

I smile in anticipation of what lies ahead. I am on the lookout for glimmers of bliss, such as the twinkling of a child's eye, a flower standing erect among the weeds, the fluffy cloud formation that resembles a dinosaur, the leaves swaying in the wind, or an embrace from my loved ones—these moments matter.

My goal is to be fully present in this chaotic and ever-changing world. I look forward to my next game of hide and seek.

IGNORE THE IGNORANCE

I must confess, I have a bad case of wanderlust. I relish the sensation of being in a new place. My heart quickens, my head spins, and all my senses feel heightened. It's as if someone has toggled my settings to high alert . . . and I love it!

Is that strange? The reason I ask is because oftentimes I feel like I am the only one who enjoys this aspect of venturing out into the world.

I was delighted when, during a recent social gathering, the conversation shifted to travel. It is my favorite thing to talk about! Vancouver, Glacier National Park, Willamette Valley wineries, and various Tahitian islands were popular places being discussed on the overcrowded outdoor patio.

There was a pause in the conversation and an acquaintance turned to me and said, "You're always going somewhere strange. Where are you off to next?"

I smile inside. I have actually been preparing and packing for a fourteen-day adventure with my husband. We will be wandering aimlessly through the Balkan countries without an itinerary, much less a tour guide.

I hesitate for a moment before saying, "Slovenia." Then, before I could get another word out, a smugly self-assured-looking fellow remarked, "Why? Where is it, again? Isn't it communist?"

I felt my husband's hand lightly brush my lower back, his way of telling me to be calm and not react to the gentleman's snarky tone. I took a breath then proceeded to inform him that "Slovenia borders Austria, Croatia, Hungary, and Italy. You may be remembering when it was part of the former Socialist Federal Republic of Yugoslavia."

I quickly continued to share our partial itinerary. "We will be heading towards Lake Bled, Triglav National Park, and the old town of Ljubljana. But what really excites me is the Cow Ball Festival! There is actually an annual festival—complete with food, drink, and folk music—to celebrate the return of the cows from their highland pastures. Sounds fun, right?"

Instead of waiting for a response, I kept going. I wanted to squeeze in one more little detail, just for him. "We are also stopping in Bosnia. I am really excited to see the city of Sarajevo."

I took a sip of my diluted mango margarita. The expressions on their faces were priceless.

"Why there?" my girlfriend asked.

"I hear it's not safe," alleged that same smug fellow.

Bosnia intrigues me with its rich history. Its religious and cultural diversity has led some to dub it "the Jerusalem of Europe." My neighbor Walt, who visited just a year ago, told me about this nuclear bunker hidden inside a mountain, which was recently converted to a modern art exhibition. Who wouldn't want to go?

The next morning, my girlfriend sent me a text. "Where else has that gypsy friend of yours traveled?" the snarky man probed after my husband and I left.

It made me think, why do I need to explain why I visit these "exotic places?" I am used to people questioning me, but I still tend to get reactive and overly justifying. Sometimes I think maybe I should just ignore the ignorance and continue doing my own thing. But maybe I can help change people's perspectives by swapping out the negative stories they have heard with my firsthand experiences.

I feel fortunate to explore the globe. Our news outlets often overlook all the good in the world. I remember how my grandmother used to become engrossed in domestic and international chaos. She was often unable to separate the fear of what she saw from the potential benefits of going somewhere new. She had no interest in travel, not even to visit her granddaughter in California! Her instincts told her to play it safe, remaining cozy and confident in the safety of her home and small, rural community.

For years, I tried telling her how rewarding the unfamiliar can be. Though I admit, when I am in my own pocket of paradise, sunny San Diego, it is dangerously easy to think, "No way, I am not leaving. The world is an unsettled mess and there is too much danger. I'm staying safe and comfortable right where I am."

But I made up my mind never to let fear prevent me from venturing into uncertainty. Self-transformation and personal growth always seem to happen when I realize I am not in control, and that is something travel continues to prove to me.

Plus, there is always more to learn. It isn't easy to debunk the myths that society has sensationalized about other peoples and places. There is always another side of a story. Crossing cultural lines has taught me many lessons, but the biggest one is that people are far more similar than we are led to believe.

So, I am off to the Balkans with an open heart and an open mind. I feel my senses gearing up for new experiences, whatever they might be. Seeing new sights and learning about new places is always valuable, but even more so is coming home with "new eyes" that see the world without the barriers and divisions that a lack of knowledge can build up.

THE MAN I MARRIED LIKES TO TRAVEL

Looking out the window, I see the expansive ocean peeking out from a layer of cottony clouds. Instead of enjoying my usual Americano with extra hot water prior to boarding, I've decided to wait and order a glass of wine once we're in-flight.

Tim and I will celebrate our twenty-first wedding anniversary tomorrow. We are traveling together—just the two of us—to Croatia. Usually it's a family trip with a detailed itinerary. Both of us are extremely organized, but I admit my hubby has a special flair for finding amazing travel deals and creating exhaustive Excel spreadsheets filled with hotel timelines and comprehensive air schedules.

Two weeks ago, we were officially diagnosed with empty nest syndrome. Our life's itinerary has shifted. My head is spinning and my heart is heavy. I want some time to relax, be quiet, and reflect on our newfound normal. I've brought a book about daring greatly in this next season of my life.

I sip the white wine I've ordered. It's not good. It's not even the kind I sort of like, but who cares. Its airplane wine, I remind myself, and it's doing the job—mellowing my hyper, overly anxious, constantly analyzing mind.

I look at Tim beside me, beginning to close his eyes. He is a hardworking man, linear and systematic. I press my hand on his arm, feeling the warmth of his skin under a soft blue polo shirt. He gives me a smile, squeezes my hand, and returns to his slumber. This trip is not about revitalizing our relationship but rather spending uninterrupted time together without our now fully-grown children or a specific travel plan—a healthy and spontaneous second honeymoon.

* * *

Resting my head against my seatback and closing my eyes, I travel back twenty-one years. Relaxed as he was, the justice of the peace was a little bothered by our misbehavior during his serious speech about wedding rings and what they symbolize. Honestly, I wasn't trying to be ill-mannered . . . I just wanted a peek at my ring! The design of my wedding band was a surprise and I was overcome with childlike excitement. Who could blame me?

"I pronounce you man and wife. You may now kiss the bride." Tim held me and kissed me, energetically and tenderly, the same way he still does with such warmth and enthusiasm. Two decades later, our public displays of affection often irritate our two teenaged sons. "Get a room," they quip. Yet they themselves mimic similar fondness with their own lady friends.

We walked back down the aisle all smiles—full of glee and innocence. Maybe a smidgen naïve as to what we were getting ourselves into. Well, I was anyways. And so, our life began.

Because, for me, my life truly did begin when I married Tim.

* * *

"Whom can you trust?" my therapist asked me years ago.

"No one, really—except myself," I said. My father died when I was eleven, my mother remarried a dud only to eventually divorce him. Life was not dependable, nor were the people closest to me. My childhood was spent in survival mode.

"Then that's your answer," she whispered.

Yes, I had my answer. I would have to trust my gut. I married a man not knowing for sure if I could trust him not to hurt me or leave me. But my instincts told me that Tim was honest and good. We shared so much in common. We both understood abandonment and how to mask the pain of feeling unloved and alone.

"He lets me be my crazy self," I told my therapist. "He has a selfless heart and soulful eyes. I think it will work. Even if he is into horseracing and the stock market. He sounds cool," my therapist observed.

Tim makes careful decisions, whereas I prefer to fly by the seat of my pants. Despite our differences, our philosophy of life is the same: if you can't have fun there's no sense in doing it. Life for me had always seemed random and risky so what did I have to lose? And at twenty-three what did I know?

I knew I adored Tim. Now at forty-five, I still adore him. I also admire him. Love requires two people who are willing to do the work and not give up. Tim is the warmest, most generous man I've ever known. He is my best friend, my comrade, and the only person I would want to navigate the road of life with. I recognized our potential twenty-one years ago. It turns out my instincts were accurate.

* * *

Our years together have been a complete whirlwind . . . and much too full to try and summarize here. Neither of us ever wants to miss anything life has to offer. Our lives are fast, always running in fifth gear. How we manage to avoid burnout I will never know. All marriages can go awry, but we work together. True communication and respect were concepts I'd never understood, let alone experienced, before Tim. We have weathered many storms and we are still solid.

Tim loves me in a way that forces me to love myself more. I remember my first Christmas gift from him. Tucked inside a white shirt box that was wrapped with a satin turquoise bow I found a black sweatshirt with "SAP" embroidered in white block letters across the front. He was reminding me of my "sappiness," one of the reasons he fell in love with me. It was his way of expressing his own extreme sentimentality—in his uniquely witty way.

What a grand gesture. (Shhh, I seldom wear it!) I pull it out every now and then to remind myself how lucky I am to have this guy in my life. This guy sleeping next to me on the plane. The guy I chose to build a family with. The guy my therapist said sounded cool. The baldheaded guy my sister made snarky comments about. The guy who would never put himself before me, unless it was to save me from a bullet or an oncoming car. The guy with beautiful brown eyes, which light up when he sees me after two days or ten days away. The guy I choose to banter with, share secrets with, drink pinot noir with, and be spontaneous with—every damn day of my life.

* * *

I'm jostled into the present as we hit rough air and seatbelt signs light up the quiet cabin. I hold onto my glass, not wanting the contents to spill all over my jeans. Flying is kind of like marriage, isn't it? Turbulence comes and goes. All you can do is hold on tight, hoping for smoother air but never really knowing what the rest of the flight will be like.

I look out at the horizon as we pass over a patch of the Pacific. As the pilot banks a turn, the horizon disappears, and shades of green and blue saturate my eyes like the waterlily pond from Monet's painting. I am reminded of our honeymoon in Giverny, France. I will never forget that magically misty day, standing together on the emerald green footbridge, inhaling fragrant wafts of wisteria.

As the pilot announces our initial decent, I glance over at Tim. I can honestly say that I have fallen in love with every bit of my partner's soul. My perfectly imperfect partner of twenty-one years. If I was not willing to risk the unusual, I would have had to settle for the ordinary. I ended up with a marriage nothing less than extraordinary!

FROZEN FRONTIERS AND FEARLESS FOOTSTEPS

Something about the remote, the untouched, the places at the edges of the world has always called to me. Antarctica, Papua New Guinea, and Easter Island are a few, each speaking in its own way, pulling me toward the unknown, the mystery, the stories woven into landscapes few have seen.

I've been drawn to Papua New Guinea for many years, the highlands where tribes live untouched by Western influence, still deeply rooted in their traditions. Twice, I tried to make the journey happen. The first time, my husband wasn't keen on me traveling alone there. The second and most recent was with my twenty-five-year-old son, who was ready to join me, but the cost to reach the interior was astronomical, as one company controls all bookings and has monopolized the market. As much as I wanted to go, I couldn't justify the price. Trust me, I love exotic adventures and am willing to pay to play, but this was a whole new level.

When I finally arrived on Easter Island ten years ago, it felt like stepping into another world. The moai stood as silent guardians, their presence heavy with mystery, their origin stories tangled in myth and history. But it wasn't just the statues, the island itself, the rhythm of the waves, the depth in the eyes of the local people, the inexplicable magic that lingers in the air. A place that imprints one's soul, leaving magical moments and memories that don't fade.

And now, Antarctica awaits, the ultimate frontier, a place of pure extremes, where ice and sky blur into endless white, where survival is raw, and nature reigns without apology. It's the only continent without an indigenous population, yet it holds a pull as strong as any ancient land. Maybe it's the isolation, the silence, the idea of standing at the edge of the earth with nothing but ice, sea, and sky stretching infinitely beyond.

There's a profound privilege and gratitude in making these treks, standing in places few will ever see, and stepping outside my world and into another. Travel like this isn't just about checking off remote destinations; it's about expanding my cultural intelligence, deepening my understanding of humanity, and witnessing the resilience and beauty of people who live in ways so different from my own. Each journey strips away assumptions, challenges my perspectives, and instills in me a greater reverence for the diversity of life on this planet. I don't take that for granted. To walk among the moai of Easter Island, to imagine what it would be like to sit with the tribes of Papua New Guinea, and now, to prepare for the vast silence of Antarctica, it's a gift, one that reminds me how vast, complex, and astonishing the world truly is.

I am prepared for my expedition, which takes place in five days, with two books in hand, *South* by Sir Ernest Shackleton and *The Worst Journey in the World* by Apsley Cherry-Garrard—both thoughtful gifts from my bibliophile friend Edward. I'll also watch Werner Herzog's *Encounters at the End of the World,* which offers a philosophical and poetic take on Antarctica, adding to my human curiosity about the adventurous souls who choose to live and work there. This journey feels like a natural extension of the awe I found in Easter Island and had hoped to encounter and experience in Papua New Guinea, knowing each place is a testament to resilience, mystery, and the untamed spirit of exploration. There is something magnetic about these landscapes and the people they draw in, perhaps mirroring my own restless drive to pursue, engage with, and understand the unknown.

RECHARGE AND RETREAT

I returned to my babe cave from a quick trip to Arizona to see my two sons and spent my last night in Sedona near the Boynton Canyon vortex. The place was private and tranquil, away from the "noise' of the city. What I took away from this experience was not only the stunning scenery but the act of disappearing, which left me inspired and invigorated.

I wanted to share a few thoughts with you.

Retreating and recharging, for me, is a necessary discipline, one I am still mastering. Throughout history, many great free thinkers and architects have had to remove themselves from civilization to connect with their work at a deeper and more meaningful level, sometimes against their wills.

Life is constantly inviting us to let go of ourselves so that we can experience rebirth. Sometimes, we are slow to recognize these moments—a death in the family, a lay-off, a divorce—but change is always happening all around us, often disguised as loss, asking us if we are sure this is who we want to be.

I stood and stared for several minutes admiring the hovering hummingbirds tirelessly whiz by me. It was the perfect ending to my trail walk and opportunity for introspection. Despite the excessive mid-air flapping of wings, these mystical creatures appear to understand the importance of conserving energy while managing their metabolic rate.

Our identity, in many respects, is an idea: a story we tell ourselves that is reinforced by our environment. When we let go of this idea, even briefly, we are free to re-imagine almost everything about our lives, including our work. Disappearance, then, will refresh a soul when done well. At the pool, later that day, I read these ancient words of wisdom from Lao Tzu, the Chinese philosopher who wrote *The*

Way of Life: A sound man, by not advancing himself, stays further ahead of himself, by not confining himself to himself sustains himself outside himself: by never being an end in himself, he endlessly becomes himself.

To endlessly become ourselves, we have to let go of what we think we are. This, I believe, is the quest of the artist, the visionary, the creator. She must go to the heart of life, tasting the sweet nectar of it, and only then may she re-emerge to talk about it sincerely.

This can be uncomfortable. At one point on my trail walk with flip flops on, I slid down a rock face. Thank goodness I did not break a bone—or my skull. The danger of the experience was both frightening and exhilarating, and that was the point. We have to find new edges; we have to go beyond what we think we can do if we want to keep growing in our work and inspiring others to do the same.

When we don't allow ourselves to disappear, we often lose ourselves in the haze of a frantic, unintentional life, settling for something less than our best. This discipline of stepping away from the outer world to access a more profound, inner one teaches me to let go of what I thought was true and allows me to access something new and altogether familiar.

Anyway, it's good to be back. Sitting in my babe cave, I remember the stillness of Sedona. I noticed a hummingbird outside my window and smiled. As I start small, I am not fretting about what the next chapter in my life entails. I will continue to explore both my inner and outer self and do what I need to let go of right now to make room for what's to come, even if I don't know what that is.

LIVE WHILE ALIVE

It's My Life's Battle Between Niceness and Self-Preservation

While running my daily miles at the gym in Taipei City, I found myself gazing out the window, watching the world go by. Down below, life moved with a frantic rhythm—people coming and going, immersed in their routines and struggles. It struck me how small we all are in the grand scheme of life and living. I often feel this when I travel, but this moment hit differently. Amidst the noise and the motion, the familiar chords of Jon Bon Jovi's *It's My Life* filled the gym; then, a few minutes later, when I put my air pods back in, what are the chances that this same song would ring in my ears again, within thirty minutes of each other. Suddenly, the song wasn't just background music. It was a wake-up call.

"This ain't a song for the broken-hearted," Jon sang, and I realized it wasn't a song for the people I had spent my life trying to please in the past, either. It was a song for me. I had been bending, twisting, and reshaping myself for years to accommodate others. I said "yes" when I meant "no," smiled when I felt like crying, and took the blame to keep the peace. But the more I gave, the more I felt empty. The more I sacrificed, the more the world and people seemed to take without much gratitude.

This life of being *nice*—a well-trained people-pleaser—had become exhausting, but it came with a cruel reward: acceptance. However, fleeting, the illusion that I was indispensable to others' happiness was enough. Or so I thought for far too many years. But Jon's lyrics, "I just wanna live while I'm alive" haunted me.

What was I doing with my one wild, precious life?

The truth is the world doesn't reward self-abandonment. People are consumed by their own struggles and their own needs. They don't notice when your sacrifices drain you. And why should they? The burden of taking care of our own happiness rests solely on our own shoulders. The chorus started to ring louder each time I heard it: *"It's my life / It's now or never / I ain't gonna live forever."*

Being accommodating felt virtuous, but it became a slow death. Each time I put someone else's priorities above my own, a little piece of me faded. I thought kindness would win hearts, but it often attracted takers—people willing to drain me dry because I made it so easy. I realized the flaw in my logic: living for others didn't guarantee love or loyalty. It only guaranteed that I would continue to keep losing myself.

Yet, breaking free of the likable persona over the years wasn't easy. It felt selfish at first. There's a line in the song that says, "Like Frankie said, 'I did it my way.'" At first, I envied that audacity . . . the courage to unapologetically chart my course, to say "no" without guilt, and to claim my right to joy.

The transformation was gradual. I began to set stronger boundaries. I started asking myself the hard questions: *What do I want? What makes me happy?* For the first time, I allowed myself to pursue those answers without fear of disappointing others. And yes, some people did and have pulled away. Others have called me self-focused, or they have quietly faded out of my life. But Jon's words guided me: *"Stand tall when they're calling you out / Don't bend, don't break, don't back down."*

The beauty of living my own life is this: I am learning that the people who matter will respect me for it. They'll cheer me on instead of trying to pull me back into the shadows of self-sacrifice. The ones who don't? They were never truly on my side, to begin with.

There's a bittersweet lesson: people are too consumed with their lives to care for yours. It's not cruelty; it's just human nature. The world won't stop for your needs and won't reward you for being a martyr. But when you care for yourself, you teach others how to treat you—with respect, not expectation.

It's My Life isn't just a rock anthem. It's a manifesto. It's a call to stand up, claim your space, and refuse to let others' demands dictate your happiness. The message is simple but strong: You're alive. Live like it. Because at the end of the day, no one else is coming to save you. No one else can live your life. And, as the song says, you can't live forever.

So, I'll indulge in some Taiwanese street food tonight at the Shilin Night Market, with over five hundred food vendors. Here I come: scallion pancakes, steamed dumplings, tube-shaped sticky rice with mushrooms, and mystery meat. My favorite to watch, make, and eat are the quail eggs with shrimp omelet bites. I may need to roll back to the hotel instead of walking, so be it. The mouthfuls of delicate deliciousness are worth it.

ROOTED: 'UP NORTH'

I'm here in Northern Michigan, nestled in a cabin in the woods by the water. The warm fall breeze brushes past as I hear the gentle waves against the shore. From my desk, a handmade creation, clearly pieced together with whatever materials were on hand, I sit here and type atop its uneven legs, tucked in the corner of a screened-in porch. I have a perfect vantage point to watch all the interesting and inspiring things nature offers. Despite the desk edges being rough-hewn with splinters, its crooked charm allows me to work and appreciate the tall trees as they begin to turn, bursts of orange and yellow peeking through the branches.

The cabin has a weathered charm, with its creaky floors adding to the rustic ambiance. Its gray shingled siding, faded from years of enduring elements, contrasts beautifully with the vibrant red trim around the windows and doors. The paint on the trim is slightly chipped, telling stories of countless seasons spent nestled in the woods. This structure exudes a sense of history, as if it stood quietly by the water for generations, offering shelter and solace to all who pass through the doors.

The sound of those slamming screen doors takes me back to my childhood, reminding me of endless summers at my great-grandparents' log cabin on Drummond Island. I can almost see the worn wooden beams and smell the pine trees surrounding us, feeling the warmth of those long days exploring the island's rugged beauty. Each slam carries echoes of laughter, family gatherings around that pine picnic table, and the carefree days and simpler times that shaped so many of my cherished memories there.

I feel fortunate to be a guest here, listening to the rustic soundtrack of my solitude. This writing retreat offers a peaceful escape, where the natural rhythms of life around me create a perfect backdrop for reflection. It is a place that encourages stillness and invites inspiration to flow freely, providing space and serenity for my words to find their way onto the page.

Northern Michigan has held a pivotal place in my life. Each fall, I return, not only to reconnect with myself and my roots but also with my father. Before his passing, we shared countless moments outdoors together. Now, at fifty, I reflect on the tangles and trauma that once felt like they would shape me forever, yet in this place, they make me feel more alive and closer to him than I do in California, where I have lived for twenty-eight years. The environment here has left a deep imprint on my soul, and I find myself reveling in my agency, choosing and claiming what is redemptive and life-giving.

As I sit here in this familiar place, surrounded by the sights and sounds woven into the fabric of my life, I am reminded of the healing power of returning to where it all began. Northern Michigan is more than just a destination; it is a sanctuary where I can reflect on the past, embrace the present, and honor the memories of my father. Each visit reaffirms the path I have chosen to reclaim what is redemptive, nurture what is life-giving, and continue writing the story of my becoming. This area remains a place of personal reflection and where much of my writing has taken shape. The quiet solitude of Northern Michigan's natural beauty provides the perfect backdrop for my creative work, allowing me to dive deeper into my thoughts and stories.

A JOURNEY TO THE EDGE OF THE WORLD

Seven Continents - One Self

Long before I ever boarded a plane, I traveled through stories. My grandmother's voice, steady and soothing, was my first passport, turning pages that took me far beyond her living room in Reese, Michigan. That early love of books sparked something lasting in me: a conviction that stories are how we understand the world and our place within it. Over the years, the gatherings I created, the space I held, and the people I met along my journey were all rooted in keeping the art of storytelling alive. Because I believe in the power of shared experiences, which enhance understanding and shape what it means to be human, years ago, while my grandmother was still alive, I set out into the world, traveling across all seven continents—not just to see, but to feel, to collect not just souvenirs, but perspective. I have returned changed and more myself than ever before, thanks to Grandma Rosie, who was always in my heart.

Antarctica is not just a place but an encounter with something greater than life. It is an immersion into silence so deep it presses on you, a vast landscape that defies understanding. The towering, glowing glaciers seem to shine from within, their jagged edges catching the shifting light. Icebergs, massive and shaped by time, drift through the cold waters, indifferent to how small I feel. Even at the height of summer, the continent stays covered in ice and snow, a place where life persists against all odds. And yet, for all its harshness, I've never felt more at peace with myself. Never so still, so completely in the moment. There are no words to fully capture the enormity of what I experienced, but I know I have been changed.

I kayaked through this frozen dreamscape, my orange vessel skimming the water's surface so clear it felt like a portal into another world. I could hear the ice shift, cracking and groaning in a slow, glacial conversation. The humpback whale's breath broke the silence, close enough that I could feel its presence before I saw it, its fluke rising in an elegant arc before vanishing beneath the surface. For five days, I lived within this untouched wilderness, moving through it as a guest, knowing that this experience was something few would ever have.

And then, there was the plunge. The moment my body hit the Arctic water, it was as if every cell erupted, an instant, intense, yet exhilarating shock. For a few seconds, my mind went blank—there was no past, no future, only the present. And as I surfaced, gasping and laughing, I felt something I never expected: complete stillness. A clarity that only happens when everything else is stripped away.

A bibliophile friend suggested I read the story of Ernest Shackleton in *South* before I arrived in this frozen realm. After reading, I was gobsmacked, so I made my husband watch the movie a few days later. Shackleton's story resonated with me profoundly because I feel it mirrors my own resilience, tenacity, and ability to overcome impossible odds. His survivor's story in Antarctica, together with his fearless leadership, refusal to surrender to despair, and ability to inspire and protect his crew, even in the most desolate and unforgiving conditions speaks to something primal within me—the part that has endured, fought, and led through adversity.

I have faced profound loss, betrayal, physical hardships, and emotional isolation, yet I've done my best never to let these storms define me. Like Shackleton, I took responsibility for myself and those around me, often coordinating survival efforts for my family, even when I was struggling. His ability to hold onto hope and move forward without knowing what lay ahead reflects my journey of breaking generational cycles, choosing self-preservation, and confronting uncertainty with unwavering resolve despite the odds.

There's also the element of the frozen, barren landscape, which symbolizes times in my life when I felt emotionally frozen and abandoned, cut off from warmth, safety, or clarity. But Shackleton's journey wasn't just about survival and getting his people home against all odds. Maybe that part of the story—the promise of return, of overcoming impossible distances, and the odds of finding a way back, especially within myself, is what touches me most deeply.

I couldn't stop thinking of Shackleton and his men while wandering this ethereal continent, and of the world they encountered more than a century ago, a world far more savage than the one I experienced. I came here wrapped in the privilege of modern exploration: thermal layers, guided excursions, and a warm ship waiting for me at the end of each day. Shackleton had none of that. He and his men were at the mercy of Antarctica in its most ruthless form, yet he refused to break. Shackleton refused to let his men break. He held them together through sheer force of will, navigating the impossible and ensuring no life was lost. It is one thing to read about it—to understand it intellectually. But it is unfathomable to stand here, feel the bite of the wind even in the luxury of my gear, and know that he survived without any of this.

His story isn't simply one of endurance; it's one of leadership, toughness, and the will to carve a path forward, no matter how impossible it seems. And in that, I think I see myself, and was deeply moved.

Yet Antarctica was not the only continent that carved itself into my soul.

Africa, with its raw, ancient rhythm, taught me to listen more deeply—not just to the sounds around me, but to the pulse within.

There, in the vastness of the Serengeti and the wild intimacy of conservancies like Lewa, I found a different kind of stillness—one that echoed with ancestral knowing. At Sirikoi Lodge, my oldest son helped prepare meals with local women—a type of cultural exchange that nourishes more than just hunger. And in those open lands where lionesses nursed their cubs and Tito the giraffe greeted us each morning as elephants strolled past in the distance, I saw the balance of strength and softness, protection and play. Africa awakened a reverence in me, not just for nature, but for the way traditions hold space for the sacred in everyday life.

Australia, sun-soaked and untamed, offered its own elemental wonder. Holding Macy the koala on Kangaroo Island and staying at the Southern Ocean Lodge felt like stepping into another dimension of wild luxury. In the Daintree, the world's oldest rainforest whispered its secrets as we moved through its green embrace, reminding me of time's unhurried passage. The Great Barrier Reef shimmered beneath us—alive, breathtaking, vanishing. My youngest son speared a reef shark and we shared a meal with a local family, connected by curiosity and gratitude. And then there was Sydney, sitting beneath the vault of the Opera House, holiday music echoing within its soaring sails, I felt like I'd stepped into a living sculpture. Bruce Chatwin called Australia a labyrinth of pathways, each leading toward a deeper understanding of nature and its origins. I now know what he meant.

North America gave me my roots—and my reckoning. It's where I learned how to survive, how to strive, and eventually, how to soften. From the golden sunsets along the Pacific Coastline to the southern hospitality that lingers in Beaufort and Savannah, this continent holds my earliest lessons in both grit and grace.

Up north, the hydrangeas and coastal charm of Martha's Vineyard whisper of summer ease, while the lights of New York City and the thrill of Broadway pulse with unrelenting ambition. Alaska, with its raw and rugged wilderness, reminded me what it means to feel both small and infinite all at once.

And then there's Michigan—my home state—a wooded wonderland where lake life set the rhythm of my summers and became a memory to my soul. Each state has its own atmosphere, its own way of seeping into my bones. From the Rockies where my childhood echoes, to the coastal roads that now feel like home, this land didn't just raise me—it revealed me.

South America stirred something ancient in me. Cusco and its colors, Machu Picchu stood not just as marvels of human endurance but as mirrors to my own internal ascent, stone by stone, step by step. It was here I learned that thin air can still carry deep meaning.

From the windswept paths of Patagonia to the thunderous awe of Iguazu Falls, this continent awakened a rhythm I didn't know I had. In Buenos Aires, I danced with the ghosts of tango and toasted with malbec under sultry skies. The coastline of Lima offered pisco sours and a kind of calm only the Pacific can promise. Santiago fed me with avocado, steak, and the poetry of Pablo Neruda, his words greeting me like an old friend etched in stone and spirit.

I traveled deep into the Amazon, where pink dolphins surfaced like dreams and traditional medicine spoke a language older than time. And how could I forget Copacabana—its beaches, its chaos, its Carnaval, a swirl of colors, costumes, and joy that left me breathless and laughing, utterly alive.

These weren't just trips; they were experiences that shaped me. Each place left a mark, a lesson, a moment I will carry with me forever.

Europe reminded me of elegance, history, and a sense of belonging. Wandering through Parisian streets, sipping espresso beneath terraced balconies, and standing in front of works of art that still breathe centuries later. These moments reminded me that beauty and struggle often coexist.

But how can I even begin to list all my experiences across this continent? I've spent countless hours here, and each place has left an imprint on me. France has completely captured my heart, from the elegance of Paris to the lavender fields of Provence, from the vineyards of Burgundy and Bordeaux to the champagne sparkle of Épernay and the aristocratic charm of Chantilly. Style, food, wine—yes, I'm smitten.

England drew me into its historic past, with Cambridge being a favorite spot—church bells ringing as I walked the academic streets and enjoyed high tea at the Ivy. Ireland felt like home—my roots in Limerick, my joy found in Dingle with its jigs and jugs of Baileys. Scotland offered its hearty hospitality with haggis, neeps, and tatties, while Austria and Switzerland provided the kind of beauty that makes you believe in music and mountains. Munich was all about beer steins and warm pretzels, with celebration in every bite.

The spice market in Istanbul captivated my senses, and the apple tea was a quiet revelation. And Budapest—remembered as the place where I sat in an opera house with my sons and husband, marveling at a world that somehow felt like mine.

Each country I've visited has become part of who I am. I still pinch myself while riding the Eurostar, Belgian chocolate in hand, dreaming of the yellow waffle truck in Brussels. Europe hasn't just shaped me; it keeps calling me back, whispering in a thousand accents that I belong.

Asia drew me into a contrast, with temples beside skyscrapers and incense trailing behind bullet trains. Amid its rituals and fast pace, I found peace in the paradox. Whether walking the ancient Silk Road or sipping tea in a quiet courtyard, Asia reminded me to stay still, even as the world spins fast.

The Great Wall of China is a marvel not to be missed; just avoid the days of tomb-sweeping when the traffic rivals the crowds. Cambodia gave me a moment I'll never forget: a man I call the "Happy Man" emerged from the rice fields, soaked and smiling, handing me a bouquet of lotus stems with a joy so pure it left an imprint on my heart. The people of Cambodia are some of the kindest I've ever met.

Thailand was a feast of sensations, bustling streets, fragrant food stalls, and unmatched generosity. It was there I received the best massage of my life, delivered with care and precision that felt more like healing than luxury.

Japan left me in awe. Every detail, every gesture is purposeful. My own sense of order and formality felt amateur compared to their graceful discipline. Walking the Philosopher's Path in Kyoto, surrounded by cherry blossoms, felt like stepping into a dream. A sober visit to Hiroshima offered a quiet yet powerful recognition of the toll of conflict and the resilience of peace.

South Korea captivated me with its vibrancy, though I couldn't shake the eerie feeling of being close to the North while standing in the tunnels. Still, the people were friendly, and the culture fascinating.

Malaysia offered yet another layer... lush, untamed beauty and gentle surprises. "Hellman" has my heart, and I can still see the glowing dance of fireflies in the mangroves, a moment of magic I hope to relive again.

There are too many places to name, too many moments to recount. But what I carry most from Asia embodies the quiet depth of cultural intelligence, the rhythm of rituals, and the daily reminder that we are all bound by stories, struggle, and a search for meaning. Asia didn't just show me the world—it softened and sharpened me all at once.

Sometimes, I hesitate to share my experiences. A part of me worries it might sound like bragging, as if traveling is a luxury beyond conversation. But I've realized that others like me exist, people drawn to the world's vastness and eager for exploration. They might not always be in my close circle, but they are there. I've learned to embrace my wanderlust openly, understanding that my stories are not just about places but about moments that have shaped me in ways words cannot fully express.

Standing on all seven continents has been more than just a journey; it has been a transformation. Every place I've visited has left a lasting impression, changing how I see the world and, more importantly, how I see myself. Travel, with all its surprises, has been more rewarding than I ever expected. The memories are embedded in my soul, the stories are endless, and the lessons are invaluable. Each experience shaped a part of me. But it was Antarctica that truly made me whole.

CHASING FREEDOM

An Expedition Across the World and Within

Travel is more than just a journey through places—it's a journey into myself. Every destination has a spark, reminding me of who I am and who I'm becoming. From sipping Sancerre and eating pâté in the vineyards of Chablis to truffle hunting in Tuscany with four generations of my family, including my eighty-eight-year-old grandfather and my twenty-something sons, I've felt the deep connection of life's interconnectedness. These moments are more than memories—they're proof of life's beauty, spontaneity, and freedom.

I've stood on the wild tundra of Alaska at Winterlake Lodge, sharing stories with DeeDee, a legendary dog musher who has competed in the Iditarod over twenty times. Her grit and grace echoed the wildness of the lakes and land around us. I've wandered through tea plantations in Sri Lanka, where chance encounters with strangers turned into meaningful, heartfelt conversations. Whether in the wide-open spaces of the Serengeti in Kenya, the peaceful charm and oysters of Prince Edward Island, or the icy wonder of Kiruna's Ice Hotel, I am reminded of the true meaning of freedom: it's not just a place—it's a feeling.

This sense of freedom carries me across continents, fueled by a wanderlust that propels me forward. Is it about running away from something or toward something? I wonder if I'll ever truly know. What I do know is that these experiences weave together a patchwork of gratitude and purpose. I recently achieved my goal of visiting all seven continents, and I can't help but reflect on the why. Why do I need to explore, connect, and feel?

Maybe it's because travel provides clarity, stripping away life's noise and revealing the raw, untamed truth of existence. Whether I'm sitting in hours of traffic in China while tombs are being cleaned on the way to the Great Wall, counting tunnels in Croatia with my husband, seeing bullet holes in buildings in Bosnia, or meeting remarkable women on a walkabout in Bali, there's an undeniable sense of kismet in these moments. Am I blessed and grateful? Yes, deeply. But gratitude isn't passive—it's a responsibility. It's about using these experiences in the most beautiful way possible, honoring them, and letting them change me.

With every step on foreign soil, every glass of wine shared with family, and every unplanned meeting that feels like destiny, I feel humbled by life's vastness and empowered by my role in it. Life may be larger than me, but I am the one charting my path, chasing freedom, connection, and meaning. For now, that is enough.

VAGABOND OF THE SOUL

"Where are you off to *now*?" they ask, eyebrows raised and smiles that don't always reach their eyes... "Can't you just settle down and stay home?" I believe it's not meant to wound, but it lingers—an undercurrent of judgment wrapped in curiosity. Still, I've learned not to bristle. Instead, I breathe and answer: "I have a vagabond soul."

It's not because I'm running from something but because I'm running toward something—toward understanding, toward meaning, and toward the golden thread that connects all things when we're willing to look closer. My next journey, in two weeks, takes me to New Zealand and Tasmania—not for the postcard views and wines (those call me too!), but for what they might teach me about presence, reverence, and what it means to *belong* without possessing.

Some people search for a home. I search for truth, the kind that exists between places, roles, what is handed down, and what feels sacred to me. I am a vagabond of both the road and the soul, not because I am unhappy, but because I am deeply, dangerously curious.

As a kid, I questioned everything. When adults gave me answers, they rarely made sense. I wanted more—more depth, more honesty, more proof. But often, they couldn't give it. They'd say, "Don't worry about it," or "That's just the way it is." That never satisfied me. I wasn't trying to be difficult—just to understand.

In high school, I remember challenging my religion teacher: "Why do I need to believe this? Why does this version of the truth matter more than my experience of it?" Blind faith never came naturally to me. I wanted to feel truth in my body, to witness it myself, not adopt it just because someone told me to. That instinct to experience rather than assume is what still drives me to travel, to seek, to go where others don't.

People often speak with conviction about places they've never been, cultures they've never experienced, lives they've never lived. They adopt secondhand beliefs and make them their own truths. That's never made sense to me. I'd rather stand on the soil, hear the language, and feel the heartbeat of a place firsthand before making conclusions. That's how I understand the world — by being in it, fully.

My restlessness isn't caused by a lack. It's driven by longing, a desire to experience life truly, to peel back the shiny surface and press my hands against the raw, breathing core of things. I've never been satisfied with inheriting a blueprint. I want to create my own map.

Of course, vagabonding, both spiritually and physically, comes with a cost. I've felt the burden of other people's confusion, their need to label or fix me. But I've also experienced profound freedom. I've left relationships that didn't respect who I was becoming. I've let go of timelines and expectations that weren't mine. I've made room for wonder.

Living on my own terms hasn't always been easy, but it's always been true. I trust the rhythm of my growth. I struggle to settle because I've made a pact with authenticity: to observe, to challenge, to live alert and never settle for mediocrity.

So no, I am not escaping. I am arriving—again and again—in every unfamiliar place that offers me a mirror. New Zealand and Tasmania are next on the list of soul-stretching teachers. I am a vagabond not only of roads but of soul, a restless heart with a compass tuned to truth, tenderness, and the untamed. I do not seek a final destination. I strive to stay present. And if that means wandering for the rest of my days, then so be it.

The journey has become my home.

LOVE AND CONNECTION

Threads that Bind

Love is the undercurrent of everything—whether it's the love we give, the love we withhold, or the love we search for in others and ourselves. This section explores the complexities of human connection—the bonds that have lifted me, the heartbreaks that have broken me, and the moments of tenderness that have reminded me of the beauty of vulnerability. Love is not just romantic; it is the foundation of family, friendship, and even self-acceptance. It is the force that has shaped my relationships, tested my capacity for forgiveness, and, at times, forced me to redefine what love even means.

Some of these entries are grounded in the everyday sacredness of marriage and motherhood – the slow, steady rhythm of choosing each other through the seasons of joy and strain, and the fierce, protective tenderness of raising children while still learning how to raise myself. Others explore the longing for deeper understanding, the quiet fractures that go unspoken, and the unexpected ways love continues to evolve. I have learned that connection does not always look like closeness; sometimes it is the grace of letting go, or the courage to stay. These ramblings attempt to hold love in its many forms – imperfectly perfect, radiant, and resilient and to pay homage to the strands that bind us together, even as we grow and change.

GOBSMACKED—TWENTY YEARS WITH THE HUBS

I am grateful to be married to someone who *understands* or, better yet, *tolerates* my unique and unusual ways.

After two decades, I have yet to figure out what it is *exactly* about Tim Cohen that keeps me grounded despite my urge to take flight at certain times. When we met in 1997, his oversized smile captivated me, even though I had other plans in life. His persistence was endearing. His charm, natural.

It was pure kismet how we met. I was living in Michigan. He, in California. We were both attending the same corporate event at the Hilton Hotel in Orlando, Florida for our respective companies. "As any good salesman would do, the first priority is to know their client." That's Tim's feeble attempt to defend the moves he made that summer day in late June.

When Tim's playful cinnamon-colored eyes looked at me across the counter in the large commercial kitchen, it felt like his gaze went straight into my soul. For that endless moment, no one else existed. Even now, that comforting feeling surrounds me with warmth, making me feel loved unconditionally. Cue romantic music, creating complete sappiness here. Yet, the obvious answer to my question of "Why have I stayed with him all these years?" could be his genuine humility or, better yet, the way he speaks with sincerity, even when he is stressed.

Over the years, I have jotted down thoughts about our "Lofty and Loony Love" fest, but for this milestone anniversary, it felt fitting to reflect on how our love has contracted in both its wild *and* elevated aspects. Amidst the chaos of life and living, it can be difficult for two people to stay connected while maintaining their sanity in the swirling storm of chaos.

I deeply respect how we challenge each other's thinking. Our approaches to problem-solving are often different. Naturally, each of us believes our ideas are the solution, but the process becomes an opportunity for both of us to grow. It's been a great experience learning to embrace his strengths and admit my flaws, and vice versa. Like any working partnership, when each person gives their best, they are unstoppable together.

As someone who constantly seeks new information, my drive to pursue change versus sticking to the status quo is limitless. I thrive on the unknown and enjoy challenging the norm, which often includes my dear husband's perspective. Mediocrity is not a word in my vocabulary. My compassionate partner has always supported my relentless quest for satisfaction. Tim and I are opposites in that regard. He tends to be satisfied and prefers predictability. Me? Not so much.

I have come to realize that marriage involves merging and meshing two distinct personalities. My relationship with Tim has taught me patience, especially when my darling leaves the cupboard doors and kitchen drawers open. Truth be told, I *never* leave the coffee pot on or forget to clean the wad of hair out of the shower drain. If marriage is a continual game of give and take, both partners must be willing to participate, understanding that the percentages of giving and taking regularly shift.

Marriage has the ability to capture the loneliness of uncertainty, to offer a safe refuge to reside with a buddy. My hubby understands my need to be my own person and be on my own, patiently waiting for me to return, both mentally and physically. He cheers me on when creativity flows and books my plane tickets when I need to go.

I distinctly remember a conversation we had years ago when he quipped, "You are like a balloon; I get you on the way up and the way down." At first, I was offended, then I realized this clever man appreciates all my tendencies and loves me for who I am. Both life experience and becoming a mother has brought me to a different level of understanding my messy large, vibrant rainbow-colored balloon filled with "hot air" floats up and down, but I know deep within my heart Tim likes to ride in my basket. I like to tell myself he enjoys my vantage point, even though he is not fond of heights.

To this day, I am utterly astonished that twenty-plus years ago fate finally presented me a partner who understands my unpredictability. My patient husband not only celebrates it, but he also *never* attempts to reduce it. What I know, respect, and admire is his ability to accept my inconsistencies and encourage me to be myself without remorse or regret. It took me years to understand the significance of this unique trait.

In his college fraternity days, Tim and his Sigma Alpha Epsilon brothers memorized "The True Gentleman."[1] He is truly the quintessence of this creed. I marvel at this empathetic fifty-something man who consistently orders vanilla ice cream over the other 31 flavors, has an uncanny ability to be a human calculator in a matter of seconds, and launches the quickest and wittiest retorts of any person I have yet to encounter.

Our lives have been a rollercoaster, zigzagging from the beginning. We both enjoy the unpredictable movements and weird sensations that come with thrill-seeking activities. He and I both practice compassion despite our differences as we navigate life's adventures. Learning together is a vital aspect of our relationship.

Since I love asking questions, we each separately made a list of *twenty words* that felt significant to us over the past *twenty years*. I felt a mix of anticipation and anxiety to see how many words we would choose in common. Please notice our personalities shining through the list below, and take note that Tim did not follow directions and sent me twenty-one words instead.

Shannon:

Communication. Humor. Compromise. Patience. Respect. Acceptance. Recognition. Admiration. Perseverance. Trust. Silliness. Forgive. Forget. Adventurous. Spontaneity. Partnership. Change. Optimistic. Honesty. Dream.

Tim:

Evolved. Involved. Sorry. Thankful. Handholding. Understanding. Compromise. Dedication. Humor. Respect. Patience. Silly. Honest. Fun. Laughter. Kindness. Understanding. Passionate. Partnership. Self-Awareness. Yes, Honey!

Each of us came into this marriage wanting the same thing: a happy, lasting, and fulfilling partnership. Honestly, not much has changed during our time together. I am the same person Tim married. Although right now it would be nice to have that twenty-something taut body back, but right now, I am more inclined to strive for a taut mind.

Our honeymoon period will continue to be extended yet another year, albeit not without drama or difficulties. Changes and challenges are indeed inevitable. A splash of maturity and a dash of acceptance have guided me in developing a deeper appreciation for this loving and mindful man. He will keep weathering my storms. For my part, I will work at accepting that dark clouds exist rather than resisting them. Twenty years have and will continue to bring sunny, bright days regardless.

My simple request is we keep floating together and delight in my balloon flights. Let's be truthful—sparkly stars, puffy clouds and beautiful butterflies are never at ground level.

Up, up and away Tim Cohen. Let's keep making life more magical together!

[1] "The True Gentleman is the man whose conduct proceeds from good will and an acute sense of propriety, and whose self-control is equal to all emergencies; who does not make the poor man conscious of his poverty, the obscure man of his obscurity, or any man of his inferiority or deformity; who is himself humbled if necessity compels him to humble another; who does not flatter wealth, cringe before power, or boast of his own possessions or achievements; who speaks with frankness but always with sincerity and sympathy; whose deed follows his word; who thinks of the rights and feelings of others, rather than his own; and who appears well in any company, a man with whom honor is sacred and virtue safe." – *John Walter Wayland*

THINKING LIKE A MOTHER

There's no universal template for a child's happiness.

Happiness, this is what I wanted, yearned for, and dreamed of growing up . . . and believe it is what my boys want, yearn for, or dream of—but it's not my job to figure out how to attain it for them. Who they are and what they want is only something they can figure out. Each may blame me thirty years later when various dysfunctional discussions with their therapists arise. Oh well!

Motherhood has taught me plenty.

Lying in my bed next to the window overlooking a lush treescape, I would write out the life I planned to lead when I grew up and gained control. That battered, lavender-colored notebook in which I plotted my future is tucked in a plastic storage bin somewhere in my garage. It took me years to understand that, at any point, only I could claim that steadfast confidence in my ability to change my circumstances.

For a long time, trusting people was not my superpower, but trusting myself always was. I grew up in a broken household. Let's be honest, we all had some form of deviation from social norms swirling around our dinner tables. Even as a young child, I believed in my mind, my resilience, and my ambitions. I have never been afraid of many things in my life, but the fear of not acting and achieving was one of them.

Becoming a mother at the age of twenty-five forced me to think about all the things I would never do as a parent. All the ways I can improve and do better. I had a determination to create the home life for my children I'd wished for and wrote about growing up.

My identity as a mother is never fixed. In fact, it's likely to change in ways that surprise and delight daily. Having children has taught me to see beyond my suffering. The person I turned out to be after the first year of motherhood is not the same person I became after the second, twelfth, or twenty-first year. With both boys grown and flown, and in honor of Mother's Day, it felt right to reflect on how my messy and gloriously complicated story showcased the identity of my motherhood.

Children are like seeds of possibility. I heard this in one of those weekly church services my mother dragged me to. This statement resonated with me later when my role of a parent became clear. I was to help them understand it is possible to do the things they want in life and be who they want to be. It took time for me to eliminate the need to be picture-perfect—to have all the answers.

No matter how much I loved my boys, I would make many mistakes, some that may somehow scar them. Many mistakes, I most likely would not even know I was making. That confident control I had exercised over my entire life felt halfhearted when I became responsible for raising two human beings. Both witnessed me and all my flaws daily, as their own personhood was being formed. No pressure to perform there! Empathy entered for my adolescent parents, and I recognized everyone is doing the best they can with what they have been given.

Motherhood can be a community of helping hands, but sometimes we must reach out for them. In our DNA, are hundreds of mothers who came before us. We stand ahead of hundreds more, because we too will survive this challenging time, and our children will inherit our choices.

I learned that asking for help is not a sign of weakness. There is no shame in asking for support. It takes a special kind of bravery that can only come from humility and surrender. Which is where the African Proverb *it takes a village to raise a child* must have originated from.

Over the years, I have tried be of help and to ask for help. There have been wise women and a handful of emotionally intelligent men that I have entrusted with my vulnerabilities and shared my burdens. I once wrote in my journal what motherhood had taught me: it was everything I had dreamed of becoming and having – but what I had not realized was that it was never meant to be done alone. It has been those shared moments, the quiet support, and the unexpected sisterhood – and, of course, in continually motivating myself – that I found the strength to keep going.

This Mother's Day and every other day, I tell both boys, rather fully-fledged men, how much I love them, how much they mean to me, and how each have changed my life for the better. I also own up when I make mistakes and embrace my past. I hate to dishearten them, but the dim hum of reality is that disappointment is a normal dysfunctional family behavior. To me, shaking that need to be perfect has been one of the most memorable moments of being a mother.

I am content when I see my boys smile. When I see them happy, I'm happy. This is what thinking like a mother looks like to me. We are all in this together.

TOGETHER IN BLOOM

I am married to a gentleman who grows with me. A tenderhearted soul who reminds me with his everyday actions of what really matters in life.

This gentle man, my life companion, took my breath away today—he arrived home with a magnificent bunch of my favorite flowers. An abundant spray of French tulips, hydrangeas, ranunculus, and orchids was given to me, bound tightly together. They present a remarkable cluster of coloration, and individually, they exhibit their own unique splendor.

The bouquet of beauty he offered symbolized something deeper and greater. His gesture brought me such joy that I paused to consider an interesting analogy. This spontaneous act of kindness, especially because it included flowers, led me to reflect in an abstract way on how our life together resembles the growth patterns of a plant. I have always admired the process of life and living. My husband's act of affection gave me an opportunity to explore that admiration further. As I sat gazing into the beauty of the flowers, my curiosity longed for a deeper discussion.

My thoughts became as vibrant as the medley of blooms tucked together inside the container. I surmised that each period in our partnership has passed through and embodied a different stage of evolution. The delicate transformations that gradually occur in nature also happen in our relationship.

Allow me to explain.

My husband and I try every day to enrich each other, like how a seed must germinate for a plant to slowly emerge.

Our intent as companions is to grow and expand. We have shared eighteen years together and our objective has always been to flourish.

When our environments mingled together, we communicated to each other our desire to be together. In time, we each produced a copy of our genetic material in our two sons. This is also an essential stage for a plant, as it reproduces through fertilization, creating new seeds for future growth.

Likewise, my partner and I have continued to evolve into distinct individuals with shared fundamentals. As we age, the goal is to have lived our lives to the fullest, individually and together, with no regrets. Always awakening towards the sun and retreating to each other for comfort and warmth in the evening. My life companion anchors me like the root system anchors the flower against the wind. He has helped bring back to life a wilted flower, attempting to withstand the outside forces. Our love has learned to sustain the winds and storms in life just as the flowers and trees stand against the gusts and gales of nature.

As we remain entwined, each season in our union has been nourished. We locate and gather the proper nutrients to enter our system and continue the growth cycle.

Structurally, we are the same people as we used to be, but we have stretched our perspectives and knowledge base together through admiration and adaptability. There must be constant fertilization and scattering of sunshine and rain along the way. It takes sunshine and rain to continue the course through our blooming cycle. Without both, we would only be able to sit to the side and watch our union shrivel up and never blossom again.

I need to write him a thank-you note for bringing me flowers. He must know how much I appreciate his gesture. As well, I must say the following to the world:

> *This man understands me. I understand him. All our past frustrations, pains and discontents subside when we open up to the sunshine that radiates all the way to our roots.*
>
> *His feeling of warmth calms me and my irrational reasoning and balance.*

In his existence, there is a gentle and tranquil breeze.

I am confident this man will walk through life by my side. He loves me for all that I am . . . despite all that I am.

He likes my messy mind.

He adores my magical moments.

This man encourages my curiosity.

Frequently, he understands my wants and needs better than I do.

His intuitive sixth sense is able to untangle my tangled root system.

He finds sensibility in my unusual scenarios.

This amazing individual sees the greater picture of my unique landscape and appreciates the beauty it exudes, even when I cannot.

He continues to help me find ways of exploring the outside world and the world inside myself.

We both have realized that, to admire and emerge as a flower, each person must let each other be their own flower and then, even though surrounded by the weeds of the world, it will remain a lovely flower. This fruition in bloom is an experience that alone is doable but together is better.

Yes, I am beaming. Yes, I am blessed. Yes, I will continue to bud and blossom in every growing season of our togetherness.

What more is there to want in this life cycle?

GROWN AND FLOWN

As a parent, I quickly realized that life is one long series of letting go. These extensions of my genealogical and genetic tree quickly crawl, walk, run, and drive away. However, I was not prepared for the flood of emotions that came with the college chapter.

My first-born son leaves in one day to attend Northern Arizona University. Even though I've been feeling weepy for the last couple weeks, the actual, imminent separation is devastating. I am hopeful that the lump rising in my throat, the random outbursts of tears, and the nauseated feeling I get when I imagine walking by his empty room will wane.

My heart is so full of love for him that it aches like a physical pain, and it's that unbearable fullness that brings tears to my eyes. I will miss him terribly and the way we were. Things will now change between us, yet again. We will always be mother and son, but our time together will now come in broken up intervals. The light and life he brings into our home will now be sporadic.

I will worry about him because I desperately don't want him to ever feel lost or alone. But I am certain that he will experience those "lost and alone" days, as everyone has them. I am confident he will self-soothe with his emotional intelligence.

I am not at all worried that he will fail. In fact, it's just the opposite. I have no doubt that he will be successful, because he is motivated and intellectually capable. He is walking into this bright new chapter of his life—where the possibilities are almost endless! I too must start my own new chapter. But I will be holding him in my heart, always, as that little boy and young man whose smile melts my heart and whose silliness makes my cloudy days bright. The tenderness of those moments will never leave me. There are endless ones to reflect on . . . and smile.

It is emotionally exhausting thinking about not physically having him here. But I take comfort knowing all our time spent together—which simultaneously seems like a lifetime, and the blink of an eye—will carry me through my state of sadness.

Sharing him with the world sucks. But his wingspan is wide and strong. He is beyond ready to fly. We will all soon adjust and I will see his grown and flown condition more clearly, as a beginning for both of us—not as an end.

With our family of four now driving away a family of three, I look back and hope I've done most things right, or right enough, that he will make wise choices, and that fortune goes his way. It is an ending and a very different beginning. This new transition scares and excites me, but most of all, right now, it makes me sad.

I will get to the other side.

But for now, I am mourning.

CHEERS TO THE HEART'S TRUE COMPASS!

When I reflect and explore my relationship with my husband, I find a common theme: Love, Curiosity, and Solitude.

To date, I have often asked people, "What is your definition of love?" Most offer up some hokey Hallmark-type answer to pacify my inquiry. Although I recognize that there is no one universal answer to what love is, I am always looking to delve deeper into relationships and, ultimately, the space between trust and love. Why? Well, within me has always been the need to question everything, an insatiable curiosity to understand my own emotional inner and outer landscape, not to mention human behavior—my own included—intrigues me. My easy-going husband gets the brunt and burden of it, but placates and partakes.

It was evident that I was the girl who likes adventure and will always take the road less traveled. My hubs proved he was up for that. I went into our marriage curious rather than feeling bound. In fact, my honorable husband and I are celebrating twenty-three years of wedded bliss. With over two decades together, I have noticed we steadily grow together rather than apart. Perhaps not at the same speed or style, but in those moments of "holy hell," we are not on the same page; we take the time to listen deeply and ultimately find our way back to the same page together. Bless him, well, and me, too, for not only going the distance and building a life together but understanding that relationships are complicated and not always easy.

There is an investment of time, the process of learning together, and the continual commitment that we will endure through tough times and, of course, the good. We both learned to love, together and on our own. The balance of intimacy and independence can be daunting and demanding. I have learned that love is listening and apologizing when one of our remarks is unfounded. Love is trusting each other's truths, even if we see it through a different lens. We have done our best to see each other as whole and separate beings and hold each other up when weaknesses seep into the conversations. We have learned the impact of being honest to our core even when it might hurt. Love is accepting each other for who we are, but most importantly, love is genuinely a non-attachment to our old ways.

Love is being deeply seen and listened to while having the ability to surrender to love as an escape from our loneliness. To care for one another, we had to understand our whole being, with all the strength we have gathered and garnered over the years of being alone with our misdirected thoughts and feelings. This counter-courage we each had to display at varying times allowed our relationship to surpass our sovereign solitude, not to turn codependent or have a form of mutual helplessness towards each other. For this, I am incredibly grateful. This includes his random silly faces and one-liners when I am not in the mood to receive them.

The essence of love is thinking about what makes life worth living. Both my hubs and I have, over the years, compared our childhoods. Our capacity to connect and reveal what inheritance of trauma we each bring to the relationship was vital for the evolution of our relationship. Tender and timeless as these ponderings are, I feel they continue to be prudent and worthy of discussion on the eve of our anniversary.

What we each carried into our instant connection to each other on that balmy eve in Florida was solitude. There has been significance and salvation in internal isolation for both of us. I can attest to the emotional detachment from people all my life, both needed and natural. To date, I spend hours in my babe cave reading and writing, traveling alone to foreign lands, or sipping wine fireside with candles lit while the house is uninhabited. For some, solitude is not easy to bear. It can come, and all you want to do is exchange it for togetherness. But loneliness is what my husband and I learned growing up. As hurtful as it felt, it was healthy to be alone in our blanket forts.

The feeling of tremendous inner solitude is about going within and learning to speak your truth first to yourself, then others. Since I experienced this growing up, having a partner who appreciates that I needed this sort of separation made the relationship much more whole. We both watched all the adults in our lives living their lives without us. At the time, I could not understand what was happening. Now I recognize how and why I learned to escape from my emotions, which was an escape also from myself.

As children, both my hubs and I could see out of the depths of our inner worlds. Little did we know, this vastness of our solitude ultimately became our saving grace, and we would find a counterpart in love. Together we have grasped how the busyness of life can be heartbreaking and desolate despite the thrill of the commotion churning around you. We watch those near us miss moments of being alone with themselves and disconnect from life to lose those they love eventually. We have learned the importance of harmonizing curiosity with the interplay between our solitude and togetherness in love, as they both enrich each other and magnify the totality of each of our spirits.

Love is not about merging; instead, it is about differentiating. To become ourselves in a world that responds to another. Our two solitudes continue to protect and be each other's most prominent advocates. Love is being with someone and their human vulnerabilities while having the courage to change but remain yourself in social surroundings or solitude.

In gratitude for having you, hubs, as my life partner.

Happy Anniversary—twenty-three and counting!

BOTH BOYS, ONE BORDER AWAY

I didn't think my heart could stretch any further after sending my firstborn off to college, but here we are. Son number two is officially off to ASU, and our house, once pulsing with chaos and noise, now hums with a strange quiet.

We are, as they say, *empty nesters*. But honestly? It doesn't feel "empty." It feels… full. Full of memories. Laughter. Empty water bottles by the bed, inside jokes, loads of laundry, and socks with no match. Late-night fireside chats, and the soundtrack of a family growing up, and navigating life together.

Letting go the first time was a crash course in surrender. The second time feels like a soul-level final exam. Not because I doubt him, quite the opposite. He's more than ready, strong, steady, and self-aware, funny, sharp, and deeply loved. But that doesn't stop the heartache.

I find myself walking past his room and instinctively touching the doorknob, as if I might catch him in the middle of a laugh, sprawled on the bed, or walking down the street with his surfboard, texting me that he's running late for dinner. But no. That chapter has closed. And I'm trying not to dwell on the past too much. But the days of him in those yellow rainboots and wanting to be held are gone. Our meetups for sushi after his shift at Hansen's surf shop and our DoorDash nights at Luna Grill will be sporadic. My heart hurts, but I remain happy for his next chapter.

This moment is bittersweet. We did it and raised both, giving them roots and wings. And now… we watch them fly. Yes, I'm still a mother, always will be. But motherhood is no longer front-and-center; it's background music now, playing softly, lovingly, as they write their own symphonies. And maybe this is where I begin to rewrite mine, too.

Part Two of Flown and Grown isn't just about their launch. It's also about *my* becoming. A rhythm reset. A boundless love, unbroken but evolving. So, here's to the new season of all our lives, to late-night FaceTimes instead of footsteps down the hall. The endless worry will never wane, but now I take monthly plane rides to Arizona. I will miss my sweet baby boy in the best way possible. Now I begin to find myself again in the quiet.

The nest may be officially empty.

But the heart?

Never fuller.

ENERGY MEETS DEPTH

Why Effort + Dialogue Still Matter

In a world that often prizes speed over sincerity and performance over presence, I find myself drawn to something quieter but infinitely more powerful: relationships rooted in reciprocity and real connection.

I deeply value spaces, whether with a friend, a partner, or even a stranger at the bar; where energy is matched, and conversations are more than just casual noise. Showing up doesn't have to be grand, just consistent and sincere. Because effort in relationships isn't measured in how often someone checks in or how loudly they express care. It's felt in the small, steady gestures—thoughtfulness, emotional availability, honest listening, that remind you: *you're not alone here.*

Genuine connection thrives where effort and energy are mutual. When someone meets you with equal presence and intention, it creates a foundation of trust and shared safety, a space to be fully seen and fully human. For me, this shows up most vividly in conversation. I crave depth, not just dialogue for dialogue's sake, but the kind that invites reflection, curiosity, and a willingness to explore the unsaid. Whether across a dinner table, on a long walk, or at a bar on a Tuesday night, I'm not afraid to ask the deeper questions or share the honest truths. Because in those conversations, something real unlocks.

I know not every interaction will go there. Some people don't have the bandwidth, or simply prefer lightness, and I respect that. Small talk serves its purpose. It buffers energy. It fills space. But even then, I find myself wondering: *What's your story? What's underneath?*

Because what I've learned is this: when effort meets emotional depth, something remarkable happens. We evolve, not just individually, but together. We remember what it means to be connected in a world that often pulls us apart.

So, yes, I still want more.

More realness.

More reciprocity.

More conversations that leave us changed.

And I'll keep seeking them.

Because for me, that's where meaning lives.

RELEASING RESENTMENT

What I am learning about resentment is that it often grows in the space between expectation and reality—when I keep hoping things will change, but deep down, I know those who have harmed or disappointed me are not equipped to do so or have the desire to change. That has been my most challenging and complicated "truth" to accept.

And now, I face the following, which is acceptance: how do I carry this "truth" without letting it harden me and send me deeper into contempt?

I know resentment can wane, but only if I can process and release it. It lingers when I ignore it—leaving it unexplored or unchecked—subtly influencing my emotions and interactions with those involved. I've learned that one of the most enormous consequences of unresolved resentment is how much it shapes my reactions and responses, often without realizing it. It took time for me to recover from that realization and even longer to recognize my part in the problem. Healing isn't just about acknowledging the hurt; it requires understanding the root of it—whether that's unmet expectations, betrayal, or repeated wounds that never received closure.

My inner peace is mine to attain, and part of that means recognizing my own needs while also accepting the limitations of others.

Can I accept being shortchanged, or do I need to shift the dynamic? That is not easy, trust me, as that shift could mean adjusting my expectations, setting firmer boundaries, or perhaps the hardest one for me—less conversation about feelings and pulling back emotionally to protect myself. This is where effort and energy come into play.

I find immense value in relationships where effort and energy are reciprocated in healthy ways. In a world that often feels rushed and transactional, there's something profoundly grounding about being in the presence of people who genuinely care—those who can and have the capacity to meet me where I am while holding space for me to feel truly seen and heard.

Effort in relationships isn't about grand gestures or constant communication. It's in the small, consistent acts of care, attention, and presence. It's in the moments that remind me I am not alone, in the spaces where I don't have to fight to be understood. And yet, effort without sincerity is meaningless. It's not about how much energy is given but rather the authenticity behind it.

Relationships built on mutual effort create a foundation of trust and connection. They thrive when both individuals show up—not just for the big moments but in the quiet, everyday ways that cultivate real intimacy. When energy is matched, it becomes a force that enriches rather than depletes. The challenge, then, is knowing when to invest and when to accept the limits of what another can give.

Forgiveness isn't always necessary—I've learned that acceptance is often enough. Accepting what happened, what cannot be changed, and the reality of others' limitations allows me to move forward. It's not about excusing anyone's behavior but about releasing the grip of resentment so it no longer dictates my energy. Ultimately, I must decide where to place my energy and effort, how much to give, and when to walk away. Inner peace comes not from controlling others but from honoring my boundaries and embracing the "truth" of what is.

Adulting is not for the faint of heart.

WHAT IS LOVE, REALLY?

One can feel love or not, depending on how you view it today. Due to Valentine's Day's commercialization, today's true meaning is likely lost in translation. I see the day differently and have decided to feel different about it.

Valentine's Day is often rooted in courtly love, but I want to dig deeper and not measure this feeling from outside influences. The pressure of the day brings a certain level of questioning into what love should look like, most notably in a loving relationship.

After twenty-seven years with the same Valentine, a few things come to mind. In the early years of any relationship, adoration is uncomplicated. Loving someone felt simple and natural—a narrative we create that makes sense in that moment. Even through the struggles, each person plays a role in the relationship and values what is right, familiar, and important, individually and as a couple.

When one moves forward in the relationship, years pass, experiences occur, and life lobs some absurd humor your way. Social expectations continue, yet the narrative is somehow different. I have learned to veer off script with my Valentine in these next chapters of my life.

In the chaos of many years of change, I continue to scramble to disrupt how I see myself and my partner in those "relationship roles." The ways familiar and old, the comfortable no longer applies.

Loving is no longer "as easy," and things, life, and living cannot return to how they were. We cannot go back to what is "normal," . . . even though I never liked what the word *normal* signifies. As I surrender to my truth, the only everyday things available now are change, movement forward, and innovation.

Valentine's Day is no longer about love, fluff, chocolates, and flowers, although my partner sent me a charcuterie board with heart-shaped cheese and salami roses. This Hallmark holiday is another day to surrender to the truth that we must stop resisting. We need to love the unknown and love each other's flawed nature.

Life wants to guide us. We must stop resisting and release what we know to be true. I continue to learn that it's never too late to start a new chapter, a new life, uproot, and take on the newness of normal. My partner and I started a new adventure this year, using only our intuitive nudges as the map. We will keep open and brushing up against the discomfort of disruption, shedding our old habits and ways of being that no longer apply to this new version of our relationship.

Only curiosity today, on Valentine's Day, comes in the box of life's sweet new beginnings. As I emerge, I surrender my need-to-know what flavor my baggage is left behind, and I clear a space between me and my Valentine of twenty-seven years to come closer together yet again. As life connects us to our earlier chapters, it makes sense again. This is the type of heart day I want to celebrate.

REDEFINING MAN

The Trials, Tribulations, and Truth Behind the Alpha Male

After being a wife for twenty-six years and raising two now-adult sons, I've come to a staggering realization—I might finally understand what it means to be a man. No, I haven't suddenly grown a beard or developed an inexplicable fascination with tools I'll never use, but I've started to get a glimpse front row to the trials and tribulations that men, like my husband and sons, face daily. And let me tell you, the journey to this epiphany has been anything but straightforward.

For years, my judgment was colored by my past encounters with manipulative men. You know the type—the self-proclaimed alpha males. From childhood to adulthood, I encountered them in various forms: The boastful, the controlling, the I-can-fix-everything and the I-am-never-wrong types who made it seem like vulnerability was reserved for "weaker" species, like goldfish. I became convinced that all men fit into this box and were born and bred as aggressive, emotionless, and perpetually always right and in charge.

So, let's talk about the term "alpha male." It's a phrase we use with carelessness. The idea of an alpha male stems from our observations of chimpanzees, our closest primate relatives. The alpha chimp rules the troop, exuding confidence, power, and leadership. Sounds familiar, right? Except, it turns out we've been interpreting even the chimps wrong. The "alpha" doesn't just lead through dominance and aggression; he builds alliances, shows empathy, and protects the group. He might even share his bananas!

Part of my correlation stems from listening to ninety-year-old Jane Goodall on Julia Louis-Dreyfus's podcast *Wiser Than Me,* where she spoke about the hierarchy of chimps, their behavior, and how it influenced the mothering of her human son, Hugo.

Somewhere along the way, though, we humans latched onto only part of this picture—the part where the alpha male flexes his muscles and commands respect, whether he's earned it or not. This perception spilled over into our culture, shaping the way we view men and how men view themselves. Cue the impossible expectations: be tough, never cry, and never ask for directions. Society turned masculinity into a survival-of-the-fittest contest, where the fittest isn't necessarily the strongest, but the one who appears to care the least. Charles Darwin, the father of evolutionary theory, believed it was the most adaptable person who survived, and I agree.

As I've learned through my marriage of over two decades and watching my sons grow into twenty-something men, the problem with this stereotype is that it ignores the truth: Men, just like women, are deeply emotional creatures. They feel pressure—immense pressure—underneath that carefully curated exterior. They are told to "man up" when the world weighs them down, yet they are just as susceptible to heartache, self-doubt, and vulnerability as anyone else.

The only difference is they've been trained to hide it.

What our culture misses—and what I missed for far too long—is that the depth men have is as vast and rich as any ocean. Their ability to care, connect, and be tender is there, often simmering beneath the surface. But showing these qualities can feel like crossing an invisible line, stepping into territory where judgment and ridicule await. Why? Because we've categorized emotions as a feminine trait, and heaven forbid a man to be "soft."

Yet, in the privacy of my home, I've witnessed moments where my husband, the so-called alpha of our family, has been raw and real, even admitting his shortcomings. I've witnessed moments where our sons, as they strive to navigate the expectations placed upon them, reveal their fears and insecurities. In those quiet, unguarded moments, I see the complete picture of what it means to be a man, an image far more nuanced than the rugged, stoic figure society projects.

Perhaps this is where I, as a woman, tap into my masculine energy. Whether born with it or developed through my experiences, I've had to harness a certain toughness to protect myself and stand up against injustice throughout my fifty years. Whether I was fourteen or forty, I've never shied away from a towering, angry man regardless of his physical strength or ability to manipulate intellectually. And, yes, I learned early on that being vocal, standing my ground, and speaking my mind were often seen as "masculine" behaviors. And it's true—being a verbal woman, unafraid to call out the truth, is frequently met with disapproval from men (and women, to be honest). But I've always believed that power lies in truth-telling, no matter how uncomfortable the conversation.

For the three men in my life—my husband and my two sons—maybe it is time and exposure that have conditioned them to the "uncomfortableness" of authentic expression, or perhaps they understand that my voice is not something I will ever hide. It is a significant part of who I am. They allow me to be me, without feeling threatened by my assertiveness, and I'm grateful for that. I am pleased that I fully know this is our family norm. Our home is filled with raw, honest moments that may feel intense at times, but through these moments, we forge authentic communication and connection. These moments allow us to adapt and grow. And isn't that what real strength is, the ability to adapt?

To learn not to suppress emotion or avoid tough conversations, to be unafraid to face truths together, and to break patterns of bad behavior.

So, I ask myself: What does "being an alpha male" mean? Is it the bravado? Is it dominance? Or, perhaps, it's the courage to step outside those rigid confines and say, "Hey, I'm not okay." I think it's the latter. The actual alpha male does not suppress emotion, but the one who embraces it, the one who understands that leadership doesn't come from force but from compassion and understanding. Being a man is not about taming the world; it's about taming oneself. It's about navigating a landscape where vulnerability is feared, yet essential to be a whole and nuanced human. And, as I've realized, it's a trial far more challenging than I once thought.

In redefining what it means to be a man, I have come to understand that strength isn't measured by dominance or silence, but by the ability to show up authentically, to feel deeply, and to embrace the full spectrum of human emotions. As a wife and mother, I've witnessed this vulnerability in the men I love, and it's challenged me to rethink the narrow definitions we often assign to masculinity. It's time we give men the space to be more than society's caricature of an alpha male and recognize their emotional depth and capacity for connection.

Maybe, just maybe, redefining manhood is the ultimate evolution, one that starts when we raise our sons. I want to give all men the space to go beyond the narrow confines of alpha and let them be human. And now, after writing this, I hope my neighbor, Walt, who has given me a hard time for years about writing women's stories and lifting their voices, can finally be content.

Walt, this one's for you, now you know I've written about men, too. I support them the same; we're all together, striving for understanding, connection, and a more compassionate world.

LOVE IS . . . A VERB.

Being with someone for over a century of my life, I have learned that love is not a permanent state of enthusiasm. For me, I often get bored and need constant stimulation of some sort. I realized a pattern was emerging. When I would pursue something new, whether that was a job, hobby, relationship, or even with my schooling, there were a few months of being in seduction mode. I then would find myself bored, disinterested, disappointed, and even looking for the next person to come along.

Why? I began to ask myself and eventually my therapist. Did I have attachment issues? Was I not willing to give all of me? There is always the fear of being hurt or let down. It's not that simple; I learned once I began my search to sort out this conundrum.

Love, desire, connection—all things that make me want to stay and go deeper with someone—are not always induced by that other person or activity. They are co-created. Instead of asking whether I've found the right person, I began to imagine what it would be like to be in a relationship where both partners are mutually interested in being good for each other.

After twenty-plus years, I have to recognize it's not the other person's responsibility to woo me, or vice versa, to maintain attention, heal and help each other grow. Love can do a plethora of things, but it can't do everything, nor can our partners. Love is an ongoing collaboration, and it takes everyone in the relationship to sustain and grow it. This was refreshing to realize. I am not sure I believe in the true love story—that to me is too Disney-esque. The dazzling, the adventures, and infatuation will wane.

So, we continue to build this life story, brick by brick, truth by truth, even when the storms come. Especially when they come. Real relationships are not the glossy Disney versions that many of us grew up believing. They don't resolve in ninety minutes or end with a single kiss. They require work and compromise. Showing up when it's messy, not just when it's magical. Love, I have learned, is not just something you feel; it's something you do, or don't. And in the end, the story we write together will be shaped not by perfection, but by the willingness to keep turning towards each other, again and again.

RELATIONSHIP RESET

Relationships are not easy. They demand patience, compromise, and a willingness to evolve. They test us in ways we don't expect and challenge us to confront our deepest fears, frustrations, and insecurities. And yet, despite the struggles, they offer connection, growth, and shared joys, if we are willing to put in the work.

Being human is complicated. Our emotions, experiences, and personal histories create intricate dynamics between us and those we love. No relationship is static; we are constantly changing, whether we realize it or not. After nearly twenty-seven years of marriage, I've learned that maintaining a strong partnership requires continuous effort.

Open communication, the courage to face uncomfortable truths, and the grace to accept each other's differences are all essential. When I married my husband at twenty-four, I was a different person. I've spent decades on a journey of self-discovery, healing, and growth. As I like to say, I'm in a high-powered speedboat, cutting through the water at full throttle, while my husband, whom I affectionately call "Hubs," follows in my wake in his rowboat. Our paces may not always match, but we've always moved in the same direction.

The past few years have been particularly stressful, shaped by family dynamics—his and mine—while trying to keep our nuclear family intact. From the start, we both agreed we wouldn't raise our sons, now twenty-five and twenty-six, the way we were raised. That shared vision grounded us through some of the most challenging times.

Middle age brings a different kind of reckoning. A chance to recover, to reconcile, not just with others, but with us. I've always been an agent of change, speaking out against injustice, but these past years have permitted me to reset yet again. Not just once, but continually. I'm on Shannon 12.0 by now. With each reset, I've come to realize that shedding outdated beliefs and expectations is essential. I've had to let go of the people-pleasing persona I once relied on, the version of myself conditioned by obligation and guilt. It's like placing an old identity in a box on a shelf labeled *Outgrown Self*—a reminder of who I no longer need to be.

Writing my manuscript in memoir form—letters to my dad from the time he died when I was eleven up until I turned fifty, brought an unexpected revelation: I had spent years operating from the mindset of a hurt, lonely, and scared little girl in survival mode. That version of me served a purpose, but she no longer needed to be in control. The patterns of survival I once relied on, protecting my mother and sister after my dad's death, fighting for justice when my mother remarried a deeply flawed man, navigating relationships with people who weren't willing to grow, kept me in a cycle of seeking validation from those who could never give it.

But one person did—Hubs. In his way, in his own time, he showed me his love and devotion. Did I push for more? Absolutely. Did he always meet my demands? Not even close. But he stayed. He listened. He loved me, even when we struggled in our ways.

A turning point came recently when we found ourselves at a crossroads. I was emotionally exhausted and fed up with his idleness. He, in turn, was retreating into himself, protecting himself from feeling too much. Both of us—Little Shannon and Little Tim—were in survival mode. But neither of us wanted to walk away. We both longed for a marriage that neither of us had witnessed growing up.

So, we put in a lot of hard work. We had awkward, brutally honest conversations. We sought therapy. Tristen, our trusted therapist, became a bridge when our words failed. And we started the process of resetting.

Then, in a grand and unexpected gesture, Hubs planned a trip to Antarctica—my seventh and final continent. A place of raw, untouched beauty. Just the two of us, with no distractions.

Antarctica reset more than just our perspectives. It reminded us of what truly matters. The silence of the ice and the vastness of the landscape put everything into focus. But of course, in true Shannon style, I still found ways to share my opinion but kept it in check. Even with Tristen recently reminding me to be less of an air traffic controller and more of a passenger. Yep, that behavior is still a work in progress.

Hubs, however, surprised me again. He added an excursion to our itinerary: kayaking in the icy waters, surrounded by glaciers and humpback whales. At first, control set in, and I resisted; visions of being swallowed whole by a whale (thanks to a viral video) were less than appealing. But I went to the briefing. And something shifted when we pushed off into the water, just the two of us and another couple.

As we paddled through the frozen wonderland, I let go. I trusted Hubs, not our guide named Haman. I allowed the experience to be bigger than my fear. It was hands down one of the most breathtaking moments of my life, surpassing even my polar plunge and stepping onto the continent itself.

Hand in hand, oar in oar, we rediscovered something essential: laughter, love, and the simple joy of being together. Relationships challenge us, but they also provide a foundation of companionship and support. They hold up a mirror, forcing us to see ourselves in new ways. They push us to adapt, to grow, to find our way back to each other—again and again.

Antarctica was our reset. However, the truth is that resets aren't once-in-a-lifetime experiences. They are necessary, ongoing, and vital. They are the conscious decision to stay, to listen, to evolve. For us, resets make our relationship and our life together worth every effort.

DEAR ME

The Me Who Loved Them First,

Did I even know, back then, what I was doing?

When their little boy hands were impossibly small, and their world was safely nestled inside mine, did I realize I was quietly shaping the men they would become?

I think of those long nights—checking their angelic breathing, watching their chests rise and fall, soothing tummy aches through tears, and managing brotherly quarrels with gentle reminders like, "Give your brother two put-ups for the not-so-nice behavior you just showed him." My body was aching with exhaustion, both mental and physical, but still, I showed up.

I remember the car rides, filled with questions, silences, singing to music, unusual travel destinations, and shared moments that stitched the years together with memory after memory. The tiny notes I tucked under pillows, hiding their Easter baskets in weird locations, Valentine's Day coupons, all little reminders of my love. I made whispered prayers for their safety and the happiness of finding themselves. I still do. And trying hard to make the birthdays and holiday traditions magical, even when I was barely holding myself together.

They're 24 and 25 now. Men. Kind, generous, thoughtful, and equipped with knowledge to navigate the world. And still, I see flickers of the little boys they once were, in their brown eyes, gestures, and how they sometimes reach for me without even realizing it.

They will never fully know how much I doubted myself; no mother's manual existed. How deeply I feared getting it wrong. I learned and somehow survived by not repeating past patterns of behavior. Or how fiercely, relentlessly, I loved them, even when I didn't fully understand how to love myself. I loved them and would walk to the end of the earth for them. No one tells you how much of motherhood lives in the shadows. The sacrifices were never spoken of. The ache that lingers even as they grow. The way a mother's heart stretches, breaks, and still finds the strength to say yes—again and again.

But here I am. And somehow, through the mess, beauty, heartbreak, and joy, I did something lasting. I raised good men. In the process, I found pieces of myself, too. The things I couldn't change have changed me. I can't rewind time, but there are many moments when I look at myself in the mirror and wonder: How did I make it through? How do I keep going?

And then I remember, I'm no longer the woman I once was. And I'm still becoming the woman I'm meant to be. Motherhood has reshaped me in ways I never expected. And the memories—oh, the memories are etched forever in my heart. Raising my two boys has been the greatest accomplishment of my life. Nothing else compares. What a ride we've been on together. My heart is full of love, pride and contentment.

With all the grace I can muster,
Me

LOVE: MYTH, MIRROR OR MEANING?

Love, at its purest, is often talked about as if it were a destination, something we find in another person, something we earn, something we cling to tightly so it doesn't leave. But what if love is less about possession and more about perception? What if it's not the reward at the end of the story, but the story itself, one shaped long before we ever have words for it?

I've spent much of my life trying to understand what love *is*, only to realize I first needed to understand what love *wasn't*. I inherited stories about love through tone, gesture, absence, and silence. My family didn't always openly talk about love, but we expressed it through actions. We feared losing it, clung to its approval, and confused control or sacrifice with its proof. Like many, I absorbed these early messages unconsciously, unaware of how much my adult idea of love was shaped by blueprints passed down through generations, including some tender moments and many fractured ones.

Intergenerational trauma subtly but powerfully influences how we love and believe we should be loved. It's in how my mother modeled me to be small and accommodating for peace, which I could never fully do. It's in how my father withdrew emotionally from my mother and let his own demons overpower him, or how my grandparents think that providing necessities is the same as caring. These patterns became my emotional inheritance, both visible and invisible, and I felt them deeply.

For a long time, I chased myths about love. That it should save me. That it should look like the movies. That if it hurt, it meant it was real. But somewhere along the way, usually during the unraveling, I began to realize that love is not a myth or a transaction — it's a mirror. It reflects our sense of worth, our willingness to be seen, and our capacity to hold space for someone else without losing ourselves in the process.

The harshest truth I had to accept was that I couldn't receive the love I desired until I learned to give it to myself. Not the superficial kind of love promoted by bubble baths and self-help books (though those can help at times), but the tough, deeply rooted kind, the kind that supports you through heartbreak, seeks you out when you're hiding, and reminds you that you are already enough.

This shift didn't happen all at once. It came in pieces—through therapy sessions, journal entries, uncomfortable confrontations, and quiet epiphanies when I realized I was reenacting someone else's story instead of writing my own.

Now, when I think about love, I no longer look for a single definition. I ask myself: Is this love a myth I've inherited? A mirror reflecting something I need to heal. Or is it a more profound meaning I'm still learning to live within? Because maybe love is two flawed people trying to move forward, figuring it out together, because it isn't just what we give or receive, it's what we remember, reclaim, and redefine. And you, what version of love have you been taught, and is it the one you truly believe in?

LETTERS AND MUSINGS

Notes to Self and the World

Some thoughts don't fit neatly into a theme. Some moments are best captured in a letter, an observation, or a stream of consciousness that doesn't seek categorization. *Letters and Musings* is where those pieces belong—the intimate notes to others, to myself, to the universe. These words have come unfiltered in quiet moments of reflection as I process both the simplicity and the vastness of life.

This section contains the echoes of unsent letters, late-night wine, fireside realizations, and a few unspoken truths that never found a home elsewhere. Here, the lines blur between past and present, between what was said and what was felt. These entries often appeared without structure, written in the margins of journals on days when something moved inside me or when language seemed like the only container large enough to hold what I couldn't yet explain or understand. Some are gentle. Some are searing. All are genuine.

What binds them is not the subject matter but the intention to speak freely, to remember more fully, and to create that space where thought and emotion can coexist without apology.

WHY I TELL MY STORY

I have embraced my role as a truth-teller. Sharing my truth helps me understand what's happening around me. However, I have also discovered that many people aren't comfortable discussing certain parts of their lives, often because of fear. Fear that others won't accept them. Fear of criticism. Or fear that revealing the truth might break the image others hold of them.

Shame grows in silence. For me, sharing my story has become a powerful way to release that shame. Each time I open up, whether in a conversation, in a journal, or during a quiet moment with someone I trust, I hear a familiar phrase: *"Me too."* It shows that we're all carrying something. Some of us are dealing with it now, while others have been there and come out the other side. But without sharing, we'd never realize how connected we truly are.

That said, choosing the *right* people to be vulnerable with is crucial. Not everyone can handle the weight of someone else>s truth. I have learned this the hard way, especially within my own family. Avoidance can seem safer than being honest for some. And I've had to accept that it's their choice if they're not ready to face or heal from what's been left unsaid. Still, I've also realized this: I no longer feel obligated to keep others comfortable at my own expense.

My history with complicated family dynamics has shown me that releasing shame also means letting go of the pressure to protect those who were part of my pain. Some people may never be ready to face uncomfortable truths. Some might say, *"It's your family—just keep it together,"* or *"That's just how it is."* But I disagree. Because here's the truth: real, meaningful relationships can't be built on silence. They can't grow where there's only performance, not presence. Sharing our stories, especially the hard ones—is how we begin to feel seen. It's how we invite others to see themselves. It's how we stop enabling patterns that keep us small and disconnected. And it's how we reclaim the parts of ourselves that shame told us to hide.

That's why I write stories about women. It's why I have created an epistolary memoir—a life review told through letters—to speak truth and to explore the many versions of myself that once felt fragmented or lost. I see them now as shadows cast against the wall of truth. And I want to walk up to each one with a smile and say, *Thank you.* Thank you for not giving up, even when I know you wanted to. Thank you for finding your voice, even in silence. There's a quote that speaks to me deeply: "To discover new land, we must be willing to lose sight of the shore." That has become my guiding principle. I am learning to let go of the emotional attachments to people I once made feel special by keeping their truths hidden inside me. Now, I understand that detachment reveals truth. And in that space, I am free to build something more honest, more aligned, and more whole.

We don't share the truth to destroy others. We share it to free ourselves.

THE ERA OF UNBECOMING TO BECOME

For years, I thought the path to peace meant keeping the peace. I learned early how to deconstruct myself, adjusting to the emotional climates around me, absorbing others' moods, and tolerating behaviors that made my soul wince. I believed those were what love and family required. What being a "good daughter," "good sister," and "good wife and woman" signified. But what I was doing was silencing myself to stay chosen, or at least, not be abandoned.

And then I began to wake up. Slowly, painfully, powerfully. Call it therapy, growing up, or survival—either way, I started reverse engineering my own life. I didn't realize at first that that's what I was doing. But I began observing patterns, listening to the deeper language, and tracing the roots of my reactions and why I kept accepting versions of love and loyalty that drained me.

I stopped asking, *"Why are they treating me this way?"* And started asking, *"Why did I ever think this was okay?"* That question took me everywhere, back to childhood dynamics, early beliefs, and the quiet agreements I made with myself to accept dysfunction for the sake of family, friendship, or familiarity. And once I started reverse-engineering my relationships, there was no going back.

You start seeing clearly. You begin noticing who makes you feel safe and who makes you feel small. You recognize who only liked the version of you that didn't ask for much. And you stop blaming yourself for outgrowing dynamics that were built on your silence.

Were these relationships healthy for *them*? Maybe.

But as for *me*? Absolutely not.

This season of my life isn't about reconstruction, it's about realignment. It's about honoring who I am without shrinking from who I'm not. I am not repeating what hurt me, nor downplaying what healed me. I am done negotiating with those who only love me when it's easy. No more chaos, only clarity, and a continued curiosity for what is real. This is my era of psychological reverse engineering. And damn, does it feel good.

HUSTLING HARDER WITH MY BURNING HEART

"No one hustles harder than a woman who had to painfully learn she couldn't rely on the people she once trusted." Hi, that's me! This quote I came across today really resonates with me deeply, though I'm not sure of its original source.

Early on, I became familiar with hyper-independence—a survival tactic I later realized was a trauma response. When the people meant to support and protect me failed, I had no choice but to take charge, trusting only my instincts to get through. There have been several situations over the years that I won't bore you with, which have shaped me into someone who, for better or worse, rarely asks for help. If something needed to be done, I took care of it myself. As an adult, that drive to handle everything alone led me to overextend myself, causing resentment to build. Still, the thought of relying on anyone and facing disappointment or betrayal kept me silent, trapped in a cycle I created out of necessity.

Throughout my pre-teen years, *Rocky IV* was my favorite movie, with a soundtrack that reflected my struggles and ignited something inside me. "Eye of the Tiger" was my anthem, but it was "Burning Heart" and "No Easy Way Out" that spoke directly to the girl fighting battles far beyond her years. Watching Sylvester Stallone as Rocky face his own inner demons was like watching my own fire that fuels my soul's actual fight. The inner strength needed to conquer life's most brutal battles doesn't come from muscle alone, but from gritty, fierce determination deep within —the unwavering drive that keeps one moving forward even when the mind screams to give up.

Recently, during one of my early morning runs, those familiar Robert Tepper lyrics from the song, "No Easy Way Out," hit me differently: *"A quest for answers with an unquenchable thirst and unmistakable fire . . . no surrender as the body says stop, my spirit cries 'never.' Deep in my soul, a quiet ember knows it's you against you."*

As a child, these words captured my daily fight for survival, navigating a world where support often came with strings or didn't materialize. Now, as an adult, I realize how deeply that battle has defined me—the drive to push, to rise, to fight the odds, even when it feels like me against everything. There's a unique kind of loneliness in realizing you can only depend on yourself. It becomes both armor and a cage. That self-imposed isolation, born from necessity, gave me strength and kept me from reaching out.

Beneath the hustle lies a heart that longs for care, protection, and genuine support. The flame that fuels my drive—the *"unmistakable fire"* from the song—isn't just ambition; it's a desire to prove that I am more than my hardships and disappointments. Yet the most complicated truth I've had to confront is that breaking free means risking vulnerability, allowing myself to trust, to lean in, and to be seen, not just as someone who carries it all but as someone willing to let go, even if it means facing the fear of being let down again. I bravely hope and know there is so much at stake. Still, for me, it is about that inner freedom, where resilience grows, from daring to believe that my "burning heart" can carry both strength and vulnerability without shattering, and if I need to do it alone, I am capable of it.

DEAR DAD

Dear Dad,

I recently realized that I had forgotten how your voice sounds. How wonderful it would be to have a recording of it. I remember Mom always reminding you to answer the phone properly. You never bothered with a time-honored "hello," it was always just "yeah." This was one of Mom's pet peeves, but it still makes me giggle. I remember thinking how cool it was, that you did the opposite of what everyone else did.

I think of you often, but especially around this time—August 30, 1985, the anniversary of your death. There are so many moments that I have grown to cherish throughout the thirty-five years we have been apart. I think about Mom's dismay when you would take me on your "boy sprees." You taught me how to ride my bike at the age of five and drive a four-wheeler at nine. I can see you smiling at me with that genuine grin you flashed when I would follow you up the sand dunes on my four-wheeler or when I hit a golf ball with ease. I remember us wrestling in the living room until I would shout the magic password ("Acapulco!") for relief.

I never told you this, but it made me feel miserable that your yearly "prize deer" was killed for sport. I still enjoyed our time together. I remember the meat locker that made me shiver, with cold and excitement, knowing I got to join you and the butcher while you skinned and slaughtered the animal in the stockroom at the grocery store you managed. And I did enjoy the taste of fresh venison jerky and that spontaneous snap when you bite into it.

I appreciate how patiently you allowed me to play beautician, placing countless clips in your curly hair and beard while you watched television or read the paper. How quickly things changed for us after that routine visit to the doctor. You were complaining about headaches and neck pain. How could we have known it was cancer, Non-Hodgkin's Lymphoma to be exact, and that we only had two more years together?

How did you cope? At twenty-eight years old, you were still trying to understand who you were or what you wanted to do in this world. What was your first thought? Were you scared? Did you think you could beat it? Did you cry? The only time I remember you having a negative attitude about your disease was our last Christmas morning together. Mom bought you a traditional camouflage hunting outfit with pants and a matching jacket. I remember the image of you standing in it so clearly, after Mom snapped your picture. You sank back into your tattered, tan recliner and said clearly, "I will not need this."

Sometimes I try to picture the situation for myself, imagining how I would handle a toxic cloud of cancer hovering over me. Your pain must have been unbearable with the radiation and chemotherapy, not to mention the pain from the tumor itself. I respect your strength and everything you did to protect us from the turmoil you must have been feeling deep inside.

Sometimes life's small problems can feel overwhelming. I often think of you to put them into perspective, reminding myself and others that you would happily be forty and have wrinkles, fifty and need cholesterol medication, sixty and require a colonoscopy, or seventy and deal with memory loss. All of these would be better than dying from cancer at the early age of thirty.

I feel sad for you and for myself. For thirty-five years, I have missed having you in my life. There have been countless times I wanted to share my victories and struggles with you. I used to imagine you coming to my grade school basketball games at Trinity Lutheran, spotting me on the court in my baby blue uniform and white Nike high-tops, running fast just the way you taught me. All those free throws we practiced in the parking lot of the Catholic church paid off. My high school coach told me my form was pure.

High school bored me, but playing sports kept me out of trouble. It was my coach who helped me recover after I tore my ACL in my junior year and learned I wouldn't be able to play in college. After that, I didn't know what path to follow. I wish I could have talked to you. I wonder if you would have been a good listener. You always seemed to be when I was young.

I always trusted my instinct, even when it seemed to lead me nowhere. I made some bad choices, but when I focused on my gut feeling, I could fix them. One time this was true was when I nearly married the wrong person. We weren't a good match, complete opposites. But I liked the attention he gave me, and his affectionate family was something I longed for. Still, I stayed true to myself. That was something you modeled for me.

I've never stopped wanting to make you proud. That desire has been the fuel that propels me forward. I had to be more persistent, more driven, and motivated to succeed. I kept fighting, knowing you would want me to be strong like you were until the very end. You believed in me and wanted me to believe in myself, which is the greatest gift a parent can give their child.

So much has changed that I wish I could share with you. I married a man who delights in treating me like a queen. You both share a similar zest for life and a witty sense of humor. He has been my rock, Dad. He has given me a peaceful place to find myself and the freedom to be me. We have two remarkable boys who evoke emotions in me that I have never experienced before. So many of their characteristics remind me of you—their charming prankster ways, especially! I think you would enjoy watching me be a parent. And recently, I found my inner girl. I always felt like your princess, but now I enjoy dressing up and playing the part too. I wonder what you would think of your fashionable, feminine tomboy.

I miss our shenanigans. As I raised my boys, I instinctively recreated the fun times we had together. I incorporated some tough love, like you did, but always much more affection. There have been many moments when I knew you were still with me in spirit. One particular time comes to mind. I was feeling overwhelmed with parenting my four- and five-year-olds, and on the way to their preschool, a regal-looking buck appeared by the roadside. I stopped. He stopped. And we both stared each other directly in the eyes. At that instant, I felt you telling me what I needed to hear: "Never give up, Buttercup!" See you in the funny papers, Dad.

Forever Your Fan,
Me

DEAR MOM

As I sit and stare at this blank sheet of paper, I often wonder what our story would be if we could imagine it ourselves. Surely, we would have chosen a plot twist or two. But with those changes, we might not have ended up where we are now, forty-plus years together through a kaleidoscope of experiences.

Over the years, situations arise, and we often wish for a reset button. What surprises me about our connection is that we have restructured our relationship with an open-door policy of honesty and respect. This has pushed us further into the mother-daughter relationship that fiction writers aspire to depict. There have been many rocky paths that neither of us wanted to navigate. We have shared tender moments together through long conversations about self-improvement. We have also exchanged heartfelt disclosures about our silenced feelings over the years. I look forward to the many memories and life lessons we have yet to experience together.

It seemed only natural for me to share how in awe I am of your resilience and perseverance. The struggles you've overcome, even before I knew you, are truly extraordinary. You continue to impress me with your optimism, boundless energy, and ability to create an environment that feels effortless. To anyone who meets you, they may not realize the constant battle you've fought and won to earn your place in this life we call living.

Your pain must have been unbearable to protect me from the intense agony you were likely experiencing in every part of your being. I admire your strength in shielding me from your internal turmoil and external instability, along with various side effects and symptoms of being a victim of domestic abuse, not to mention the pain from the mental and physical attacks themselves, let alone all the secrets you had to carry growing up from your mother.

There have been many times in my life when I have encountered women who have gone through similar stories and little did I know, my own mother was suffering in silence. I can only imagine the countless times you wanted to share your pain, humiliation, and anger, hoping someone would willingly make it all go away. Over the years, the choices you've made are directly influenced by your experiences, and for that, I now understand and respect you for having the courage to keep going with a brave face, even though you were scared inside. I hold you in high regard for not wanting to tarnish my father's image. You've always maintained a neutral stance, and this must have been easier said than done. Thankfully, our conversations over the years provided you with a safe space, free of judgment, where you could express the secrets you had kept locked away for years.

The main point I want to convey is that we have control over our choices. It was your decision to live with this anguish for decades, letting others think you were the weak pillar of our family when you were the cornerstone. I praise you. I admire you. I thank you. We both had to mentally adjust our thought processes by making small changes to our behaviors, which we regularly practice with each other, our family members, and friends. We understand that breaking habits can be difficult. However, what continues to impress me is your persistent desire to change your current behavior, allowing for growth to occur.

Transformation cannot happen unless we are willing and able to accept the responsibility that comes with change. You have done this over the years at your own pace. There were times I wished it had been at my pace, but time and maturity helped me realize that it is not for me to judge. We both have learned there are no magic pills that can fix the paths we've taken together or separately. Personal progress is what shifts the gears toward the outcome one desires.

Learned behaviors from parental practices passed down through generations can be difficult to break. The constant verbal abuse you've endured from various people in your life is inexcusable. The physical abuse inflicted on your spirit was unjustifiable. Despite these negative experiences, you have repeatedly felt responsible and guilty for them, which has carried over into my life. You must understand that these experiences have enabled me to create change. They forced me to make the best of each situation that comes my way, even when I didn't know what would happen next. You gave me the space to enjoy the unknown, find comfort in uncertainty, and realize that once the discomfort and vulnerability pass, you can find pleasure in this new way of living. I hope you can find peace within the relationships you have that still bring agony.

One of my favorite quotes by Kurt Vonnegut states, "We have to continually be jumping off cliffs and developing our wings on the way down." Thank you for showing that I have the strength to do many things, but I must believe in myself to get there. Over the years, you didn't always believe in yourself, but I always believed that you had immense courage. Your deep desire to leap from unstable situations to find solid ground couldn't have been easy. Take comfort in knowing that watching you over the years has made me realize what it takes to be a survivor.

You have taught me many things. The only way we can move forward in life is by firmly refusing to retreat. You are a shining example of this. I will continue to honor you. You must celebrate yourself and let go of those who have haunted you over the years. In short, Mom, my wish is that you raise your expectations for happiness and let go of the past to make room for your full potential to flourish.

With deep love and admiration,

Your firstborn daughter.

NAVIGATING NARCISSISM

I used to always seek retribution, but as I grew older, I learned a few more tricks and tips for life and living. I have come to realize that shitty people usually end up sabotaging themselves. That said, I understand that the closure I need in many relationships is that I deserve better. I wrote this piece to make sense of the senseless, realizing I was made to be the villain in someone else's story because my truth and reaction to their disrespect weren't what they wanted to see.

It is worth noting that navigating conflict in healthy relationships is a complex skill that I am still learning, a skill that I believe we continually hone and improve throughout our lives. Yet, as essential as this skill is to a healthy relationship, it's nearly impossible to apply within an unhealthy relationship, precisely one where narcissistic tendencies prevail—manipulation, triangulation, lack of empathy, shifting of blame, and superficial connections where you serve their needs to then be discarded or ignored once you are no longer useful to them.

This is where I find myself on a trail with manipulative masterminds, also known as narcissists, who keep infiltrating my sacred space. While it's been an ongoing lesson for me to understand and navigate these situations that have surrounded me, my ability to do so has finally reached a level of toxicity that is unhealthy to manage or even attempt to manage.

In the past, I have never been shy about expressing my feelings and thoughts when injustice occurs. I believe in healthy and honest relationships, so speaking up and sharing my perspective is essential. I've appreciated this openness and honesty in others, believing that genuine connection and understanding grow through mutual respect. Communication is vital, even if it means agreeing to disagree.

Listening is crucial for understanding and seeing beyond oneself. Sadly, all of this becomes unclear when narcissism comes into play. They tend to flip the script I've learned—making their bad behavior your problem.

Twelve-plus years ago, I sat in a therapy office with a spirited pre-doctoral intern who was finishing her hours to obtain her Marriage and Family Therapy license. Tristen, with her no-nonsense approach to problems, quickly introduced "narcissistic behavior" to me after I shared a short situation about my father-in-law, who at the time was making me feel like my feelings about "his behavior" were my fault. Manipulative behavior can do that.

"Narcissists will not tolerate anything that threatens them," Tristen said. Put another way, they cannot tolerate anything that threatens their self-esteem. "They are incredibly clever in order to hide the feelings of inadequacy they feel deep inside," she told me during that same session. The zinger was when Tristen ended by saying, "You are a threat to their self-worth because you are aware of who you are." And here I thought it was the opposite, as these manipulative minds knew the right words and ways to make me question myself and deny what I was feeling or doing with conviction, making me stop and think, *did I hear what was said right?*

Now, at this stage in my life, all I can hear is Tristen's voice reminding me, "They are overt and covert, and this behavior will cut into the core of who you are if you let them—ripping your kind and empathetic heart in two, not once, not twice, but multiple times." Still, I struggle to understand what being a narcissist really means. Lately, my inner Rosie tells me that my honesty and heartfelt actions simply can't reach the mindset of a narcissist. I think what I have finally learned and absorbed is that the people in my life who show these self-absorbed tendencies (narcissistic traits) seem to be allergic to accountability or healthy self-awareness. This realization is key to breaking free from the merry-go-round of self-doubt that narcissists try to fuel inside you.

Am I the lunatic? Am I misreading the situation? Why is my assessment of reality so different from theirs?

Narcissistic people thrive on trying to undermine your competence, actions, and skills. They want you to doubt your memories, experiences, and understanding of events to invalidate you.

As difficult as it has been over the years to unpack this behavior from the different people in my close circle, I have realized that distancing yourself from a narcissist is the only way to protect yourself and maintain well-being. Narcissists do not like being dismissed.

In a windstorm, I have learned to see myself as a solid oak tree. The more rooted I am, the more connected I feel to myself, and the firmer my boundaries are, the less impact the unruly wind will have. I know there will continue to be uncomfortable storms that blow in at times, but I will not be pushed over or fall apart. Not out of family guilt or obligation, either

One of the most disheartening outcomes of dealing with a narcissist, besides the pain of lost love if involved, is the damage their behaviors can cause to others in your circle. Triangulation is a tactic narcissists heavily rely on to try to stay relevant when they feel threatened. By bringing in a third party, or even more, they use a manipulative strategy to reinforce their distorted view and maintain control. They will do whatever it takes to keep the triangulated parties apart and uncommunicative, aiming to divide and conquer with an us-versus-them mindset. I have seen this far too often, in my own family system and that of my husband.

As I continue to navigate narcissists around me, I am freeing myself from unbalanced relationships, noticing that none of them like when I go "no contact" (remember, narcissists hate nothing more than dismissal). It is okay for them to ghost me, perhaps even preferable. But having strong boundaries infuriates the narcissist. This skill (of setting boundaries and distancing) is the sovereignty needed when trying to manage a narcissist.

Tristen recently told me that "water does not affect fake flowers." This changed my entire perspective on relationships that manipulate.

This insight has helped me redirect my energy from trying to convince or prove my reality to a narcissist—since it's futile—toward recognizing when self-preservation is the only option. Narcissists simply do not listen to words of reason.

And so, I walk away with only the words that might matter... "It looks like we see things differently." This letter I wrote below could be sent to several people I have learned possess narcissistic tendencies.

Dear Narcissist,

I need to express some things, and I believe writing them down is the best way to make sure my thoughts and feelings are communicated clearly and without interruption.

Over time, I have gained a deeper understanding of our relationship and how it works. I have observed a recurring pattern of behavior in you that has made it harder for me to connect with you genuinely. It's become clear that your actions and words often focus on your own needs, desires, and perceptions, sometimes at the expense of others. Your lack of accountability blocks any real connection.

My efforts to communicate honestly and openly often meet with defensiveness or manipulation. This continues to create an unbalanced relationship and an environment I don't want to be a part of. (As mentioned in a previous conversation, cut me out if I am the villain in your story.) I can't stay in a relationship where my feelings are ignored, and the focus is only on your perspective. Meaningful relationships are based on mutual respect, empathy, and understanding are vital for any healthy and fulfilling connection.

My only goal in writing this letter is to promote clarity and inspire change. I believe everyone has the ability for growth and self-awareness—myself included—and I hope that sharing my perspective will encourage you to reflect on our interactions and their effects on us and those around us.

While I accept that you may not realize the pain you cause, I will simply say that there are limits to what love can overcome. I don't believe that one can continually hurt another and expect their connection to endure. Even those of us with big, empathetic hearts have boundaries; our energy for conflict diminishes, and our ability to maintain a problematic relationship weakens. Ultimately, relationships are forever changed and damaged.

While empathy for others is a value I cherish, there comes a point when self-care must come first for my mental and emotional health. I need to set boundaries and focus on my well-being. I genuinely hope you can understand how your actions affect your relationships, but I know I need to create some distance between us for now.

Love,
Me

BUILT FOR ANYTHING

Life doesn't give me what I want, but what I need. Every experience, every person who has helped, hurt, loved, or left has shaped me into who I am meant to be. That's a hard truth to swallow but resisting it doesn't change it. Pain has been my teacher. Rejection, my educator. Loss, my guide. Life has been the school I've attended for nearly fifty years, and it's about time I stopped ignoring the curriculum I've been handed.

I used to play small, thinking it would protect me. But giving up my dreams didn't make me happier. Being angry didn't bring back my dad. Justifying my losses as reasons to stay stuck only kept me from moving forward. If I don't release the pain, if I refuse to let go, I let it be my excuse for not stepping into the unknown. And yet, I've realized something: my expansion and growth don't care about my feelings. My soul, relentlessly calling me back to life, will do whatever it takes to get me to answer its call. Every door starts to open, but only after I choose to turn the knob.

Life has a way of forcing us to confront our wounds through relationships. Our past traumas will resurface repeatedly, played out in different scenarios with various people, but always with the same familiar echoes. And here's the truth: healing doesn't happen in isolation. It occurs *in connection.* Each relationship challenge I've faced has, in some way, been a blessing, a test, or an opportunity to rewrite the past by choosing to respond differently.

This journey isn't just about overcoming obstacles. It's about proving my past wrong. It's about reconnecting with my power, turning setbacks into stepping stones, and becoming a guiding light for anyone who has ever felt lost in the dark.

I've been pulling myself out of that place alone since childhood, and if these years have taught me anything, it's this: I am built for and capable of anything. Go on, bring it!

CHOOSING TRUTH OVER TOLERANCE

There comes a moment in every story and relationship when clarity hits, and a choice must be made. For me, that moment arrived after years of trying to navigate the deeply dysfunctional dynamics of my husband's family.

It was crucial for me to finally understand that not everyone is willing or ready to grow. Despite my best efforts over the past twenty years to foster connection and understanding, I often faced resistance instead of openness. I filled gaps with love and compassion, hoping to change the dynamic, but the reality was ongoing disconnection. This was not a reflection of my worth or efforts, but a choice made by others. Recognizing this was a turning point for me. I realized that my well-being and that of my children had to come first. It was time to stop striving for community harmony at the cost of my emotional health. Protecting myself and my family became the focus, allowing me to nurture relationships that are mutual and truly supportive.

What I've come to realize is this: after years of being gaslit, scapegoated, and emotionally manipulated, even the strongest parts of you can begin to doubt your own reality. I was the pot-stirrer, the outsider who simply couldn't conform. But the truth? The only thing I was guilty of was refusing to play a part in their broken act.

And now, I'm done. If I can stop enabling my own family, I can surely do the same with my husband's. I've made it clear that I am no longer willing to tolerate behavior that insults my integrity or undermines my worth. Nor am I interested in managing others' dysfunction to keep the peace. I've made peace with being misunderstood because I now fully understand myself.

After a series of events, I reached a point where continuing to tolerate unacceptable behavior was no longer sustainable for me. My limit was reached, and I read the following words aloud to my husband's stepmother, a woman who, for years, echoed the sentiments and manipulations of his late father. His father's death in November 2022 left behind more than just grief for his children; it also caused a trail of emotional wreckage and financial disarray that needed to be navigated. Speaking these words wasn't about changing her. It was about unburdening myself. It was closure, not confrontation.

Fireside, one evening, I read aloud the following letter (shortened and edited for publication) I had written to her:

> *I've watched this family struggle forward for years. I tried to help, not by controlling, but with kindness. I aimed to demonstrate good communication, compassion, and responsibility. I attempted to shield my children from the toxicity, and in doing so, they gained empathy and resilience, not because of this family but despite it.*
>
> *You both have had, and still have, a relationship with them because of me—because I protected them and believed, even when you both hurt me, that the love they felt was worth saving, even if it was limited. I now see that I betrayed myself and them in that process. Even when I spoke up, you never defended me, and his destructive behaviors were ignored. For too many years, I watched manipulation and nastiness while listening to how much "family matters," as the lack of presence and connection continued for far too long.*
>
> *I will no longer pretend. I will stop acting the part I fell into. From now on, I will be neighborly but not nurturing. Civil, but not complicit. My boundaries are no longer flexible for a family that has never truly seen me and has had to be told how to love. I resign from being the villain in this story. And I reclaim my role as a truth-teller in my life.*

What followed was not a reckoning but a release. I didn't need a response or expect a revelation; I spoke those words for myself. Whether she wanted to change or meet me halfway was up to her. I know I was kind to him and her and endured behaviors toward me that were unwarranted.

The truth is, I tried harder than anyone should have to. But now I realize: some people simply aren't built for accountability. And that's not my burden to carry. My focus is on protecting my peace, my family, and myself from further harm. This isn't about revenge. It's about reality. We teach others how to treat us by what we allow. And I've reached the limit of my patience and tolerance for being the bigger person.

The takeaway for everyone, including myself, in sharing this part of my story is to stop shrinking myself for the comfort of others. I'm no longer engaging in emotional gymnastics to keep up a façade. I'm choosing truth over illusion, boundaries over burnout, and peace over performance. I share this not out of bitterness, but out of awareness. Maybe someone else needs permission to stop tolerating the intolerable. Perhaps someone else needs to realize they're not alone in untangling from a family system that was never safe to begin with.

To them, I say:
You're not crazy.
You're not dramatic or sensitive.
You're done.
And that's not just okay, it's empowering.

DEAR GIRL GANG

Dear Girl Gang,

There's nothing quite as powerful as emotional support. It's the invisible force behind bold dreams, daring decisions, and the quiet courage needed to face the chaos life throws our way. When my ground shakes or the hallway goes dark, it's the presence, real or remembered, of my gal pals that gets me through.

To my fellow women on a mission: we know the path isn't always illuminated. We walk it anyway. Sometimes we run. Sometimes we crawl. Often alone. And if luck is on our side, when we emerge, there's someone on the other side offering a hand or simply holding space.

I've never believed that men are stronger than women. Growing up surrounded by flawed male role models, I learned early on that strength isn't about size or muscle; it's about resilience, self-awareness, and feeling. While gender bias affects everyone, women often shoulder most of it. We're told we're too sensitive, too emotional, too much.

But I've come to believe our "too much" is exactly where our power lies. We are magnetic. Lunar. We are literally synced to the moon. We create and carry life, yet we're expected to stay small, quiet, and unfazed. But we weren't born for smallness. We were born for magic, mess, and meaning. Can I get an Amen?

In my late twenties, I read *The Alchemist* by Paulo Coelho, and one quote has always stayed with me. "And, when you want something, all the universe conspires in helping you to achieve it."

That line became a tether during my darkest times, when faith flickered but never fully went out. With the universe behind me and intuition in my bones, I kept going.

And here I am, fresh off the launch of another volume of *S.H.E. Share Heal Empower,* my third book that features twenty-two courageous women and twenty-five incredible artists. It's more than a collection of stories; it's proof that healing happens when we share. That we rise by listening. That our stories don't divide us—they connect us forever.

What I've learned repeatedly is that creativity thrives when we're connected to something bigger. For me, that means the universe... and a few fiercely honest, deeply loving humans. It's why I believe so strongly in the importance of a girl gang.

My crew—Tristen, Danette, Linear, Jenine, Paige, Linda D—are straightforward. They bring honesty and compassion. They tell me what I need to hear, even when I don't want to listen to it. They keep me grounded. They remind me I am not crazy, and I am not alone.

We don't all need the same kind of tribe, but we do need *someone*—a witness, a challenger, a mirror, a soft place to land. Because let's be honest: we carry so much. We move through the world multitasking like machines, checking boxes, holding space, and making magic happen behind the scenes. And sometimes, it's just too much. We crack. We cry. We need backup. That's what we do for each other. We may be cosmic creatures, but we're still human. Life is hard, but I feel much better with my girl gang.

And if you don't have one yet, build one, borrow one, or be one. Because none of us were meant to do this alone. Together is better.

With love, fire, and fierce loyalty,
Me

EVERYDAY PATHWAY

To allow my senses the opportunity to consume life all around me is one of the greatest gifts I can give myself.

I walk to the beach just about every day, along a trusted path that has become reliable and revealing. While I set my pace, I wander past nearby houses, each providing a familiar feeling. Overgrown green hedges with dainty blue flowers intrigue me, ruby red geraniums in pots electrify me, and tattered prayer flags draped around a palm tree quiet me. An unruffled tabby cat named Murphy saunters beside me. I meander on past a broken, brick pathway and a little green gate. The two-foot wide and two-foot-high gate always puzzles me, as it seems to serve no function. Who would use it?

My stride is steady, but the uneven asphalt in my neighborhood keeps me alert to each step. After stepping onto the concrete walkway, it quickly leads me into a busy intersection. Suddenly, I feel irritated by the rush of motorized vehicles speeding past. My peaceful neighborhood is left behind, and now the noise of activity pulls me out of my thoughts.

Once I make my way past the noise disturbance, a canopy of Torrey Pines shelters me from the sun. I stroll past a stylish beach hotel with aged stone pavers. Vacationers are pampered with strawberry smoothies on the pool deck lined with Crayola-orange canvas. My inner compass guides me to follow the winding path filled with wildflowers and native grasses. The pathway veers right, and I slow my pace as I descend nineteen sandy steps with a rusted railing for support. An old train depot appears on my right, sparking thoughts of untold stories and decades of families crossing the same path to enjoy a playful day at the sea.

I sneak across the train tracks to cross the two-lane coastal route in front of me. I stop and grin. My destination peers at me with its shimmering beauty. An expansive stretch of aqua-blue water greets me, while the wind whispers a soothing tune. The scent of salty sea air pulls my gaze down from the clouds to the beauty of reality.

Seagulls squawk as the ocean rolls and roars in real-time music. The rhythm of the waves hitting the shoreline syncs with the laughter echoing from beachgoers. The sandpipers move forward and retreat with each change of the waterline. The coconut-laced aroma of sunscreen drifts me to the tropics. My toes touch the sandy beach, and my soles are soothed.

Along the shoreline, some of my favorite finds are sand dollars, moon shells, flat scallops, and knobby whelks; all slightly submerged and not looking to be found, only admired. These marine mollusks lie and lurk, asking nothing of me. I think about their daily journey. What familiarity did they leave behind, and why? As their shells all tell a story of travel, I wonder what created their outer beauty. What commotion did they experience to arrive at our shared destination? I admire each detail on their sturdy, protective outer layers. Their presence creates movement in my mind.

It's up to me to find the randomness in this routine walk I take each day. I keep moving forward and notice the uncomfortable conversation I start having with myself. Life and death naturally remind me to stay alert. Sometimes it's to notice what hasn't changed, and other times it's to see differences. Change is part of all living things; whether I like it or not, it happens with or without my consent. It might be something small—like a rusty nail or a tourist asking for directions—or something significant—like a dolphin washed ashore.

As a writer, this walk provides clues when I feel stuck. Meaning is often found in the most modest places. I am motivated daily to find importance in each moment and openly accept the certainty and uncertainty it offers. This everyday path, my path, continues to spark ideas within.

RANDOM RANTS

Unfiltered Growth — Ranting,
Evolving & Owning My Journey

Most of what I focus on is understanding what happened, why it happened, and how I can move forward in a way that benefits me. Do I question everything? Yes. Is that healthy? For me, absolutely. Breaking down false beliefs about myself and past situations helps me build a solid personal foundation based on my truth. That foundation provides me with peace of mind, stability, and a deep sense of self.

I've learned that when something—or someone—doesn't align with my values, I say, *No, that isn't for me.* The more I reflect on who I am and what I need, the more empowered and freer I feel. That said, my one toxic trait, I still get upset about old pain, even if I've moved past it, because I still don't understand why I deserved it. And maybe I never will.

You must catch me while I care. Once I stop, I become a different person. There comes a point in the healing process when you stop trying to convince others to do the right thing. Instead, you just observe their choices, understand their character, and decide if they still belong in your life.

Or maybe the journey isn't about transforming into something new. Perhaps it's about *unbecoming* everything that isn't truly me so I can finally become who I was always meant to be. I like the "She is We" idea. She is not perfect. She doesn't have all the answers. She struggles with self-doubt and overthinks everything. She can be harsh on herself. But none of that matters because she is still bringing all her dreams—and more—into reality. She is unstoppable, simply because she says so. She is me. She is you. She is us.

We don't need to know what's coming next. We don't have to have everything figured out right now. We are living, growing beings, constantly changing and learning. And that's exactly what life is: a journey. If we knew what was coming, it wouldn't be a journey at all. Life doesn't end; it just changes. And that uncertainty? It can be haunting, but it's also beautiful. It allows us to expand, grow, and stretch beyond what we once thought possible. The only thing that truly matters is being here, now.

So, live peacefully within yourself. Let your heart not be disturbed by your mind I learned in Puerto Escondido, Mexico when a shaman named Dante looked me straight in the soul and said, "Less head, more heart." He had just done something, I'm not sure what exactly, pressed or pinched a point between my eyebrows so deeply that it left a mark. It hurt like hell, but it cracked something open. As I lay there, the muggy air heavy around me and the sound of the ocean crashing in the distance, I felt a sense of lightness. Not healed, not whole, but somehow more awake. Like my third eye had been pried open just enough to let some light in.

Everyone develops at their own pace, and some may not develop at all. I try to keep that in mind. I've learned the hard way that not everyone recognizes their struggles as a problem. And if they don't see something as a problem, they won't be open to a solution. Even if my advice is wrapped in compassion, if someone isn't ready, it's just white noise. Without the life experience to understand what I'm saying, they won't hear me. So, I'm learning to leave people alone and let them wade through their own puddles and play and splash only in mine.

Meanwhile, you'll find me staying in my own lane, maybe ranting, but minding my own business, evolving, and embracing the journey as it unfolds with a red mark on my forehead.

MY SWAN SONG

For as long as I can remember, I've worn myself thin trying to be everything to everyone, slipping into roles as effortlessly as wine fills my vino vessel. I've prided myself on this, convincing myself that if I could be enough for everyone else, I would surely be enough for myself. But now I realize that in doing so, I was slowly chipping away at the core of who I am—stretching, straining, and contorting until I was depleted. The person who was once vibrant and deeply rooted in her essence has begun to feel like a distant memory, a faint outline hidden beneath the layers I'd worn to survive.

The weight of this journey, the habit of carrying others' expectations and conforming to their needs, left me on the verge of something that felt like ruins. My soul felt cracked and bruised from years of being twisted and reshaped. I reached a point where I could no longer maintain the facade. The demands of being everything to everyone had robbed me of being true to myself.

And now, on the verge of a comeback—a return not to what I was but to who I truly am—I face an unexpected obstacle: my old identity, the very version of me that has endured so much in order to feel loved, valued, and needed. It clings to me, insisting I stay where I am, whispering that this is where I belong, that I can't possibly change now. There's comfort in the familiar, even when that comfort comes with chains.

Yet I know this shift will ripple through my relationships. As I shed the layers of what others have known me to be, I realize that some may feel unsettled or threatened by this change. The balance of those connections might falter as I let go of the parts of myself that once catered to others at my own expense. Some relationships may grow and change with me, while others may resist, and through this transition, I'm learning to accept that I can't control how others will respond. I can no longer silence these fiery feelings that have grown fiercer and fuller.

But in this moment of reckoning, I feel an undeniable pull to shed that skin. Deep inside me, a voice continues to call out, urging me to stop fighting myself and start honoring the part that knows I am enough just as I am. To have a bright and true future, I must let go of the weight of others' expectations and trust that my own will guide me where I need to go.

This is my swan song—a final bow to the version of me that once served a purpose but now holds me back. The path forward requires courage, not to be more than I am, but to be exactly who I am. So, I let go of the need to be everything to everyone, and in doing so, I am finally free to become fully, unapologetically, myself for my own good and for the future self who deserves to live untethered.

STILLNESS IN SOLITUDE

Solitude can be a strange and powerful experience. For some, it might evoke feelings of loneliness, but for me, it serves as an invitation to reconnect with the parts of myself that often get lost in the shuffle of daily responsibilities. Sitting on the dock, overlooking Lake Charlevoix, I'm reminded of the beauty of quietude, of being alone without feeling lonely. There's a certain freedom in it, freedom from the need to be anything or anyone.

It's just me, the water, and my thoughts. There's a unique stillness as I look out at the water. It's as if time slows, and I no longer feel bound by everyday demands and others' expectations. The noise fades away, replaced by the gentle lapping of water against the shore behind me and the occasional rustle of wind through the changing colors of the trees. In this moment of solitude, I feel more connected to myself than ever.

I often reflect on the simplicity of nature. The water doesn't rush; it ebbs and flows at its own pace, completely unconcerned with schedules or expectations. There's something deeply comforting about that. It reminds me that I, too, can be still, without always needing an agenda or deadline. In a world that constantly urges us to be productive and purposeful, sitting on the dock feels like a quiet act of rebellion —a friendly reminder that I am enough, even when I am simply being.

My stillness and solitude on the dock give me space to process my emotions. In the busyness of life, it's easy to avoid confronting what's going on inside. I distract myself with writing, with people, with endless to-do lists. But here, with nothing but the sound of water and wind, there's no avoiding the thoughts and feelings that surface. Sometimes, they come gently, a soft tug of contemplation from the past. At other times, emotions surge like waves, demanding my undivided attention. And in that solitude, I allow myself to meet whatever comes.

Being alone this way also helps me realize how much I've been conditioned to fill every moment with noise. Whether it's the hum of social media, the constant barrage of news, or the endless stream of tasks, there's always something pulling my attention. But sitting on the dock, none of that seems to matter. There is no urgency, so there is no need to respond or engage. The world keeps turning without me, and I find peace in knowing that I can step away from it all and return to myself.

In these moments of silence and solitude, I find clarity. It's as if the water reflects not just the sky but also my own thoughts. The answers I've been searching for, those I didn't even realize I needed, seem to surface. Whether it's a decision I've been struggling with or a feeling I've been trying to hide, the stillness of the dock gives me the space to listen to what's really happening inside.

Ultimately, sitting on the dock in solitude is a form of self-care. It's a way of reminding myself that it's okay to pause, to breathe, to let go of the need to be constantly doing. It's in these quiet moments that I realize the importance of stillness in solitude, not as something to be feared or avoided, but as a necessary part of the human experience. It's where I find myself again, stripped of all the distractions, just me and the gentle rhythm of life unfolding around me.

THE POWER OF LISTENING TO ONESELF

As I reflect on the past twelve months, I find myself going through a series of recurring lessons—some new, some revisited—that have shaped my year. Themes like my tendency to fix things (especially relationships), the lingering effects of my people-pleasing habits, and my habit of overexplaining myself and overthinking interactions have all come up. These habits have often left me drained, wasting energy on people and situations that didn't deserve it.

I could easily stop here, listing all the things I still need to work on. However, that wouldn't truly capture what this year has taught me - endless lessons that, while hard-earned, have been transformational.

The first and possibly most important point is this: people can only meet me as deeply as they are willing to meet themselves. This realization hit me hard. I spent too much time trying to connect with people who, for their own reasons, were simply not capable or willing to engage at the level I hoped for. My repeated efforts, the same disappointing results, only led to my misery.

But 2025 will be my year of awakening. While I called 2024 the "year of taking care of me," I only truly understood what that meant through trial and error. I learned that repair and reconciliation are only valuable in relationships where honest conflict can exist, where both parties are willing to accept and process difficult truths, even when it's painful. Relationships built on a façade of "dishonest harmony" (something both my family and my husband's family often rely on) only lead to stagnation.

It's been eye-opening to see how many people can't handle the truth, whether it's subjective or objective. For someone like me, who thrives on truth, this has been a hard pill to swallow. I welcome critique, hard facts, and even criticism if it helps me grow and improve. To me, truth is a gift, not a threat.

This clarity has inspired my focus for the upcoming year: *accountability*. I will hold myself responsible for my actions, my behavior, and my growth. I will continue to face challenges head-on, refusing to ignore or avoid what feels uncomfortable. I've decided I won't tiptoe around the elephant in the room; ruby-red lipstick, a glittery tiara, and a pink tutu glaring for all to see.

Moving forward, I realize that perspective has been my greatest ally this year. I've adopted a broader outlook on life, prioritizing meaningful connections with people who share my values of accountability and growth. My mistakes will remain my teachers, but only if I'm willing to listen to myself, others, and the lessons life presents. Interestingly, my writing this year has been one of my best teachers. I've been reminded of the power of flexibility and humility through the editing process, with its red marks and strikethroughs. There is always another way to express ourselves, think, and grow, but only if we listen carefully and stay open to learning.

As I close out this year, I move forward with gratitude for the lessons learned, the clarity gained, and the relationships that have shown me the value of truth, accountability, and listening to myself. Here's to continuing the growth journey, one hard-earned realization at a time.

WHISPERS FROM GRANDMA ROSIE

The older I get, the closer I feel to my grandmother, Rosie. She has always been my favorite person, my second mother, and my anchor. When I was little, I didn't fully understand the quiet strength she carried. I only knew I felt safe with her. I loved our time together; simple, steady, sacred. But now, with time and perspective, I see her with new eyes. I notice the storms she weathered that I was too young to understand back then.

She lost her mother, her husband, and her son—*my father*—all within three years. These three blows would typically break most people, but not Grandma Rosie. She persevered and lived life on her own terms. I remember overhearing her sister and others say, "We invite her… but she never comes." Yet, when she did show up, she was radiant with hair done, lipstick on, warm and chatty as ever, until, just as quickly, she'd slip away. When she'd had enough, she left with no apologies. As a child, I thought she was just private. But now I realize she was *free*. Living alone wasn't lonely for her; it was a sanctuary. I understand now.

As I get older, I see myself in her. Or perhaps I see her in me. The peace found in solitude. The quiet joys of puttering, reading, and writing. The beauty of being still. People assume I'm an extrovert, and maybe I am in certain situations, but a part of me longs for silence. That values the slow moments, the unscheduled hours. The small rituals that ground and nourish me.

Grandma Rosie used to borrow stacks of books from the library. She would mow the lawn with her rusty push mower, tend to her garden, or sometimes buy vegetables and fruits she could can. I still taste those juicy peaches and delicious applesauce. She kept an ear on the Detroit Tigers game and quietly checked her perfectly cooked New

York strip sizzling over a tiny Weber grill she propped on the hood of her white Oldsmobile Cutlass Supreme. Then Grandma Rosie would settle into that teal-colored plastic-webbed porch chair that left criss-cross marks or caused me to slip through as a child. She didn't need company to enjoy her evening; she had herself. She had her rhythm, and she didn't care what anyone thought about it. There's such dignity in that. Such power in knowing who you are and living like you mean it.

Years ago, I named my inner compass after her, Rosie, my north star. The part of me that always knows what matters. The part that says, "It's okay to do it your way." The part that reminds me that I come from resilience. From grace. From a woman who knew how to stay true to herself, even when the world didn't understand.

And sometimes, when the house is quiet and the light is soft, I feel her presence. Not in a loud or dramatic way, just a whisper. A gentle nudge that says:

Keep going, sweetheart. You're doing just fine.
Do it your way.
Live the life that fits you.
I did… and so can you.

HOW I OUTRAN MY DREAM

I attest that outrunning a dream is complex,
but definitely doable.

~SHC

My dream was to become a writer and surround myself with words. For twenty years, I forgot how to make choices for myself. Much of what I did during those years wasn't truly what I wanted to do. I was complacent and accepted my circumstances. Sound familiar? Plotting a different course and taking on the challenging task of living my dream felt overwhelming. Many times, in my life, I wanted to understand and unravel my emotional obstacles, but my uncertainty, circumstances, and poor choices stood in my way. I did not find pleasure in the path I was on. Maybe I wasn't meant to let my life lead me—I was meant to lead it.

Why do I share this? Because it matters. We all have dreams, and most of us fail to act on them.

Well, without realizing it, I outran my dream! How did I do this? Very easily. I failed to follow through on what I had set out to do. I gave up and went on to other ventures that were not making me happy. For many years, I neglected to give myself the freedom and permission to follow my fancies. My days of daydreaming disappeared. Life, with its responsibilities, put blinders on me. I missed my turn to capture my bliss. I was sidetracked by adult duties and dashed right past my dream.

I had to turn around immediately. Without hesitation, I stopped letting myself get distracted. It was hard to ignore the different ideas everyone else had for me. When I tuned out their input, it was clear their advice suited them, not me. Figuring out what was best for me was confusing. I wasn't sure if purpose in life was something we're born with or something we find and foster. Whatever the answer, I was not going to let my dream pass me by again, despite my adult responsibilities pressing on me. I stopped playing by society's rules and those of my generation and created my own playbook. I no longer wanted to feel stuck, lost, or unhappy. My apathy disappeared. I began to realize that my perceived failures and the changes in my life choices were just minor speed bumps on my way to achieving my dreams.

No fancy tricks, just determination and desire this time. Being alone with my thoughts. Learning new things. Making a difference with words. Feeling no pressure to perform. These four things helped me understand there was an inconsistency between my wants and needs. They were strides toward my dream. I was finally chasing my dream. My dream is to write and be surrounded by words. These small units of language bring me happiness, contentment, and satisfaction. At the end of each day, I have been truly honest and open with myself. It was a wise decision for me to return to my dream. Today I am living it, and it gives me immense pleasure and purpose. Do not make my mistake and run past your dream; catch it the first time.

DEAR LIFE

Dear Life,

You never gave me an easy path, but you gave me *my* path. You took my father too soon, along with any illusion that life was fair. At eleven, I became the one who stayed alert—the protector, the peacekeeper, the early adult in a world that suddenly felt unpredictable. I learned that love doesn't always last, safety is never guaranteed, and I'd have to forge my own way forward.

And I did. But not without detours. Not without bruises, scrapes, and scars. I gave my heart to men who mistook it for a mirror, wanting to see themselves in me, not truly see *me.* I over-gave, over-functioned, and over-accommodated. I confused approval with connection. I kept shrinking in plain sight. But somewhere along the way, I stopped molding myself to be held. I began building a life that fit me, not just them.

Then you surprised me. You brought me a man who didn't want to fix, possess, or manage me.

He listened. He laughed. He softened. He became my first friend—my equal, my partner, my steady. Through him, I saw that love can be calm, honest, and gentle without breaking under pressure. With him by my side, I mothered two boys into men. And in that becoming, I found a fierceness and a tenderness I didn't know I had. Motherhood cracked me open in new ways—and it also stitched me back together. But the healing didn't stop there. You called me out into the world. To walk beside the dying. To share stories. To stand in silence on an ancient land. To let faraway skies and unfamiliar customs reawaken parts of me I'd forgotten.

From Antarctica's stillness to Paris's poetry, I've answered the call for *more.* Not more possessions or status, but more meaning—more truth—more that can't be measured but can always be felt. I'm fifty now, and I feel both ancient and newborn at the same time. I've lived many lives in this one lifetime, and I'm finally living *for myself.* You've taught me that there is no final destination—only deeper unfolding.

And I've stopped asking for directions from people who were never headed where I'm going. So, thank you for the ache and the awe, the heartbreak and the homecoming.

We're not done yet, Life. Not even close.

Love,
Me

POETRY

Verses from the Soul

This book ends with poetry—a reflective and emotional conclusion that condenses my experiences into something more basic and visceral. Drawn from nature, love, longing, and the complex, beautiful journey of being human, these poems invite you to feel deeply, contemplate, and connect with the core of what I have seen and felt along the way.

Poetry has always been the language I turn to when prose falls short—when emotions demand rhythm instead of reason. These verses emerge from the undercurrents of my life, often arriving unexpectedly: during morning beach runs, in the stillness of sitting by the lake, or in the in-between spaces where reflection often sneaks in. Some come from joy, others from ache, but each poem is a fragment of truth caught in motion.

As Prolific Preambles comes to a close, this section serves as both a gentle landing and an open door – an offering of presence, breath, and beauty. I trust these poems will meet you wherever you are. Just feeling, just being – a final whisper before the page turns and life moves on.

CONQUEST OF CONTENTMENT

Together we are dynamic
Alone we are different
Together we demand devotion
Our great love story takes action

Connection to the other's soul is the prize
Together we are energized
Alone we are resilient
While our alliance offers, no lies

What is this mysterious warmth?
Fictitious stories have encrypted themes
Allowing room for self-rule and growth
Separate natures, merging into one team

Your vivid smile continually sways me
Deeper levels of emotional empathy appear
Alone changing our strides
Together hearts ascending with pride

Hold me firmly
Together we are one
Alone our lives go into darkness
Together let us say, we won!

Love together beams
Love together is bright
Love together is brilliance
Never a need to alone take flight

FREEDOM TO FLOAT

Why do I lead with my heart?

Despite the drama
Which often carries ample trauma

Life will tease
It is not my place to please

My past provided plenty of rope
Now unrestrained to find new hope

A man I met who preferred to elope
Brought light and delight to areas remote

Confinement of my soul no longer exists
Next up—discovery of bliss

Excuse me, I do not mean to gloat
Learning to love has been my *freedom to float*

LOVING MYSELF AS IS

Loving myself as is.
It's a tricky act.
Loving oneself, as is.
Now.
In my body and all its glory.
In my mind and all its quirkiness.
In my spirit and all its wanderlusting ways.
Without the journey, I would never start.
To uncover.
To unravel.
All the magic, burning deep within me,
Honoring my mess.
Honoring my lessons from life.
Surrendering to the process.
Playing my part.
Falling in love, over and over.
With the art of becoming.
Myself as is.
Pure joy.
Pure freedom.

CURED BY THE SEA

One gulp of clean salty air, and I stand lured by a roar of the sea, by no means planning to plunge. Simply a means by which to restore.

As I exhale slowly being surrounded by the sea, my heart stirs. While soul searching and rescuing, my mind spews, as I relinquish the control, I impart.

Setting my turmoil free, no longer ignoring the essence of me. The deep-sea rumbles, once more reminding me I cannot force things to be, allowing my instincts and natural elements, to guide me.

It is here I observe the slow and steady rhythm of life. Each step I realize my stride increasing resembling the pace of a sandpiper fixed on finding the reward beneath a sandy shoreline.

As the sea foam skitters across the sand I too, dance.

As the sand dollar appears mysteriously on the shore,
I too, resurface.

As the castle-like structure of wet sand is stately.
I too, stand grand.

Her waves of truth are a form of therapy, self-discovery in my sea sanctuary, compassion in the currents of my life and patient with who I continue to become.

Determined not to sink while sculpting my selfhood, to feel underwhelmed is good, to not be burdened by my mind is better. A safe harbor for an unfinished self to settle.

A joyful journey only accessible on my own, the sea cures me, an oasis offering endless possibilities, a continual surfacing and submerging to the ever-changing me.

MY MEANDERING MIND

Mysterious wishing
Away with the garbled thoughts
Coming my way

It is imperative I learn
A way to make them stay
For only myself will I betray

They often lead me astray
What will they convey as I find my way
It is important to not disobey

Interpretations will display
A scenery that reminds me of a parfait
Layers upon layers of my past with a blink of today

I begin to slowly overplay
My mysterious wishing
Recognizing my desire to overstay & never stray

It is my soul I must repay
For it was I who disobeyed
Gradually beginning to decay, this was not okay

Perchance I become versed and conscious on how to convey
My jumbled ways of receiving & reasoning
With this awareness, now I shall strut and sashay

LOONY LOVE

Is a contradiction,
An ability of being human.

The work of true love
Is never conflict-free.

Flawed and full of fears,
Foolish conduct occurs
With attempts to lather in lotion.

Yet a unique bond forms
With a protective role,
Despite the stubbornness and
Creases within a fatigued face.

Activating a highly difficult balance
And delicate dance
Between a version of loony and lofty love.

No normal patterns,
As we twirl to our tune of *Loony Love,* daily.

Learning to love can be demanding.
Frustration occurs.
Annoying habits, hard to ignore.
Finding a friend for life, eventually follows.

Truth is, loving can create acceptance.
An exposure,

Re-examining the view of self-love,
An improvement involving the singular versus the shared.

Loony Love is a gamble.
Desired outcome, unpredictable.

Two flawed individuals, injured and misplaced.
Finding hope in common and contrasting storylines.

Delving into complexities,
Negotiating differences intelligently,
Teaching and finding the best version of each other,
A lifetime project of betterment.

Loony Love is not for the feeble of heart.
It challenges our core.
Igniting emotions, aggravating and possibly annoying.
Enduring our own and our partner's weaknesses,

Building better behaviors.
Fewer blame games.
Dissolving sullenly silent times.
Each taking responsibility for missteps.

Disengagement is dangerous.
Going bonkers is typical.
Putting the puzzle pieces back, together.
Building better behaviors.

Yes, this is *Loony Love*.

A spinning of two hearts.
Tired and twisted.
Often times, out of control.
Waiting and wanting to be wooed.

Similar to spun sugar,
Delicate to touch,
Delicious to taste,
Easy to scald.
Crafting a stunning web of glossy saccharine strands,
Yet, taking years of practice and perseverance to master.

Celebrate crazy.
Complex layer by layer,
Succumb to madness.
There is no normal in love.

Discovering splendor in calamity,
Cultivating chaos and control,

In everyday life.
Always together,
Despite the drama.
Tilting toward antipathy, then tipping back to empathy,

I feel saner and happier
By reexamining my very view of love.
Realizing the real work of love is not in the falling,
But in what comes after,

Love is in the little things.

Unless it's mad, passionate and extraordinary,
With mutual weirdness, it's a waste of your time.
There must be, must be *Loony Love*
For it to be long-lasting.

TO DISAPPEAR

To Disappear.
From the known of a familiar touch, taste, sound and smell of living.
To be different.
Not heard by the same ears or seen by the same eyes.
To the unknown.
The road I must go.
To silence.
As I search for aloneness.
To whisper my way into another existence.
Another conversation.
Another culture.
Igniting my instincts.
Trigger my intuition.
Departing distress.
Searching for the other side of sadness.

THE MOON IN UBUD

The moon in Ubud.
Walking in the moonlight,
I am startled by sparrows leaving the banana leaf branch.
Listening, the croaking frogs concur.
Smelling the sweet smell of the rice fields promise success.
Beyond the shadowy clouds, star twinkle.
Walking in the light of the moon, a couple raindrops sprinkle.
I hear pipits shrill in the sticky midnight breeze.
Passing a bamboo and stone structure alongside a village temple.
Where wafts of incense permeate and bring pause.
As the winding narrow path leads me to my hut.
Nestled near the center of this lush jungle.
My eyes feel complete, enough now.
As I close them and drift into a dreamy slumber.

DEEP WITHIN

Deep Within.
We all have it.
You have it too.
The sophisticated, street smart, soulful, savage and spiritual thing about you.
Take time to understand it.
Go capture it.
The depths of its reach are endless.
The journey is all yours.
STOP ignoring, suppressing, and devaluing.
Feed your senses.
Capture your heart and mind back.
Love who you really are.
YOU matter!

LOFTY LOVE

Surrendering my shield
Impacts me.

Unfolding past patterns of behavior
Frees me.

Doing away with division
Heals me.

Breaking down hand-built walls
Transforms me.

Giving myself completely to love seems scary,
Preoccupied with fear,
Emotionally wary,
Vulnerable.

Swerving past individual differences,
Understanding complexities,
And encouraging reverence,
While gently removing layers of life.

An exquisite paradox,
Complicated yet carefree,
Challenging yet compassionate,
Empowering never encapsulating.

I learned lofty love with my partner
Who sways back and forth,

With me,
Supporting my inner and outer worth.

An affectionate hustle,
With a rhythmic, unspoken link,
Rising between us,
Resembling an unassuming eye wink.

He elevates my character and spirit.
He shifts my thinking towards tenderness.
He entangles my senses and thoughts.

We go beyond the beyond,
With our similar soul vavoom.
As the lotus flower unfolds in murky water,
We also discover a deep place to feel safe and bloom.

To give and receive love,
Teaches us,
We must be our own,
Before we can be each other's.

A return to innocence.
Playfulness,
Communication,
Coming together.

Crossing chasms,
Identifying new vantage points,
Sometimes with sarcasm,
But always together.

Hand in hand.
Heart to heart.
Cultivating our version of lofty love.

ME AND MYSELF

Me and Myself
being brave
waking each morning, open to what life has to offer

Demands of everyday living can be challenging,
the busyness of being
the never-ending swirl of noise,
whether coming or going, my life is in constant motion.

I walk along the sea and welcome a new day
shining stars are stationary,
moonlight illuminates my way.

There is silence in the air
reflection, a serene time of mindfulness.

The darkness lifts, and I sense an exchange
an opportunity to see and receive a new day.

The world is waking; there is complete calmness
strolling the shoreline
sea birds peacefully mingle
tides leave their mark in footprint-free sand
waves stir without occupancy, creating a rhythmic sound.

My aloneness is short-lived
as morning solitude becomes a souvenir,
a tranquil reminder with every step
inner and outer silence can exist.

My walks with me provide time for restoration.
Mastering the art of stillness
is a gift the sea has given me.

PATH OF ENLIGHTENMENT

My load limit is often full.
Finding freedom within and giving in
makes me feel good.
My life gets complicated.
Simplicity in nature can be surreal
and habitually heal.

* * * *

As I stroll down these serene surroundings,
my perspective is refined.
My feet move forward, yet my body and mind
want to wait.
I offer myself another moment.
To pause.

* * * *

I stand mesmerized by natural beauty
and marvel at its pureness.
As sunlight radiates down through the trees,
it filters my mind.
I follow the light leading me through this wooded wonder,
reminding me of what?
I am to be audacious as I step on
each square stone.

* * * *

I appreciate silence; society rushes me.
Concealed within this wondrous walk,
while basking in freedom and fresh air,
I organize my reality and stay committed
to my heart and natural surroundings.

Taking time to contemplate on wooden benches
discovered along the pathway,
I understand that being lost, yet found,
is an art form that transcends all ages.

* * * *

I respect this refuge, admiring the diverse array of colors it presents.
Seeing symbolic significance, as the Sakura flowers emulate pink snowflakes, falling gently on the ground.
I delight in this visual and sensual treat,
marking an end or beginning to the next stage in life.

* * * *

I am alive and awakened to the reflective quality of a one-mile route.
Finding my senses, it feels appropriate to acknowledge the great sages and confluence of magical minds surrounding me.
I observe an abundance of bumblebees, perhaps disguised as the ancient greats.

* * * *

I should decipher their messages, held in the hollows of aged cherry trees.
Relishing the rhythmic stirring of the water in the canal below, I recognize its resemblance to my inner restlessness.
A discovery of bridges that bring thinkers together provides refuge on this communal route.

* * * *

I am no longer feeling void of life's uncertainties;
a smile and joy emerge inside and out.
Captivated by a confetti of emotions,
sprinkling like pink petals on the water,
I found a place of pure rejuvenation,
which will never fade from my mind's eye.
As I snapped numerous mental pictures,
this springtime tradition will last a lifetime.

* * * *

I connected with the harmony and
energy this path projects, feeling
relaxed and understanding my liberated presence.
I now recognize that seasons change and
the fragility of life exists, yet I feel whole again.
There is awe and inspiration in my capacity
to bloom at varying times in my life.

* * * *

I have this life to appreciate exquisite scenery that lies in different
pockets of the world and within me.
To be aware of how infinitely connected
we are is a gift.
As I glean philosophical wisdom from the past,
I forge forward to the future.
Year after year, remembering the stroll down Philosopher's Path in
Kyoto, Japan, in the flowering season of my forty-second year.

LOVE TOUR

I release myself.
In trust and shelter, in my partner's soul.
Understanding nourishes belonging.
Feeling free to be me.
We tour time together.
To feel understood, what a gift.
Suspended in love.
Sacred intimacy.
Secret trust.
Finding the special someone.
With the capability to awaken and free the possibilities within me.
Forever my soul friend.
All things change.
We come together, we part.
My lifelong companion is never lost.
Even when his lonely lovebird flies.
Soaring high in the sky.
Next to the clouds.
Where stars shimmer and shine.
Across the Milky Way, we meet again.
Embracing Earth's love scene.
Our love tour is tender.
Flowing like a stream.
Often feeling like a dream.
No need to stay side by side.
Love is always nearby.
Touring together.
Night and day.
Out of loneliness.
Out of exile.
Home to the house of belonging.

HIS VOICE; MY CLOSURE

It was not my voice she finally heard—
it was his.
Unleashed like thunder
against the silence I'd carried for too long.
He said what I never dared:
called out the lies, the betrayals,
named her truth aloud—
the one she kept burying under charm and spin.
Lying. Cheating. Whore.
Not as a weapon,
but as a mirror.
A mirror she never wanted.
And now, that's all she sees—
not the decades of loyalty,
not the saving,
not the late-night rescues
or the thousand small forgiving's.
Just the sound of truth finally breaking the surface.
Truth, unleashed.
Justice never whispers.
A reckoning she never thought would come—

and certainly not from him.
But reckonings do not ask permission.
They arrive when silence can no longer hold the weight.
Let her spiral.
Let her reword the narrative.
Let her emotional immaturity shine.
Let her ghosting prevail to avoid the truth.
The record stands.
This is my closure—
No more shield.
No more silence.
No more protecting the very person
who never protected me.
And no more wearing the villain's mask,
in the story she keeps rewriting.
I have laid it down—
and I am walking away clean.

ALCHEMY OF LIFE AND DEATH

The tides of the ocean
Rise and fall
The lives of you and me
Rise and fall

As the tides fade back into the deep sea
Leaving their watermark
We, too, consume life and then fade back into the unknown
While leaving our imprint on the hearts of those we love

Traverse through life with an open heart
Attach to optimism
Detach from the toxins
Love your now

Life can be glorious
Death can be unkind
The alchemy of life and death
It is a molecular movement through time

Truth against truth
Tides shift, plans and people pass
Devour the now
For all we know,
Life may be a dream

FATHER'S FLANNEL

Worn and soft, the threads still hold,
A warmth that lingers, quiet and bold.
Plaid like the days he'd spend outside,
Wearing it with pride while golfing or mowing.
Old Spice lingers, familiar and sweet,
Like dust from the trails beneath our feet.
Four-wheeling wild, his laugh in the air,
Mischievous smile, free without a care.
I see him sitting on the dock, drinking a beer,
Sun on his face, summer drawing near.
That worn red flannel, faded and thin,
Faded like the pictures of him.
Will I ever stop missing him?
Though he's gone, the fabric remains,
A silent echo through life's refrains.

DROPPING THE MIC ON MIDLIFE

I used to think midlife meant fading into the background — softening the edges, lowering the volume, making room for what's "next."

Not anymore.

Now, I know better.
Now, I know this is the arrival — not the conclusion, not the comedown — but the *becoming.*

And perhaps the most sacred part?
I don't need to have it all figured out.
I'm finally okay with the mystery.

I am not diminishing myself—I am arriving.
Fully. Fiercely. Finally.

I've lived five decades — not quietly.
I've burned bridges I needed to.
I've rebuilt from ashes others feared.
I am not fragile. I am forged.

This is not just the second act.
This is the main stage — and I've got the mic.

In my fifties, I will no longer audition.
For love. For approval. For space.
I take up room with my grace, grit, and gravity.

I've outgrown performance.
I've retired from pretending.
I've made peace with the parts of me that once felt too much,
too loud, and too tender.

I protect my peace like a woman who knows its cost.
I wear wisdom like jewelry, with no polish needed.

I no longer chase relevance because "I am" relevance.
My life is my resume. My joy is my protest.
And my story? I'm telling it all the way through — raw,
real, and unfiltered.

I'm no longer afraid of not knowing.
There's beauty in the unfolding.
There's strength in surrender.
I don't need all the answers — I will trust the rhythm of becoming.

So here's to the woman becoming and
embracing her main character energy.
The one who no longer waits for permission.
The one who lets life be sacred and untamed.
The one who walks boldly into the unknown, hello Paris
….because she knows mystery isn't something to fear,
it's something to dance with.

Let them watch.
Let them wonder.
Let them witness what happens when a woman reclaims her voice,
her time, her truth, and surrenders, fully, to the unfolding.

Mic officially dropped!

POEM OF PERSEVERANCE

Beneath the weight, I bend but don't break,
Each step forward is a choice I make.
Through Midwest storms that howl and rage,
And sunny California skies that bleed in chains of a gilded cage.
No longer allowing the sandpaper to my soul,
I shield negativity, and only my light keeps me whole.
Trusting my inner Rosie, with grit and grace,
I find my strength in every space.
Despite the deflection, the manipulation, the scorn,
In a world where hearts are often worn,
The path is long, and the night is deep,
Yet still, I climb, though shadows creep.
Self-love and compassion, the keys in hand,
Unlock the peace where I choose to stand.
For in my heart, a flame will burn,
A quiet strength at every turn.
When doubt arrives, I stand my ground,
In trials' echoes, resolve is found.
For every fall, I rise once more,
A soul unyielding, steadfast to the core.

AUTHOR'S CLOSING NOTE

The Page Turns, but the Story Continues

If you've made it this far, thank you for walking alongside me through these fragments, reflections, and revelations. *Prolific Preambles* was never meant to be a tidy memoir or a perfect map. It's more like a constellation: scattered points of light, moments of darkness, and the lines we draw to make sense of it all.

This book began as a digital diary, a quiet space for my thoughts to take shape. However, over time, it evolved into something more—a testament to growth and transformation. I didn't set out to be profound. I set out to be honest. To give form to the swirl of thoughts and emotions that so many of us carry but rarely name. And in that process, I found that writing doesn't just preserve memory—it transforms it. It softens, sharpens, and sometimes even heals.

If even one sentence made you feel seen, understood, or simply less alone, then this collection of my musings and ramblings has done its job.

The truth is, we are all writing and living our lives in preambles—setting the stage for the next thing, the next version, the next awakening. As you close this book, I invite you to keep writing, reflecting, and, above all, listening to your inner voice, sharing your stories, and honoring the stillness between them; all these magical moments matter.

This is not the end—just a pause.

Until the next page.
—Shannon

ABOUT THE AUTHOR

Shannon Hogan Cohen writes to make sense of the world. From a young age, she filled notebooks with reflections, always searching for meaning, connection, and the hidden threads beneath life's surface, an instinct shaped by her childhood love of Nancy Drew mysteries. Whether it's finding patterns in chaos or truth in tangled relationships, storytelling has always been her compass.

A freelance writer with work published across community advocacy platforms, travel magazines, and personal essay outlets, Shannon gives voice to the often unspoken. She writes with heart, humor, and an unapologetic splash of truth-telling. Shannon Hogan Cohen, author of the *S.H.E. Share Heal Empower* series and the epistolary memoir *Love, Me,* is a freelance writer whose work appears across community advocacy platforms, travel magazines, and personal essay outlets. Her writing gives voice to the often unspoken, with heart, humor, and an unapologetic splash of truth-telling.

When she's not wandering the world and championing legacies, you'll find her in her beloved "babe cave," savoring quiet moments of reading, writing, and sipping a cup of coffee or French white wine. She lives with her family in Del Mar, California.

www.ingramcontent.com/pod-product-compliance
Lightning Source LLC
LaVergne TN
LVHW091249110826
845146LV00002BA/576